100 WONDERS of the World

This edition published by Parragon in 2012

Parragon
Queen Street House
4 Queen Street
Bath BA1 1HE, UK
www.parragon.com

Original edition: Natalie Blei/Petra Hammerschmidt, alex media, Gierstorfer, Ferstl & Reichert GbR, Augsburg
Concept: Michaela Mohr/Gerhard Klimmer/Michael Kraft
Illustrations: Evgen Lutskevych
Picture acquisition: Michaela Mohr/Michael Kraft

US edition produced by: APE Int'l, Richmond, VA
Translation from German: Dr. Maureen Basedow,
Editing of US edition: Tammi Reichel for APE Int'l

ISBN 978-1-4454-9023-6

Printed in China

Front cover images on folder and book cover L-R:

Row 1:
Australia,Northern Territories, Ayers Rock© Doug Armand/Getty Images; Akashi Kaikyo Bridge©/Getty Images; USA, Alaska, Alaskan Range, Aurora Borealis illuminate night sky© Johnny Johnson/Getty Images; Mayan ruins of Tikal by night© Sergio Pitamitz/Getty Images; Maldives, Baa Atoll, aerial view© Sakis Papadopoulos/Getty Images; Moai statue, Rapa Nui (Easter Island), Chile© Sergio Pitamitz/Getty Images; Sand dunes, rippled pattern on sand, Sahara© Hugh Sitton/Getty Images; Miyajima Otori Gate© Sean Pavone/Getty Images;

Row 2:
Saudi Arabia, Hejaz, Mecca, al Haram mosque, elevated view© Nabeel Turner/Getty Images; Abu Simbel, Egypt© Nicholas Pitt/Getty Images; Lava flow, Kilauea Volcano, Hawaii Volcanoes Nat. Park, Hawaii, USA© G. Brad Lewis/Getty Images; Terracotta Warriors, Tomb of Qin Shi Huang©Tom Till/Getty Images; Rapid City, South Dakota. South Dakota's famed Mount Rushmore National Monument©Joel Sartore/Getty Images; Khajuraho, India© MIXA Co. Ltd/Getty Images; Turkey, Cappadocia, Nemrut Dagi, statues and tombs© Laurent Parrault/Getty Images; Detail view of The Colosseum©Gary Yeowell/Getty Images;

Row 3:
The Öresund bridge©Ove Jansson/Getty Images; Tibet, Lhasa, Potala Palace, dawn© Michele Falzone/Getty Images; The Parthenon, Acropolis,Athens© Visions Of Our Land/Getty Images; Cambodia, Angkor, Siem Riep, Angkor Wat temple complex© John W Banagan/Getty Images; The palace of winds©Melinda Chan/Getty Images; The Alhambra© WillSelarep/Getty Images; Greece, Ellas-Evvoia, Delphi, Temple of Apollo© Steven W. Jones/Getty Images; Egypt, Cairo, Giza, Pyramids of Giza© Stephen Studd/Getty Images;

Row 4:
Egypt,Luxor,West Bank,Valley of the Kings,Temple of Hatshepsut©GavinHellier/Getty Images; Australia, New South Wales, Sydney, Opera House and Harbor Bridge© Robert Mort/Getty Images; California Redwoods© Ron and Patty Thomas Photography/Getty Images;View of Great Wall China©Grant Faint/Getty Images; Sea lion with young, Galapagos Islands©Steve Winter/Getty Images; Argentina,Patagonia,glacier Perito Moreno,two onlookers in foreground© Rhonda Klevansky/Getty Images; Wildebeest crossing the Serengeti at sunset© Alex Bramwell/Getty Images; Hoover Dam at night©All Rights Reserved C Tomgamache Com/Getty Images;

Row: 5:
France, Ile-de-France, Versaille, statue of Neptune and Palace© Stuart Dee/Getty Images; Great Barrier Reef© Grant Faint/Getty Images; LEANING TOWER OF PISA IN TUSCANY, ITALY© Paul Trummer/Getty Images; The Rio Negro river and the Rio Solimoes river joining to form the Amazon river, Brazil© Digital Vision/Getty Images; Giant's Causeway, Antrim, Northern Ireland,UK© Slow Images/Getty Images; Statue of Liberty ©Scott Dunn/Getty Images; Old Faithful In the Evening© Universal Stopping Point Photography/Getty Images; Taj Mahal,Agra, India© Tim Graham/Getty Images;

Row 6:
The Eiffel Tower from Ponte d'Iena© Martin Child/Getty Images; Low angle view at Empire State Building©Travelif/Getty Images; The Forbidden City©John Wang/Getty Images; Petronas Towers, Kuala Lumpur, Malaysia© Robert Harding/Getty Images; Machu Picchu© Rob Kroenert/Getty Images; Jordan, Petra, El Khazneh© Derek Richards/Getty Images; Falls Series© Hannes Steyn/Getty Images; Barcelona Sagrada Familia dawn light golden stone reflected Catalonia Spain© fotoVoyager/Getty Images;

Row 7:
View over Wailing Wall at Dome of the Rock© Neil Beer/Getty Images; Nankoweap Canyon, Marble Canyon, Colorado River, Grand Canyon National Park, Arizona© Ralph Lee Hopkins/Getty Images; Daily Life In Iraq During A Crisis©Scott Peterson/GettyImages; Stonehenge,aerial view©Image Hans Elbers/Getty Images; Golden Gate Bridge, San Francisco©Can Balcioglu/Getty Images; Rice terraces in Banaue, Phillipines©Dave Samboulis Travel Photography/Getty Images; Italy, Rome, Vatican city, St. Peter's Basilica© Jean-Pierre Lescourret/Getty Images; Japan, Honshu, Mount Fuji, Motosuko Lake© Gavin Hellier/Getty Images.

DVD front cover images. Top - Bottom:
Egypt, Cairo, Giza, Pyramids of Giza© Stephen Studd/Getty Images;
Machu Picchu© Rob Kroenert/Getty Images;
Lava flow, Kilauea Volcano, Hawaii Volcanoes Nat. Park, Hawaii, USA© G. Brad Lewis/Getty Images;
Detail view of The Colosseum©Gary Yeowell/Getty Images;
Statue of Liberty ©Scott Dunn/Getty Images;
USA, Alaska, Alaskan Range, Aurora Borealis illuminate night sky© Johnny Johnson/Getty Images;
View of Great Wall China©Grant Faint/Getty Images
Sand dunes, rippled pattern on sand, Sahara© Hugh Sitton/Getty Images;
Australia,Northern Territories, Ayers Rock©Doug Armand/Getty Images;

100 WONDERS of the World

From man-made masterpieces to breathtaking surprises of nature

MICHAEL HOFFMANN

ALEXANDER KRINGS

Parragon

Bath • New York • Singapore • Hong Kong • Cologne • Delhi
Melbourne • Amsterdam • Johannesburg • Shenzhen

Table of Contents

Foreword

What exactly is a "wonder"? According to encyclopedias and dictionaries, a wonder is something that defies the laws of nature, any event or series of events that is difficult to explain. Where religion is concerned, wonders are seen as testimonies of the power of faith and proof of the presence of divine forces in the world. It's not surprising that in many languages "wonder" also means "miracle".

In everyday use, wonders are often understood in a less philosophical, mythological or religious manner. At the most basic level, a wonder is simply something that astounds us, inspiring spontaneous applause or a gasp of disbelief. Wonders may be big, bigger and biggest, but their most defining characteristic is an unceasing ability to amaze.

There are wonderful things to be discovered all over our blue planet. Indeed, no part of the Earth is without its share of them. Our world is full of wonders because nature is a superb master builder, never ceasing to inspire and astound.

In addition, many outstanding artists and architects – human ones – have also left their mark on the world in the form of incomparable, wonderful buildings and structures. Although most of the natural wonders presented here are millions of years old, and some of the manmade variety were built less than a thousand years ago, both are nonetheless magnificent and worthy of our admiration.

This book presents 100 of the grandest, most beautiful and esteemed wonders from various parts of the world, every one of them among the sights most worth seeing on the planet. The final section looks at very special wonders – we could call them "global" – that don't fit easily within the standard geographical divisions. Even this superb collection is only a small sample representing a largely subjective point of view. What these wonders have in common is that they stand far above the commonplace and ordinary. In many cases, their unique, exceptional qualities are apparent at first glance, while in others, we need to look more closely to see what makes a wonder so special. Immerse yourself in the fantastic, magnificent world of wonders.

Africa was once known as the Dark Continent, both to Ancient Greeks and to nineteenth-century explorers. Its natural landscape bears witness to long-gone cultures and many unique civilizations. Africa is the last remaining natural paradise for animal and plant life, but also the site of man-made wonders representing the height of culture, the influence of which can be seen all over the world.

AFRICA

EGYPT

Abu Simbel

THE IMPRESSIVE TEMPLE OF ABU SIMBEL IS LOCATED SOME 175 MILES FROM ASWAN. PHARAOH RAMESES II, KNOWN AS RAMESES THE GREAT, COMMISSIONED THIS TEMPLE COMPLEX IN THE THIRTEENTH CENTURY BCE.

Pharaoh Rameses II – "the Great" – reigned from 1279 to 1213 BCE. His reign defines an economic and cultural golden age in the Land of the Nile, and no later pharaoh would match his achievements. Rameses governed his land with great skill leading to a period of nearly 50 years of peace between Egypt and its neighbours. The pharaoh was obsessed with leaving gigantic monuments in his image all over the land as a sign of his all-embracing power. It is easy to conclude that, in some sense, all of Egypt was simply refashioned into a grand monument of the god-king's making. One of the best examples of this is found beneath the first cataract of the Nile, where the two temples of Abu Simbel, carved out of a natural cliff face, surpass all earlier rock-cut temples in both size and importance. **Rameses II himself chose the site** for the temples, a place called Abu Simbel in Nubia. It was his desire that here, between the cataracts on the bank of the Nile, the very lifeline of Ancient Egypt, one more magnificent monument should be built to the greater glory of himself and in honour of his favourite wife, Nefertari. Thousands of workmen were commandeered for the project, fashioning this monument with the help of only the simplest bronze and stone tools. The temple was to be cut directly into the cliff

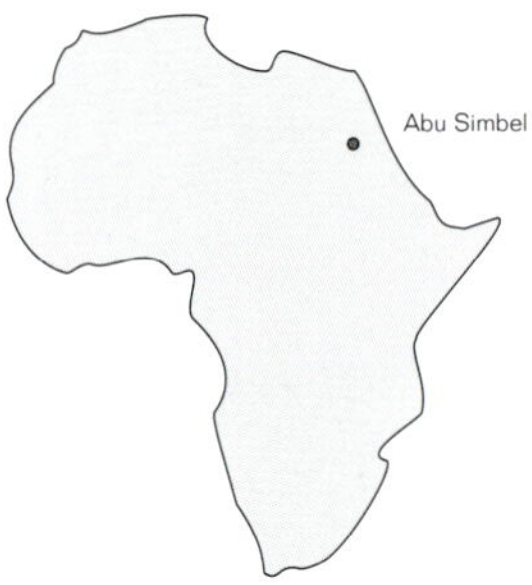

Right: The small temple of Abu Simbel is dedicated to Nefertari, favourite wife of Rameses II.

Below: The walls of the Rameses Temple is decorated with sculpted scenes from the pharaoh's life.

face, a unique plan of action, requiring the workmen to literally carve a building out of the stone. Inch by inch, they dug away, working their way slowly into the cliff. Thousands of tons of limestone had to be excavated as the workmen cut 60 metres into the mountain. Rameses II enthused about the super-human efforts of his workmen: "Oh workers, chosen ones, strong ones, with good hands, who build any number of monuments for me, who are experienced in working valuable stones, able to identify sources of granite and confident with sandstone."

Two colossal statues, 22 metres high, were carved on either side of the entrance, each representing Rameses II and inscribed with his various names and titles, one of which was "Beloved of Amon", the literal translation of Rameses, the most commonly used of his twelve royal names. The other statues refer to him as Son of Aton, Son of the King, Lord of the Two Lands, and the incarnation of the sun god, Re. The inner temple is entered through a massive tripartite hall lined by eight pillars. The relief sculpture in the great hall depicts the pharaoh's victorious military campaign against Syrians, Libyans and Hittites at the Battle of Kadesh. Four statues dominate the inner sanctuary, representing the gods Re-Harakhty, Ptah and Amon-Re alongside an image of the god-king Rameses II. This so-called "greater" temple is oriented so that twice a year, on the 20th day of October and February, the sun shines directly on these images.

Rameses II dedicated the smaller temple of Abu Simbel, built for his favourite wife, Nefertari, to the queen and the goddess Hathor of Ibshek. The smaller temple also had to be laboriously hewn from the limestone, extending 21 metres into the cliff. A passage lined with six pillars leads into a perpendicular hall with two side rooms and the sanctuary. The relief sculpture on the walls shows a coronation scene and various portrayals of Nefertari. The statues in the sanctuary, each some 10 metres high, are identified as Nefertari, Hathor and Rameses II. This is a special honour for the pharaoh's wife – her statue is the same size as that of the king! Typically, the king's consorts are depicted on a much smaller scale.

In the 1960s, when Abu Simbel was threatened by flooding due to construction of the Aswan Dam, an immense rescue project was launched. 20,000 tons of stone were sawed into 1,036 individual pieces so that the temples could be taken apart and reassembled on higher ground nearby. The work was completed in March 1968. The eternal home of Rameses II, the greatest Egyptian pharaoh, was preserved.

DATES

*** 1290–1224 BCE:** Abu Simbel was constructed.

*** 22 March 1813:** The temple was re-discovered by the Swiss orientalist Johann Ludwig Burckhardt (1784–1817).

*** 1817:** Abu Simbel was excavated for the first time.

*** 1960–71:** Construction of the Aswan Dam took place.

*** 1964–68:** The Abu Simbel temple complex was successfully relocated.

KENYA

Amboseli National Park

AMBOSELI IS A ONE-OF-A-KIND GAME RESERVE IN SOUTHERN KENYA. ONE OF THE OLDEST NATIONAL PARKS IN AFRICA, IT IS FAMOUS AROUND THE WORLD FOR ITS UNIQUE ELEPHANT POPULATION.

Amboseli National Park is the most visited of all wild animal reserves in Kenya. Originally allotted around 5,200 km² in 1948, the park was turned over to the local Masai people in 1961. Called "Park ol Tukai" in the Masai language, Amboseli spans a large variety of environments, including an extensive swamp that is particularly attractive to wild animals.

Today, the area of the national park has been reduced to around 650 km², but nevertheless remains an ideal place for a large number of wild species to live. Lying at an elevation of 1,400 to 1,900 metres above sea level and with the impressive scenery of Kilimanjaro serving as a backdrop, the Amboseli National Park at the foot of the "silver mountain" protects one of the last great natural treasures on Earth. Thanks to the Masai, who own most of the surrounding land, its unique population of elephants has survived to this day.

Known as the land of the gentle giants, Amboseli National Park is probably the best place in Kenya to get a close look at African elephants because the population inside the reserve has been able to maintain its age structure and generation lines free from outside influences for many years. This is extraordinarily rare. Most African national parks have

FACTS

✱ Name:
Amboseli National Park

✱ Amboseli National Park was founded in 1974.

✱ Area: It has a total area of 650 km².

✱ Country: Kenya

✱ Inhabitants of the national park: Its inhabitants include the Masai tribe, elephants and a large variety of animal species.

✱ Masai: The Masai are a nomadic pastoral people at home in the wide plains of southern Kenya and northern Tanzania, where their population approaches one million.

The "Silver Mountain" of Kilimanjaro reigns over the Amboseli and its inhabitants, including this small zebra herd. It is Africa's tallest mountain.

suffered through extended periods of poaching, practised regular culling or implemented long-distance relocation programmes in order to satisfy the demands of local agriculturalists who fear the intrusion of elephants into their fields. In Amboseli, the pastoral Masai keep a close watch on the park's borders, with the result that around 800 elephants of different generations have survived within its small herd, including aged cows and bulls as well as calves, teenagers and matriarchs. This permits the complex, diverse social behaviours of these gentle giants to be studied in context. The government of Kenya has devoted a great deal of effort to protecting the elephants, with gamekeepers and scientists watching over Amboseli Park all year round.

Lying in the shadow of Kilimanjaro, Amboseli is full of contrasts. Dry plains and parched savannah make up the greater part of the picture. During the extremes of the dry season, bizarre mirages appear over the dried-up Lake Amboseli. Entire villages float on the horizon, traversed by real herds of zebra and gnus. Only rarely will a hard rain fill the lake with water. The extensive swamp in the south of the park is fed almost entirely by underground streams.

In addition to elephants, Amboseli Park protects a wide range of wild species, and many other animals inhabit the reserve. Rhinoceros, Masai giraffe, gnus, zebras, hyena, jackals, cheetah, leopards and two gazelle species (Grant's and Thompson's) are at home on the savannah. In the drier parts, farther away from the swamp, live gemsboks, gerenuks and elands. The swamp itself is a virtual paradise for birds. Species that are otherwise rare in Kenya, such as pelicans and geese, gather in flocks on the open water. Kingfishers and bee-eaters lie in wait for prey in the reeds. Birds of prey include ospreys, martial eagles, grey-winged goshawks and dwarf falcons.

Above: A traditional Masai village in Amboseli National Park.

Left: Between tradition and modernity – a young Masai in traditional clothing observes elephants from behind the wheel of his jeep.

TUNISIA

El Djem

ONE OF THE LARGEST ARENAS OF THE ROMAN EMPIRE CAN BE FOUND IN THE MIDDLE OF THE TUNISIAN DESERT. THE AMPHITHEATRE OF THYSDRUS, AN ENORMOUS STRUCTURE, EMERGED OUT OF THE BARREN DESERT IN JUST EIGHT YEARS.

In 230 CE, the worthy Roman proconsul Gordianius I commissioned an amphitheatre in Thysdrus. Completed within just eight years, a structure of exceptional harmony rose dramatically from the desert floor. Bold in design and impressively monumental, Gordianus's master builder achieved something magnificent in the El Djem amphitheatre. This architectural masterpiece is completely freestanding, neither supported by a slope nor set in a depression. The reflection of the sun on its finely worked sandstone gives the amphitheatre an almost indescribable feeling of lightness, despite its great size.

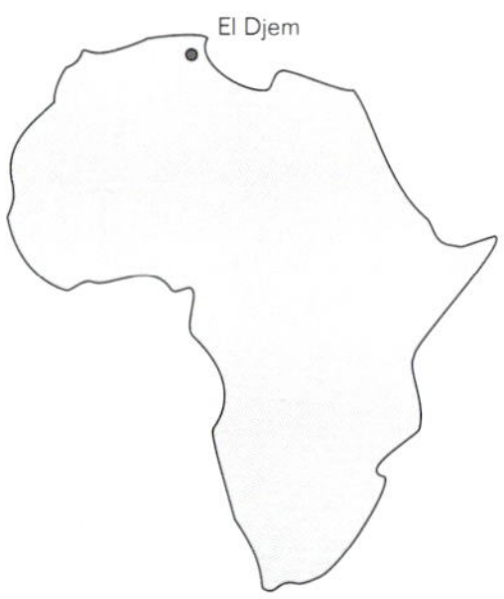

The architect designed the structure with an eye towards vistas observable both within the building and from within it looking to the distance. Light flows through the arena in all directions. Each level has 64 grand rounded arches, giving the building a highly filigreed appearance. The magnificent mosaics decorating the arena floors are unique masterpieces. At El Djem, local traditions and Roman building skills meet in a unique symbiosis.

The construction of the arena was an enormous undertaking. The necessary building materials, in particular the massive sandstone blocks, had to be transported to the site from quarries as far as 30 km away. Since sandstone is soft and friable,

Chariot races and gladiatorial bouts were held inside the arena.

FACTS

✻ Size: The amphitheatre is approximately 150 m long, 120 m wide, and is three storeys tall (about 36 m high).

✻ Building time: It was built over a period of eight years (230 – 238 CE)

✻ Building material: Local sandstone was the primary material used.

DATES

✻ 46 BCE: Thysdrus was founded.

✻ *circa.* 230 CE: Construction on the amphitheatre began.

✻ 238: A revolt was put down by troops of the Thracian-born Roman emperor Maximus Thrax (173 – 238)

✻ 7th century: The amphitheatre was rebuilt as a fortification by the Berber chieftain Damia Kahina during her fight against the Arabs.

✻ 1695: The structure is partially destroyed when Mohammed Bey breaches the outer wall using explosives.

Centre: The rooms and passageways of the amphitheatre are decorated with magnificent mosaics.

Bottom: The 64 rounded arches per storey give the structure a filigree appearance.

blocks have to be extraordinarily large if they are to function as weight-bearing elements. The monumental sandstones of El Djem have survived to this day. Their warm, earthy colour absorbs the sunlight directly until they seem to glow with its warmth, giving the building a fantastic radiance that can be observed and enjoyed today, much as it was nearly 2,000 years ago.

The amphitheatre of Thysdrus was the last great arena built by a Roman Empire that was already in decline. It remains a magnificent architectural monument, fascinating due to its exceptional quality and elegant, nearly perfect harmony of forms. Marked by centuries of wind and weather etching their deep traces, the sandstone blocks of Thysdrus have survived to tell their story.

Although the amphitheatre is located far away from the sea and well off the track of all the important trade routes, financing its construction was not at all problematic. The funds came from the production and trade of olive oil. The North African coastal plain had been the olive grove of the Roman Empire since the time of Julius Caesar, and olives had been cultivated here for well over two centuries. This barren land was, paradoxically, the most important supplier of olive oil in the entire Roman world. Profits from the olive-oil trade transformed Thysdrus into a boomtown, and the economic upswing led to extraordinary prosperity. The city's inhabitants were bursting with pride and ambition. The outstanding achievement of the amphitheatre is nothing less than a declaration of independence made manifest in stone.

In the year 238, the province of Thysdrus stood at the height of its power. Self-assured and perhaps a little foolhardy, it rose up against the Roman Empire, only to have the rebellion violently suppressed when inflexible Rome struck back. Within a few years, the culture of the once splendid city of Thysdrus had come to an end. At the end of the seventeenth century, troops led by the Turkish conqueror Mohammed Bey blew up a large part of the arena, with the ruins becoming quarries for later generations. What remains is the mythus of the games that lives on, set in stone as part of the mosaics, and the ruins of the amphitheatre itself, bearing witness to the pride, passion and pugnacity that once marked Thysdrus as one of Ancient Africa's cultural centres.

MOROCCO

Fez

THE OLD CITY OF FEZ CONSISTS OF A BARELY NAVIGABLE LABYRINTH OF STREETS AND NARROW LANES LINED WITH HOUSES, SQUARES AND SPLENDID MOSQUES. IN FEZ, VISITORS ARE ENVELOPED IN AN ATMOSPHERE OF ENTICING SCENTS AND EXOTIC PLAYS OF COLOUR.

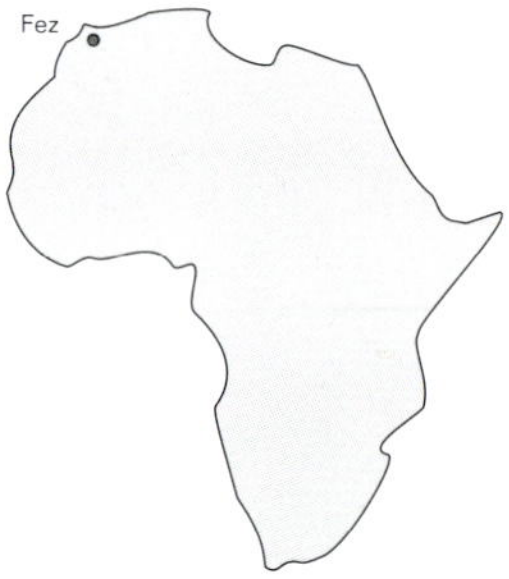

Once upon a time, nearly 1,200 years ago, Idriss I had to flee the henchmen of Harun al Rashid, the Caliph of Baghdad. His escape route led him to a river called the Fez. Here he settled and, feeling safe from his pursuers, made plans to found a city. But Allah did not hear his prayers for peace and tranquillity. The great caliph's murdering minions finally discovered Idriss's whereabouts and assassinated him. During the time he was fleeing from his murderers, however, Idriss had fathered a son, one who would be born only after Idriss's death and whose life would be spared. This was Idriss II who, boldly following in his father's footsteps, founded the city of Fez.

A fervent follower of Islam, he honoured the prophet Mohammed, praising and praying to Allah for guidance, and Allah heard his prayers. The site Idriss II chose for his city on the banks of the Fez was fortuitous. Reports of the glorious city were soon spread far and wide in songs and poems. By 817/818, a great many believers had moved to Fez to work, to pray and to share in its prosperity. In this way, 2,000 families exiled from Cairo and living in Tunisia made their way to Fez. Within a few years they built a magnificent place of worship, the Kairouyine ("Cairo") mosque, in the heart of the city. Fez quickly became

Right: The Kairouyine Mosque in Fez el-Bali, the Old City.

Below: A tannery in the heart of the Old City of Fez.

the cultural centre and religious heart of Morocco. Yet the newcomers were more than fervent believers. They also brought their technical and economic skills to the young, up-and-coming city. Its favourable location at the crossroads of important trade routes and easy access to the necessary raw materials encouraged the new city's swift rise to prominence.

The city of Idriss II grew into the most important city in Morocco. Its reputation as a centre of prosperity and bastion of the orthodox faith, a reputation it would maintain many years after Idriss's death, spread throughout the Islamic world. In the eleventh century, however, Fez was surpassed by Marrakesh, which held on to its primacy until 1250. At the beginning of the fourteenth century, Fez experienced a renewed upswing in its fortunes, with its world-famous university and its scholars accorded particular respect. During this time, the city was home to nearly 800 mosques. Then, in 1522, a horrific earthquake destroyed a large part of the city. Within a few years of the catastrophe, its many buildings were either restored or replaced by new ones, and the city shone once again with its old brilliance. To the inestimable benefit of all who visit and wonder at its beauty today, Fez would change little over the following centuries.

In 1554, Fez came into the hands of the Saadier family, who chose to rule from Marrakesh. From this point on Fez would change rulers many times as several dynasties competed for control of the Mahgreb. In 1833, Mulai Abdallah declared Fez the capital city once again. After invasion by France, Fez became part of the French protectorate on 30 March 1912. In many ways, this changed very little in Fez, which essentially remained what it had long been: a royal residence and centre of culture, faith, trade and business.

Fez has a great many magnificent mosques whose architectural and aesthetic qualities are internationally famous. Its Islamic art treasures are world-class. Visitors should be aware, however, that non-believers are still forbidden to enter the mosques of Fez. This has nothing to do with a restrictive reading of the Koran by Moroccan Moslems, nor with any particular religious prejudice. Quite the opposite: a French colonial law, still on the books, prohibits non-Moslems entering Islamic religious buildings. While Fez today is a modern city, it remains the cultural and spiritual capital of Morocco, with its markets flourishing and traditions intact. The legacy of Idriss II has been preserved, still shining in the twenty-first century with its age-old lustre.

FACTS

* **Name:** Fez
* **Population:** Fez, third-largest city in Morocco, has almost 1 million inhabitants, 99% of whom are Moslem.
* **Unique:** Fez has more mosques and Koran schools than any other city in Morocco.
* **Etymology:** The name "Fez" is thought to go back to the Arabic word for 'hoe' or 'pick'. According to legend, Idriss II used a tool like this during the ground-breaking ceremony marking the founding of the city.
* **The fez hat,** also known as a 'tarbush', is a blunted cone made of red felt with a black tassel. It was once the widespread headgear of choice in the Orient and Balkans. It was named after the city of Fez, where it was thought to have originated.

TANZANIA

Kilimanjaro

THE KILIMANJARO MASSIF IS ALWAYS A MAGNIFICENT SIGHT, EVEN WHEN ITS SUMMIT IS SHROUDED IN CLOUDS. KNOWN AS THE "SILVER MOUNTAIN", KILIMANJARO IS THE TALLEST FREESTANDING MOUNTAIN IN THE WORLD.

A famous short story written by Ernest Hemingway in 1952 is entitled "The Snows of Kilimanjaro", and indeed, the summit of the mountainous massif is covered year-round with snow, rising majestically above the East African plain between Tanzania and Kenya. About a hundred years earlier, in 1849, German missionary Johannes Rebmann was laughed at when he returned to Europe with reports of a giant, snow-covered mountain in the heart of the African savannah. Rebmann had not lost his mind, however. He was simply the first European to see, with his own eyes, what for nineteenth-century scientists was simply inconceivable: a region of permanent ice and snow cover in central Africa, right next to the equator.

In 1973, Kilimanjaro National Park was founded to better protect the natural monument and preserve it for future generations. The national park includes the Kilimanjaro massif, with its three mighty volcanic peaks. At 5,895 metres, the Kibo peak is the highest elevation on the African continent; the others are Shira (3,692 metres) and Mawenzi (5,149 metres). The park also includes six forest tracts with a total area of around 750 km^2 surrounded by a protected forest area of 930 km^2.

FACTS

✻ Name: Kilimanjaro

✻ Status: Kilimanjaro is categorized as a volcanic massif.

✻ Peaks: Its three summits are Kibo, at 5,895 m (the highest mountain on the continent); Shira, at 3,962 m; and Mawenzi at 5,149 m.

✻ Area: The area of the national park is 1,700 km².

✻ Discovery: Kilimanjaro may have first been mentioned around 100 CE by the astronomer and geographer Ptolemy.

✻ First climbed: The Leipzig geographer Dr Hans Meyer and Austrian alpinist Ludwig Purtscheller were the first to reach the 5,895-m-high Kibo summit on 6 October 1889.

✻ First ski descent: In 1912, following their third summit of the mountain, climbers Walther Furtwangler and Siegfried Konig skied down the Kibo summit at breakneck speed.

The steep Mawenzi peak of Kilimanjaro. In the foreground lies the so-called saddle, the largest tundra plain in Africa.

The predominant vegetation zones around Kilimanjaro's volcanic cone are mountain forest, upland moor and alpine tundra. Precipitation varies quite a lot by elevation, with an average of 300 mm per year in the rainforest zone, and as little as 100 mm a year near the summit. The savannah has an average temperature of 30 °C, while at the summit the average temperature is close to the freezing point, at 0 °C.

Differences in elevation also determine the types of vegetation found there. From 900 metres to 1,800 metres, fertile volcanic soil sustains the growth of trees and shrubs. From 1,800 to 2,800 metres, a mountain rainforest takes over, with fig, yew and juniper trees that can grow up to 40 metres tall. Above 2,800 metres up to 5,000 metres, there is prairie-like vegetation, including flowers such as the anemone, lily, Kenya thistle and 3-metre-tall lobelia. At around 5,000 metres, the high desert ecosystem begins. At these elevations, the air is so thin that only lichens and a particularly hardy variety of straw flower can survive. A wide variety of animal species also live in the mountainous world of Kilimanjaro National Park. Elephants, lions, leopards, hyenas, warthogs, herons, storks and coots find it a comfortable place to retreat.

But the bitter truth is now upon us! Kibo glacier is melting, and very quickly at that. Since 1972 alone, the ice cap has lost almost 95 per cent of its mass. Scientists predict that by the year 2020, there will be no more ice on the peak of Kilimanjaro, with unavoidable consequences for the climate of the region. The effects of global warming seem to be stronger and swifter-acting here and, for Kilimanjaro at least, are very likely irreversible. The silver of the mountain is changing into water. Will Kilimanjaro be a "paradise lost"?

Above: two world-famous symbols of Africa: the snow-covered peak of Kilimanjaro and a mighty elephant.

Left: View of the Kibo volcanic peak, at 5,895 m. Kibo is said to have last erupted in 1600, which is why it is not yet certain if the volcano is truly extinct.

MOROCCO

Marrakech

THE RED CITY OF MARRAKECH IS LIKE NO OTHER AFRICAN CITY. THIS IS TRULY THE PLACE WHERE EAST MEETS WEST, WHERE THE ORIENT AND THE OCCIDENT CAN BE FOUND SIDE BY SIDE WITH ONE ANOTHER.

Marrakech, founded in the year 1062 by the Berber Almoravids, is considered the most beautiful city in Morocco. The Medina, its world-famous Old City, reverberates with the rhythm of North Africa while perpetuating the history and culture of the Berbers and desert nomads.

It is hot in the city, almost unbearably so. Traders, businessmen, housewives and market women all take care of their business in the Old-City marketplace as early in the day as possible, before the Muezzin's first call to prayer, after which the city seems to fall into a state of lethargy. The people retreat to the shadows of the narrow alleys of the souk, to the artisan and business quarters of the city, and to the shelter of their houses. Only in the cool of the evening, just as twilight begins, will the streets and squares of the Old City reawaken to its usual, effervescent life.

The colourful performance that is daily life in Marrakech begins in the centre of the Old City, in the Djemaa el-Fna, the "place of the executed", where heads were still being chopped off and displayed on spikes early in the twentieth century. Tradesmen hawk their wares as artists, magicians, acrobats, dancers, snake charmers, storytellers and musicians transform the large open space into an

The 77-m-high minaret of the Koutoubia Mosque is the architectural emblem of Marrakech. Visible from afar, it presides over the whirling bustle of the Medina.

DATES

✻ *circa* 1061–62: Marrakech was founded.

✻ 1147: Marrakech was conquered by the Almohads.

✻ 1153–90: The Koutoubia Mosque was built.

✻ 1269: Marrakech was conquered by the Merinids.

✻ 14th century: Medersa Ben Youssouf, the greatest Koran school in North Africa, was founded.

✻ 1912: French troops entered the city.

✻ 1912–56: Morocco was a colony of France.

✻ 1956: Morocco gained its independence.

✻ 1985: Marrakech's Old City was designated a UNESCO World Heritage Site.

✻ 1998: Restoration of the Koutoubia Mosque was completed.

arena devoted to their art and performances. Tourists stroll across the Djemaa el-Fna and enjoy the many restaurants lining the plaza. The stalls of the herb, vegetable and fruit dealers lure both customers and passers-by, attracted by the sumptuous, colourful, exotic displays as well as by the hubbub of shouted conversations and bargaining with the merchants. The heavy, sweet smell of the Orient fills the air. An aura of A Thousand and One Nights lingers in the picturesque Old City of Marrakech.

The Medina souk branches off from the Djemaa el-Fna in a series of winding, narrow lanes. In this confusion of alleys, all possible wares and products are offered for sale – most hawked at a high volume. Blacksmiths ply their trade in their workshops with tailors, shoemakers and saddlers right next door. In the dye-makers quarter, brightly coloured bolts of cloth are hung out everywhere over the narrow streets, while coppersmiths provide percussive background music, hammering out all manner of the craftsman's art.

The Koutoubia ("librarian") Mosque is found near what was once the souk of the booksellers, whose shops stood here in a long row, giving both mosque and minaret their names. This beacon of Marrakech, with its 77-metre-tall minaret, was built during the reign of the Almohad caliphs in the year 1157. The prayer hall of the seventeen-aisled mosque is almost 90 metres long and 60 metres wide. Up to 25,000 of the faithful crowd into the rooms of the mosque for Friday prayers. The minaret, completed in 1198 and visible from a great distance, rises like a cliff out of the sea of houses in the Old City. The tower is considered to be the finest of all the famous Almohad minarets found throughout North Africa and the Iberian Peninsula.

A series of small, winding lanes lead to the Ben-Youssouf Mosque and its school, the Medersa. The Almoravid founders of the city built the mosque in the eleventh century, but its current form and appearance date to the sixteenth and nineteenth centuries. Only believers can enter the mosque, but non-Moslems are welcome in the Koran school. The Medersa was founded in the fourteenth century and quickly developed into the most important Koran school in all of North Africa. During the period of its greatest popularity, as many as 900 students studied Islamic law and theology here.

Centre: The Djema el-Fna, or "Place of the Executed", is the central plaza in the old centre of the royal city.

Bottom: This sumptuous courtyard belongs to the Medersa Ben Youssouf. Founded in the 14th century, the Koran school is a jewel of sacred architecture.

EGYPT

The Pyramids of Giza

OF THE SEVEN WONDERS OF THE ANCIENT WORLD, THE PYRAMIDS OF GIZA ARE THE ONLY ONES STILL IN EXISTENCE, AND THEY ARE AMONG THE OLDEST MAN-MADE STRUCTURES. MYSTERIES AND LEGENDS CONTINUE TO SWIRL AROUND THE ENORMOUS MONUMENTS.

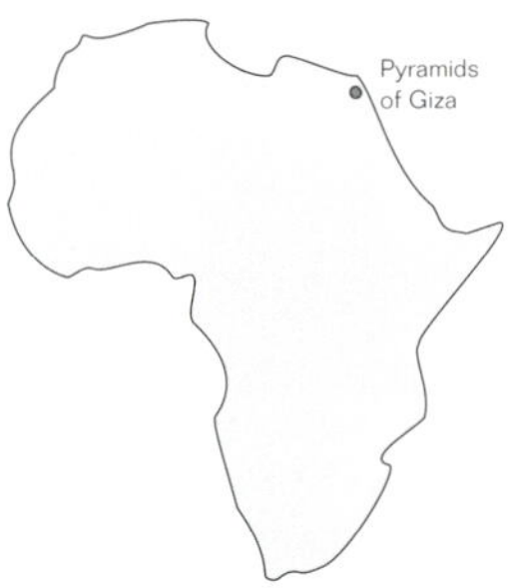

Egypt was unified into one kingdom around 2900 BCE. The rulers, the pharaohs, chose the Nile delta city of Memphis as their first capital. Pyramid building began during the Old Kingdom, reaching its peak with the construction of the pyramids of Giza. The product of an epoch of magnificence, these inaccessible structures symbolized the supreme position of the god-king pharaohs.

The largest and best known of the pyramids is the one belonging to Pharaoh Khufu (Greek: Cheops), who reigned from 2589 to 2566 BCE. The pyramid was originally clad in polished white limestone panels, of which only a few fragments survive today. The rest were broken off to build houses in Cairo.

The second of the three pyramids, the one in the middle, carries the name of Cheops' son, Chephren, who reigned from 2558 to 2532 BCE. The Chephren Pyramid appears taller than the Cheops Pyramid because its base lies 10 metres higher. It is in fact close to the Great Pyramid's height, only 3 metres shorter. The smallest of the pyramids belongs to Pharaoh Mycerinus, the son of Chephren and grandson of Cheops, who reigned from 2532 to 2503 BCE.

The Pyramid of Cheops is also known as the "Great Pyramid". It was originally 146.5 metres tall, but since 1168 has measured around 137 metres: its

FACTS

✻ The Cheops or Great Pyramid was built 2589–2566 BCE.

✻ Height: Originally 146.5 m, it is now around 137 m tall.

✻ Size and angle: Each side is 230 m long; its base area is 52,900 m². The area of each side is 20,000 m². Its angle of inclination is 51° 52' and it weighs 6.25 million tons.

✻ The Pyramid of Chephren was built 2558–2532 BCE.

✻ Height: It is 143.5 m tall, with each side measuring 215 m in length.

✻ Size and angle: Its base has an area of 46,200 m², with a slope of 52° 20'.

✻ The Pyramid of Mycerinus was built 2532–2503 BCE.

✻ Height: It is 62 m tall; each side is 108 m long.

✻ Size and angle: The area of its base is 11,600 m² with a slope of 51°.

Guarded by the Great Sphinx, the Pyramid of Chephren stands literally and figuratively in the shadow of the Great Pyramid.

limestone blocks and cladding were carried off as material for the rebuilding of the city following a great fire in Cairo. Each side of the Cheops Pyramid is 230 metres long. Its base covers 52,900 m², an area so immense that the five largest churches in the world – St. Peter's in Rome, St. Paul's in London, Westminster Abbey, the Duomo in Florence and Mainz Cathedral – could all fit within the space!

Around 2.5 million blocks of stone weighing between 2.5 and 3 tons were stacked up to build the Cheops Pyramid, bringing its weight to 6.25 million tons. The preparation and levelling of the building site alone took ten years and the labour of some 4,000 men. The construction of the pyramid itself involved at least 100,000 workers and took an additional 20 years. Since pyramid construction seems to have taken place primarily during the three-month-long, annual inundation of the Nile, when all agricultural land was covered in water, there was an ample work force available to build monuments to the pharaohs whose very existence, it was believed, made the life-giving flood possible. The individual blocks of stone were between 0.8 and 1.45 metres high, with eight workmen assigned to each block. They hauled each block out of the quarry, heaved it onto a wooden sled and transported it over a log-paved road to the bank of the Nile. There they loaded "their" block onto a bark, conveyed it to the other side and then further to the building site. They then heaved the stone block again, this time up a ramp leading to its designated position in the pyramid.

The interior of the Pyramid of Cheops is marked by a labyrinth-like system of passages and chambers, with the king's chamber located in the centre. A red granite sarcophagus was found here. Whether the pyramid was really used as a burial place remains one of the Great Pyramid's unresolved mysteries.

Above: The Pyramid of Chephren seems to be taller than that of Cheops, but is in fact 3 m shorter.

Left: The Cheops or "Great" Pyramid was originally completely covered in blindingly white limestone cladding. Most of the stone panels were broken off in 1168 to be used as building material.

SUDAN

The Pyramids of Meroë

THE MEROË PYRAMIDS LIE AROUND 200 METRES NORTH-EAST OF KHARTOUM. FOR 700 YEARS, MEROË WAS THE CAPITAL OF THE KINGDOM OF KUSH. FROM THE TIME OF THE MIDDLE KINGDOM ON, "KUSH" IS THE NAME THE EGYPTIANS USED FOR NUBIA.

The Nubian kingdom, also known as the Kingdom of Kush, extended along the Nile from Aswan in Egypt down to Karima (Ancient Kerma) in the Sudan. The first Nubian kings ruled from their capital city of Napata, near the modern town of Karima. In the year 300 BCE, they moved their capital to Meroë. In the following years, their prosperity and self-confidence grew steadily as their cultural dependence on Egypt declined. Around 150 BCE, the Nubians developed and used their own script, independent of Egyptian hieroglyphs, using a Meroitic language that still has not been deciphered entirely. It is from this remarkable phase of Nubian history, contemporary with the 25th dynasty, that we have the 50-plus pyramids known from the necropolis of Meroë.

What is called the Meroitic period began with the transfer of the Nubian capital and royal seat to Meroë. Deceased kings were buried there, beginning with the reign of King Ergamene (*circa*. 270 BCE). Over time, the new capital became home to two separate cemeteries with very steep-sided pyramids. In the Meroitic period alone, over 40 Nubian kings and queens were interred here. Ergamenes' own remains were placed in the first pyramid, and others were

Right: The steep angle of the pyramids seems to be related to their construction method.

Below: The pyramids consist of three parts: the pyramid; the mortuary temple; and the burial chambers.

reserved as grave monuments for wealthy nobles – many of whom, though not all, were members of the extended royal family. In the Kingdom of Kush, in contrast to Old Kingdom Egypt, pyramid graves were not a right reserved solely for the ruler's family. Other worthy members of society could also take part in the custom.

The Meroë pyramids, notably smaller than those in Egypt, consist of three elements: the pyramid itself, built initially from stone and later from burnt mud bricks; the mortuary temple, built in front of the entrance to the pyramid and elaborately decorated with relief sculpture; and last, but not least, the burial chamber itself, which lay underneath the pyramid because the small size and corresponding lack of interior space inside the Meroitic pyramids did not leave enough room for burial chambers inside. Kings were provided with three burial chambers, their queens with two.

It is likely that the model for the Meroitic pyramids was not the Old Kingdom pharaonic pyramid of Ancient Egypt. Their steep angle of ascent and density within the cemeteries, where they are sited much closer to one other than in Giza, suggest that they are modelled on the much later private pyramids built around Thebes during the New Kingdom. The steep angles had a technical source as well. The building masters of Kush made much use of the 'shaduf', a type of crane developed from an ancient device used to haul water from the Nile. We know this because one was sketched on a section of wall found in the Meroë cemetery. The length of the boom of this construction crane limited the base length of the pyramid's sides, which led to a correspondingly steep pyramid.

In the years 25 and 24 BCE, the Kingdom of Kush found itself in military conflict with Rome. The troops of Emperor Augustus attacked the former capital city of Napata, destroying it and carrying off most of its wealth. But the Nubians did eventually succeed in driving the Romans back, and the following years were another golden age for Kush. Its magnificent cultural resources and intensive trade with Egypt and Arabia enabled the kingdom in Meroë to once again achieve historic levels of power, influence and greatness.

In the first and second centuries CE, however, the decline of the Kushite Kingdom began in earnest. The reasons for its fall remain unknown to this day. The last Meroitic king is mentioned in 300 CE, after which every trace of this once mighty kingdom and its rulers in Meroë is lost.

DATES

* **1000–750 BCE:** The Kushite state was founded.
* ***circa* 700 BCE:** Nubia gained its independence from Egypt.
* ***circa* 300 BCE:** The capital was moved from Napata to Meroë.
* ***circa* 270 BCE:** The reign of Kind Ergamenes began.
* **150 BCE:** Roman troops attacked the Kingdom of Kush.
* **First and second centuries CE:** A new golden age for the kingdom.
* ***circa* 300:** Decline and fall of the Kingdom of Kush.

NORTH AFRICA

The Sahara

FASCINATING, DANGEROUS, INHOSPITABLE, BEAUTIFUL, UNIQUE AND IMMENSE – ONE COULD CONTINUE THIS LIST OF ADJECTIVES FOREVER AND YET NEVER QUITE SUCCEED IN DEFINITIVELY CHARACTERIZING "THE GREAT DESERT".

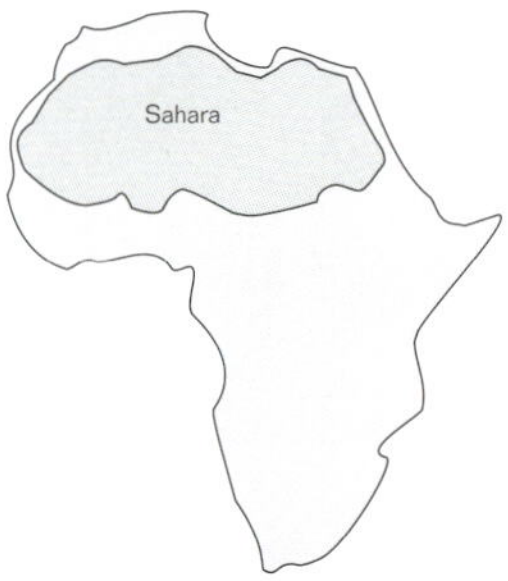

The largest desert on Earth lies east of the Atlantic, west of the Red Sea and Sinai Peninsula, south of the Atlas Mountains and, Mediterranean and finally, north of the Sahel and Niger River basin. It has been the scene of countless military conflicts, dramas and tragedies played out in its vast open spaces and rocky mountain ranges. In more recent times the desert has served as the backdrop for outstanding athletic achievements and opulent Hollywood productions. It is a focal point for all that is fascinating, a heritage belonging to all humanity.

Extending nearly 6,000 km from east to west and around 2,000 km north to south, the Sahara covers an area of more than 9 million km^2, one-third the area of the African continent. Most of the Sahara is stone, rock and gravel desert; only a very small part is actually sand, and in fact, fertile oases occupy more than 200,000 km^2. The driest part of the "waterless sea", which is what Arabs call the Sahara (in Arabic: *bahr bela ma*), is the Libyan Desert. There, the Qattara Depression at 133 metres below sea level is the lowest elevation of the Sahara and on the African continent. The highest part is the Ahaggar Massif, with its highest peaks the Erni Koussi (3,415 metres) and the Tahat (3,003 metres).

Right: The oasis of the Um-Al-Ma salt lake in the Libyan Desert.

Below: The Ahaggar Massif is a series of precipitous rock formations nearly 3,400 m high.

The Sahara extends across the borders of 11 countries: Morocco, Algeria, Tunisia, Libya, Egypt, West Sahara, Mali, Mauritania, Niger, Chad and the Sudan. The borders of the Sahara, however, cannot be clearly defined, for this is a desert on the move. Climate change and the effect of intensive agricultural exploitation, such as overgrazing of the sensitive desert ecosystem, has led to the desert's expansion, clearly observable over the course of the last millennium. As a result of this process, which is called "desertification", the Sahara has grown over an area as large as the country of Somalia in just the last 50 years. Borderlands that were once fertile farmland and semi-arid pasture are now barren and desiccated.

Despite highly adverse conditions, a flourishing and lucrative trans-Sahara trade was already well established around 1000 BCE. At that time, intrepid caravans leading oxen, carts and two-wheeled chariots regularly crossed the desert. In the third century BCE, the Cartheginians boosted the Sahara trade. Three hundred years later there was an even greater boom after the Romans succeeded in taming the wild camel so that it could be used as a beast of burden. As of the eighth century CE, the increasingly influential Arabs further emphasized the importance of the Sahara trade, which reached its highest level between the thirteenth and sixteenth centuries. During that time, the Sahara was criss-crossed by a network of trade routes and caravan paths linking the desert regions of the north with the central African economic centres. Despite all this trade activity, areas under Arab influence were not enhanced with a string of fortified trade sites. It may be that the sheer inhospitableness of the Sahara made such accommodations unnecessary. Raids on caravans, while they did occur, were a perilous enterprise in this harsh environment.

The air of A Thousand and One Nights wafts over the dunes and oases of the "Great Desert". The Mediterranean regions lusted after precious metals, chiefly gold, but also needed a source of cheap labour, making the slave trade during this period every bit as profitable as it was gruesome. Caravans brought salt, cowry shells (an important currency) and, then as now, weapons back to the south. The caravans also conveyed luxury products: the finest cloth, pepper, ivory, cola nuts, leather products and – especially valued in the nineteenth century – ostrich feathers for the couturiers and stylish salons of Europe. The end of the flourishing Sahara trade through the desert came with the arrival in West Africa of Europeans with imperialist ambitions.

FACTS

* **Name:** Sahara

* **Maximum extent:** The Sahara's maximum length is about 6,000 km east to west and about 2,000 km north to south.

* **Area:** With an area of over 9 million km^2, it covers nearly one-third of the African continent.

* **Saharan countries:** Countries within the Sahara include Morocco, Algeria, Libya, Tunisia, Egypt, West Sahara, Mauritania, Mali, Niger, Chad and the Sudan.

* **Etymology:** The name 'Sahara' comes from the Arabic word *sahra*, which is a translation of the Tuareg *tenere* (= desert, sand). The Romans called it *terra deserta* (empty, abandoned land). In the Middle Ages it was known simply as the Great Desert. The name Sahara came into general use only in the 19th century. Arabs, rather poetically, call it the "waterless sea" (*bahr bela ma*).

TANZANIA

Serengeti National Park

THE VERY NAME OF THIS PARK IS A SYNONYM FOR UNDISTURBED NATURE – ONE OF THE LAST NATURAL PARADISES. MANY PEOPLE WILL IMMEDIATELY THINK OF THE MANY FAMOUS WILDLIFE DOCUMENTARIES FILMED WITHIN ITS BORDERS.

In the language of the Masai, *Serengeti* means "wide land". This park is a one-of-a-kind natural paradise governed by the rhythm of the wet and dry seasons. The southern part of the Serengeti is covered with grassy savannah stretching to the horizon. The centre of this great plain is almost devoid of trees, while the south-eastern part of the park is dominated by the crater landscape of the Ngorono Conservation Area. With an area of 14,763 km², the Serengeti is one of the largest national parks in the world.

The wealth of species in the Serengeti is truly magnificent. A veritable Noah's Ark of animals wanders by, especially in the areas around the few waterholes. Wildebeest, zebras, giraffes, gazelles, antelope and elephants push and shove their way to the banks to gain access to the water. The numerous predators – lions, leopards, cheetahs, jackels and hyenas – are also drawn to the life-saving moisture. And then there are the birds. The richness of bird life around the waterholes is almost impossible to describe. Over 500 species of birds have been identified so far in the Serengeti. The nearly treeless plain is the preferred grazing territory for millions of herbivores, including gnus, gazelles, antelopes and zebras, but the predators are here as well, lying in wait. Some 3,000 lions

Serengeti National Park in Tanzania is a paradise for countless animal species. Around a million wildebeest roam through the savannah in the course of their wide-ranging wanderings.

FACTS

✻ Name: Serengeti National Park

✻ Area: The Sergengeti covers an area of 14,763 km^2.

✻ Status: It is the largest protected game and nature reserve in Africa

✻ Population: It is populated by around 1 million wildebeest, 7,000 giraffes, 150,000 Thompson's gazelles, more than 1,000 elephants, around 3,000 lions, over 500 different kinds of birds, as well as a great many other animal species.

✻ Highest elevation: The highest elevation in the Serengeti is the Ngorongoro Crater at 2,300 m above sea level. The diameter of the Crater is nearly 27 km.

✻ Unique: Olduvai Gorge, where Louis and Mary Leakey discovered some of the earliest remains of human-like primates, is at the eastern edge of the Serengeti Plain.

live in the Serengeti, partaking of the rich table nature sets for them.

But even the lion has some competition. Cheetahs bring down their prey after wild chases over great distances, runs in which they can reach speeds of up to 100 km per hour. In the thick-grass savannah, leopards lie in wait for victims. These elegant big cats were once mercilessly hunted, almost to the point of extinction, for their magnificent pelts. Thanks to the rigorous protection measures now in place in the Serengeti, their population has recovered.

Whatever the big cats leave behind after a meal is quickly taken care of by the scavengers: hyenas, jackals and vultures fight over the carcasses. Scavengers play an important role in the ecosystem. They are the "sanitation workers" of the Serengeti, taking care of the garbage.

Enormous hippopotami romp in the waterholes and ponds that dot the "wide plain". They spend the entire day in the water as protection from the burning rays of the sun, because hippo skin is extremely sensitive and easily sunburned. At night, they leave the water in search of food. These gourmands have been known to travel as far as 10 km in search of a delectable meadow in which to graze.

The rhinoceros is one of the most endangered animals in the national park. Illegal hunting and poaching – their horns are a costly aphrodisiac in many cultures – has greatly reduced their population.

Still, it is the elephant that reigns, undisputedly, over the Serengeti. One thousand of these normally quite gentle giants wander through the savannah and hills of the Serengeti in family groups, looking for food. The appetite of these giant herbivores is correspondingly enormous: a full-grown elephant devours as much as half a ton of vegetation per day.

During Tanzania's economic crisis of the 1870s, Serengeti National Park also suffered terribly. Desperate poachers were willing to take extreme risks to secure their victims. Illegal hunting of elephants for their ivory tusks decimated the population until only around 100 animals remained. The situation was even worse for the rhinoceros, brought close to extinction with only two animals surviving the slaughter. Since then, Serengeti National Park has profited from the economic upswing that began in the 1980s. The elephant and rhinoceros populations have been able to recover to sustainable levels.

Centre: The Ngorongoro Crater after the great rains. On account of its unique flora and fauna, UNESCO declared the Serengeti National Park a World Heritage Site in 1979.

Bottom: Not without reason, Serengeti means "wide land" in the language of the Masai.

EGYPT

The Suez Canal

EXTENDING FROM THE MEDITERRANEAN HARBOUR CITY OF PORT SAID SOUTHWARD TO SUEZ ON THE RED SEA, THE SUEZ CANAL IS ONE OF THE MOST REMARKABLE WATERWAYS IN THE WORLD.

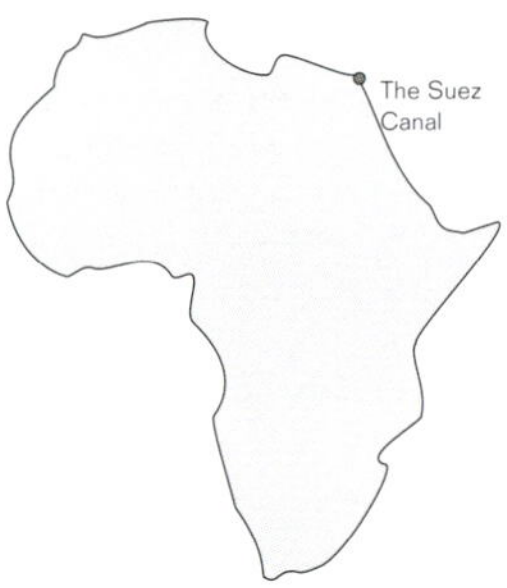

Well before the birth of Christ, Egyptian rulers had the idea of digging a canal that would connect the Mediterranean to the Red Sea. Nevertheless, it was not until the seventeenth century that philosopher and scientist Gottfried Wilhelm Leibniz brought new life to the old idea. In 1798, in the course of his expedition to Egypt, Napoleon Bonaparte commissioned a survey and took measurements for the eventual construction of a canal. It would be more than 50 years, however, before French engineer François Ferdinand de Lesseps found an ally to support his Suez Canal enterprise: the Egyptian viceroy Said. Working from plans prepared by Austrian Alois Negrelli in 1838, de Lesseps organized the project from a logistical and engineering standpoint. Finally, in 1859, the first spade pierced the soil in Port Said, breaking ground for construction of the Suez Canal.

Despite the accompanying euphoria, de Lesseps was aware that enormous difficulties lay ahead and knew that these would have to be overcome before any progress could be made. Because Egypt lacked the necessary raw materials and equipment, everything had to be imported from Europe, including all the wood needed to construct the scaffolding. In addition, they had to provide for at least 25,000

FACTS

✱ Size: The Suez Canal is 162.5 km long and between 300 and 365 m wide. The canal bed is only 180 m wide and 21 m deep.

✱ Construction: The canal was built from 1859 to 1869. Construction costs totalled £19 million.

✱ Income per year: The canal is Egypt's most important source of capital, bringing in some $20 billion a year.

✱ Capacity: Currently, only ships weighing up to 200,000 gross tons, the so-called "Suez max", can pass through the canal.

Warships pass through the Suez Canal daily. In the foreground, the American aircraft carrier USS *George Washington* continues on its way to the Persian Gulf.

workers. In 1862, 1,600 of the 1,800 camels on the site were used solely to transport sufficient drinking water for each day. The costs reached 8,000 francs per day for drinking water alone! In the end, a separate canal system had to be built to bring it in. Once the drinking water situation was resolved in 1863, work could begin in earnest. After ten years of construction the Suez Canal was finally opened to shipping, with great fanfare, on 17 November 1869. **The canal originates in the north** at the harbour of Port Said. From there it extends to the south, flowing first into Lake Menzala. It leaves the lake at kilometre 45, cuts through the El Kantara Ridge and flows 4 km further before entering Lake Balla. Then it passes the stations el Ferdana and el Gisr, flows through Lake Timsah and crosses the rising hills of the Serapeum. At kilometre 95 it reaches Bitter Lake, a large body of water with an area of 220 km^2. The lake is already affected by the tides of the Red Sea, which the canal reaches at kilometre 156 in Suez. Despite an extended period of conflict between Egypt and Israel in the 1960s and 1970s that limited traffic, the Suez Canal is the most important shipping route in the world today. Up to 15,000 ships use the waterway each year, transporting around 15 per cent of all cargo worldwide – even though the ships have to pass through in single file, travelling the whole distance in around 15 hours. The canal was not designed for ships the size of modern transport vessels. Supertankers can only use the canal if part of their cargo is offloaded in Suez, transported to Port Said via pipeline and pumped back into the ships there. The time and money saved is considerable. As of 2010, modifications to the canal should make it possible for oil tankers with a draught of 22 m to pass through, further reducing the cost of transporting the Middle East's most valuable commodity.

Above: It almost seems as if this freighter is sailing along on the sand, but behind the dunes lie the waters of the Suez Canal.

Left: Ships in the Suez Canal. They pass through the canal in single file and always in convoys.

EGYPT

Valley of the Kings

THEBES WAS THE CAPITAL OF ANCIENT EGYPT, THE CENTRE OF THE PHARAONIC KINGDOM FOR OVER 400 YEARS AND LOCATION OF EGYPT'S MOST IMPORTANT CULTS. THE NEARBY VALLEY OF THE KINGS IS THE WORLD'S GREATEST NECROPOLIS.

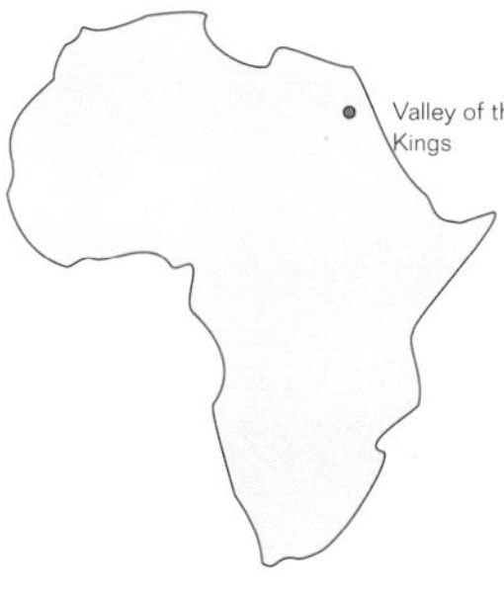

The New Kingdom (*circa* 1532–1070 BCE) – the periods of the 18th through the 20th dynasties – was the golden age of Thebes, the city we now know as Luxor. The pharaohs freely spent their unimaginable wealth and treasures to beautify their royal city on both banks of the Nile with magnificent temples and palaces. The finds uncovered here by archaeologists over the course of centuries are the stuff of legend.

History and legend swirl around the long-dead kings, weaving together fact and fiction so that one can no longer be disentangled from the other. "Thebes of the hundred gates", as the later Greek historian Herodotus described it, grew into an expansive and powerful city during the New Kingdom. Its world-famous, fantastic buildings and monuments have survived for millennia, bearing witness even today to the glory and wealth of this gigantic city of the pharaohs filled with palaces and temples. Among the monuments that still survive are the Temple of Luxor, the enormous temple-city of Karnak with its Amon Temple, the funerary temple of Hatshepsut and, last but not least, the famous grave complexes in the Valley of the Kings. The rise and expansion of Thebes into the political centre and greatest necropolis in Egypt is inextricably intertwined with

Right: The entrance to a rock tomb.

Below: The death mask of the pharaoh Tutankhamun. The discovery of his grave is a milestone in the history of archaeology.

the most important pharaoh who ever reigned in the land of the Nile: Rameses II (ca. 1298–1213 BCE).

During his extraordinary 66-year reign Rameses II guided the destiny of his country like no other ruler before or since. In this period, Egypt's economy and culture reached heights that can scarcely be believed, a zenith that would never be reached again. Rameses' skill in diplomacy gave Egypt nearly 50 years of peace with its neighbours, which freed both the people of Egypt and their extraordinary ruler to pursue other things. Rameses devoted his considerable energy to the beautification of his capital city and the construction of his tomb. Together with his advisers he put together the plans for a palace-grave, the Ramesseum. Before he could be laid to rest, however, this exceptionally long-lived pharaoh buried a great many family members nearby in Thebes, transforming it into Egypt's largest necropolis.

With the Amon Temple of Karnak, Rameses II completed the work that his father Seti had begun, but in a much more elaborate style than Seti himself had ever dreamed possible. This is the greatest of all Egyptian temples, with 134 columns, each 24 metres high, supporting the great hall. He never stopped commissioning monuments that would stand as proof of his unlimited power. The Temple of Luxor, which he enlarged with the addition of a courtyard larger than all the others, served this purpose well. Statues topped by portrait heads of the pharaoh decorated the enormous open space. Rameses also visited the funerary temple of Hatshepsut. This queen had ruled Egypt some 200 years earlier. A woman ruler was, from Rameses II's point of view, unthinkable. He had all the temple's inscriptions to Hatshepsut removed, replacing her name with his own.

Sometime around 1253 BCE, Rameses II's favourite wife, Nefertari, died. To honour her, Rameses commissioned the most elaborate grave monument in the Valley of the Queens, located directly to the south of the Valley of the Kings, where the remains of many pharoahs' wives rest in over 90 graves. Nefertari's monument is designed to be worthy of a pharoah, a female pharaoh who stood at the side of the greatest pharaoh of all.

Rameses II himself died in 1213 BCE. He left behind more than 100 children, a wealthy and prosperous land, and a capital city whose buildings have lost none of their beauty, continuing to draw admirers up to the present day. The legacy of the most magnificent pharaoh continues to impress and fascinate.

DATES

*** 1506–1494 BCE:** Pharaoh Thutmosis I had his tomb built here, defining the site as a necropolis for succeeding New Kingdom rulers.

*** 1708 CE:** Pierre Claude Sicard visited the valley, describing it as the burial place of the pharaohs.

*** 1739, 1768 and 1792:** Richard Pococke, James Bruce and William George located and identified 20 graves.

*** 1875:** The brothers Abd el-Rassul uncovered a tomb in Deir el-Bahri with 40 royal mummies.

*** 9 March 1898:** Victor Loret opened the tomb of Amenophis III, where he found another cache of royal mummies.

*** 4 November 1922:** Howard Carter entered the still mostly intact tomb of Pharaoh Tutankhamun.

*** 1995:** American archaeologist Kent Weeks discovered a tomb with more than 120 burial chambers.

*** Spring 2006:** Discovery of a burial chamber with seven wooden sarcophagi.

The Funerary Temple of Queen Hatshepsut was recently in the news, tragically, when on 17 November 1997 terrorists attacked tourists at the monument, killing 60 people.

The Valley of the Kings, the legendary valley of the dead rulers on the western bank of the Nile, is the largest and best known necropolis in all of Egypt. More than 60 tombs have been identified there so far, most belonging to New Kingdom pharaohs. The first funerary temple in the Valley of the Kings was built during the 18th dynasty. To the Egyptians, the monumental graves of their rulers were designed to be "their million-year houses".

Among the most widely known grave sites in the valley are tomb number 7, belonging to Rameses II, number 42, the funerary temple of Hatshepsut, and number 62, the famous grave of the pharaoh Tutankhamun that was first discovered in 1922. The most recent grave in the Valley of the Kings belongs to Pharaoh Rameses XI of the 20th dynasty, who died around 1070 BCE, still following the traditions of his forefathers by building his tomb at this site. For many years, grave robbing was a profitable and expanding branch of the local economy. Entire bands of thieves plundered and smashed their way through the graves of their deceased rulers, selling the valuable grave goods illegally to black-market traders.

For many centuries, the Valley of the Kings lay slumbering in obscurity known only to the local inhabitants. Then, in 1768, a French missionary priest named Claude Sicard stumbled upon the Valley of the Kings more or less by chance, setting off a wave of archaeological expeditions. His sensational discoveries inspired scientists from every European capital to uncover the secrets of the Valley of the Kings. Napoleon's expedition to Egypt marked the first systematic study in the valley, and also looting, to which the Egyptian treasures that are now housed in the Louvre Museum in Paris bear witness.

The most renowned grave site discovered so far is, without a doubt, the tomb of the pharaoh Tutanhkamun. An unimportant pharaoh during his lifetime, the contents of his monumental burial amazed and astounded the entire world. His splendid tomb, packed with lavish grave gifts, such as the pharaoh's solid-gold death mask, survives as a unique example of the magnificence of the Kingdom of Egypt. British archaeologist Howard Carter broke into the nearly intact tomb on 4 November 1922, entering the burial chamber itself on 17 February

Right: The courtyards in the Temple of Karnak were connected by splendid avenues.

Below: The ruins of the Ramesseum, the mortuary temple of Rameses II.

1923 and opening the elaborately decorated sarcophagus a day later. The valuable grave gifts and lavish furnishings from the tomb can be viewed today in the Egyptian Museum in Cairo.

Ever since the tomb was opened, rumours have circulated about the connection between the more or less mysterious deaths of a great number of those who took part in the excavation headed by English Egyptologist Howard Carter and his financeer, Lord Carnarvon, including speculation about the so-called "Curse of the Pharaohs". Is there such a thing as a curse placed by the dead rulers on anyone who violates their tombs? Did poisonous gases wafting out of the tomb after it was opened cause the deaths? Will the "Mummy's Curse" ever end?

It is said that an inscription was found over the entrance to Tutankhamun's grave chamber, and that it read: "Death shall come on swift wings to him who disturbs the peace of the King." Indeed, although similar warnings are not uncommon at other grave sites in the Valley of the Kings, they served first and foremost as a means of scaring off potential grave robbers, and are not to be understood as literal curses.

Despite the somewhat high body count among expedition members in the years following the discovery of Tutankhamun's tomb, there is a clear, reasonable explanation for nearly every death. For example, most of the 30 or so who died were already between 70 and 80 years old, including the expedition's patron, Lord Carnarvon, who died of blood poisoning following either a mosquito bite or a cut inflicted while shaving. Today, the deadly curse has been firmly dismissed by science. The purported Tutankhamun inscription existed only in the fantasies of overly excited British journalists; it is found nowhere among the many hieroglyphic texts in the tomb.

In 1973, however, a rational, scientific explanation for the deaths among members of the expedition was proposed. The grave of the Pharaoh was shown to have harboured an unusually high concentration of the spores of the fungus *Aspergillus flavus*. The metabolic processes of this fungus produce highly poisonous gases that are dangerous for humans. People with a weakened immune system can have an allergic reaction to *Aspergillus flavus* that may lead to organ failure and death. The fungus could have caused members of the expedition to be more susceptible to deadly illness.

FACTS

* **The Valley of the Kings** is a necropolis where, as of March 2006, the tombs of 63 Egyptian pharaohs have been identified. It was rediscovered in 1708 by French priest Claude Sicard.
* **The Valley of the Queens** has over 90 graves containing the remains of the pharaohs' wives and other family members. The most important tomb belongs to Nefertari.
* **The Ramesseum** is the mortuary temple of Rameses II. Its official name is "Palace of Rameses II, united with Thebes in the Kingdom of Amon".
* **The Temple of Karnak** is the largest temple complex in all of Egypt. It includes the largest sacred building in the world – the Temple of Amon.
* **The Temple of Luxor** was known as the "southern sacred enclosure of Amon". It was dedicated to the god Amon, his wife Mut and their son, the moon god Chons.

ZAMBIA

Victoria Falls

THE LARGEST WATERFALL IN THE WORLD CASCADES INTO A DEEP GORGE ON THE BORDER BETWEEN ZAMBIA AND ZIMBABWE. THE VICTORIA FALLS ARE KNOWN IN THE LANGUAGE OF THE LOCAL PEOPLE AS *MOSI-OA-TUNYA*, OR "SMOKE THAT THUNDERS".

Scottish explorer David Livingstone (1813–1873) was deeply impressed when he came upon the "thundering smoke" of the Zambesi River for the first time. The river seemed to disappear suddenly into a cloud of fine spray rising nearly 300 metres into the air. And then there was the roar and thunder of the masses of falling water: the sound of the 1.7-metre-wide racing flood falling up to 110 metres into a narrow gorge is deafening. During the rainy season in February and March, when the water level in the Zambesi peaks, up to 2,270 million litres of water per minute cascade over the Falls.

It was the custom of British nineteenth-century explorers to give an English name to every newly encountered piece of land, every stretch of river and mountain. In this regard, Livingstone usually did not follow the example of his compatriots, marking natural features on his painstakingly prepared maps with their local names. However, he made an exception for these stupendous falls, naming this overwhelming display of the forces of nature in honour of his queen, Victoria.

The origin of the falls was obvious to Livingstone the scientist. As he noted in his journal, "The Falls are no more than a fissure in the hard basalt bedrock that extends from the left to the right bank of the

David Livingstone (1813–73) was the first European to discover the "Mosi-oa-Tunya" Falls, which he named "Victoria Falls" in honour of Queen Victoria.

Zambesi River. The entire astonishing sight is the result of an earlier elevation of the ground, which left a deep cleft in the basalt lying below. The torrent of water falls down at least 1,000 paces into the resulting gorge."

Recent geological research concluded that the basalt surface traversed by the Zambesi River was formed during the Late Jurassic period. During subsequent phases of geological history, the Zambesi frequently changed its course as movements of the Earth's crust undermined the river bed, leaving behind a series of east-west fissures through which water has flowed for 500,000 years, leaving behind a visible zigzag pattern of gorges and ravines. The long sides of the gorges mark the location of the seven predecessors of what are today eight waterfalls, with a ninth one already in the works over a more recent north-south fissure. Over time, this will interrupt the flow of the east-west waterfalls and, within a few millennia, there will no longer be a waterfall of this imposing width on the site.

The border-crossing Mosi-oa-Tunya National Park was dedicated in 1972, when the protection of the falls became the special trust of the neighbouring states of Zambia and Zimbabwe, which donated around 69 km² to the preserve. The park has been a UNESCO World Heritage Site since 1989. Despite the efforts of these two nations, the conflict between preservation of this natural wonder and the desire to exploit its hydroelectric potential continues to this day. Damming the Zambesi so that its waters can serve as an energy resource is very important to the economies of all the neighbouring countries. Recently, the Zambesi River Authority announced plans to build a dam below the falls in the Bakota Gorge. This would be the third largest dam on the river, after the Kariba and Cabora-Bassa Dam and other reservoir projects already built. Nature conservationists all over the world warn of what will happen to the native flora and fauna in the gorge beneath Victoria Falls, which up to now has remained largely undisturbed. Environmentalists fear that damming the river so close to the falls will hasten the loss of a unique environment and other changes within the fascinating gorge lying below it. The question of how best to balance the natural and economic potential of the Victoria Falls remains unanswered today.

FACTS

*** Discovery:** The Victoria Falls were discovered by David Livingstone, missionary and African explorer.

*** Unique:** The Victoria Falls are the longest continuous cascading waterfall on Earth, with a height of 110 m and a width of 1.7 km.

*** Size:** As much as 600 million litres of water per minute pass over the falls.

*** River:** The Zambezi, the fourth largest river in Africa (2,574 km), originates at Luanda in Zambia some 1,500 m above sea level, draining an area of about 1.6 million km².

Centre: One can hear the "smoke that thunders" long before reaching Victoria Falls.

Bottom: The water of the Zambesi cascades 110 m over the edge, "capsizing" into an enormous gorge.

Asia, the largest continent, is full of contrasts. The European-Mediterranean flair of Istanbul meets the fairy-tale Orient of the Arabian Nights, and the exotic Far East, dominated by the "Central Kingdom" of China, contrasts with the island states of the Indian Ocean. Both the forces of nature and magnificent civilizations and religions have created outstanding wonders.

ASIA

JAPAN

The Akashi-Kaikyo Bridge

THE AKASHI-KAIKYO SUSPENSION BRIDGE IS THE LARGEST BRIDGE IN THE WORLD. IT SPANS THE BUSIEST STRETCH OF WATER IN JAPAN, THE AKASHI STRAITS BETWEEN THE MAIN ISLAND OF HONSHU AND THE SMALLER SHIKOKU.

The Akashi-Kaikyo Bridge joins the city of Naruto on the island of Shikoku with Kobe on Honshu. Its construction presented tremendous challenges from the outset; its engineers were well aware that the pervading environmental conditions made a bridge project on this site nearly impossible. The region is tectonically extremely active, with small earthquakes occurring almost daily. Typhoons with winds up to 290 km per hour are not unusual. Added to this is the fact that the Akashi Straits are the busiest shipping lanes in all of Japan. In addition, because the straits are classed as an international waterway, a 1,500-metre-wide shipping lane had to be left free at all times, complicating construction and requiring the bridge to have a centre span longer than any ever built. **Construction began in May 1988,** with the laying of the 15,000-ton steel mantel footings for the two pillars. These hollow colossi of steel were sunk into the seabed and filled in with concrete capable of setting despite being completely submerged under water. In the end, 140,000 cubic metres of concrete were poured to anchor each of the bridge's foundations. **Next, the two giant pylons** from which the rest of the bridge would be suspended were raised. It was decided that a steel frame with criss-crossed bracing

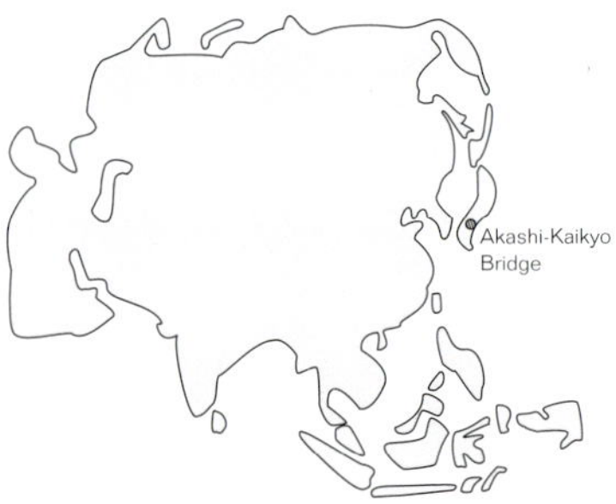

FACTS

✻ Location: The Akashi-Kaikyo Bridge crosses the Akashi Straits.

✻ The cornerstone was laid in April 1986, with construction beginning in May 1988 and completed in April 1998.

✻ Size: The bridge's total length is 3,911 m, with a central span of 1,991 m and a height of 283 m.

✻ Size of the suspension cables: Each suspension cable is 4,000 m long with a diameter of over 1 m. The space between the suspension cables is 35.5 m. The suspended roadbed hangs 71 m above the sea. It weighs over 120,000 tons.

The harbour of the bustling city of Kobe on the island of Honshu.

would provide the necessary stability while retaining the flexibility and elasticity of concrete. The pylons were designed to withstand earthquakes with a magnitude of 8.5 without damage. Each 283-metre-tall pylon was assembled from 90 steel segments, each 160 tons, piled on top of one another like bricks. Each pier also contains 20 giant oscillation dampers. These pendula stabilize the structure by immediately compensating for every movement of the bridge with a swing in the opposite direction.

The expenditure of time, material and expertise put into the earthquake-proof design proved its worth while the bridge was still under construction. On 17 January 1995, an earthquake measuring 7.2 on the Richter scale struck the region around the densely populated city of Kobe. Over 6,500 people were killed, 27,000 injured and some 200,000 buildings completely destroyed. The Akashi-Kaikyo bridge, however, not yet complete, was undamaged – this, despite the fact that the epicentre of the quake lay squarely between the two suspension pillars!

The steel cables strung across the bridge are "mega" in every way. Nearly 4,000 metres long and more than 1 metre thick, they broke every world record for size and strength. Each cable was composed of 290 bundles of wire, known as 'braids'. Each braid was woven from 127 pieces of wire made from extremely strong steel. Each weight-bearing cable, therefore, was made up of 36,830 individual steel wires. If one were to disentangle all the wire and lay it end to end, it would circle the equator seven times.

The weight carried by the main bridge cables is stupendous. Around 120,000 tons are suspended from the cables stretching between the pylons from shore to shore – 261,000 tons of steel were used to build this great bridge, a man-made wonder designed to withstand the greatest forces of nature.

Above: In 1995, a large part of the city of Kobe was destroyed by an earthquake. The Akashi-Kaikyo Bridge withstood the disaster.

Left: The Akashi-Kaikyo Bridge at night. At first glance, the filigree superstructure gives the impression of fragility, despite the massive weight of the bridge.

CAMBODIA

Angkor Wat

DESPITE EXPOSURE TO DECADES OF WAR, ANKGOR WAT, THE MYSTERIOUS TEMPLE CITY IN THE CAMBODIAN JUNGLE, STILL STANDS, BEARING WITNESS TO THE HINDU KINGDOM OF KHMER. OVER 1,000 TEMPLES SURVIVE TO TELL STORIES OF GREATNESS AND POWER.

Angkor was the capital city of the Kingdom of Khmer and the world-famous, enormous temple complex of Angkor Wat formed its core. Every Khmer ruler was a god-king and each one commissioned a temple in honour of his own divine nature, with which he expected to reunite after death. The temple complex is a massive architectural expression of this Hindu tradition. Angkor Wat was built in the twelfth century by command of King Suryavarman II, the "ward of the sun god", in honour of no lesser a god than Vishnu himself, the ruler of the world. The temple complex is designed to mirror the Khmer cosmology, itself strongly grounded in the Indian world-view. In this sense, Angkor Wat was designed as a precise representation of the cosmic universe.

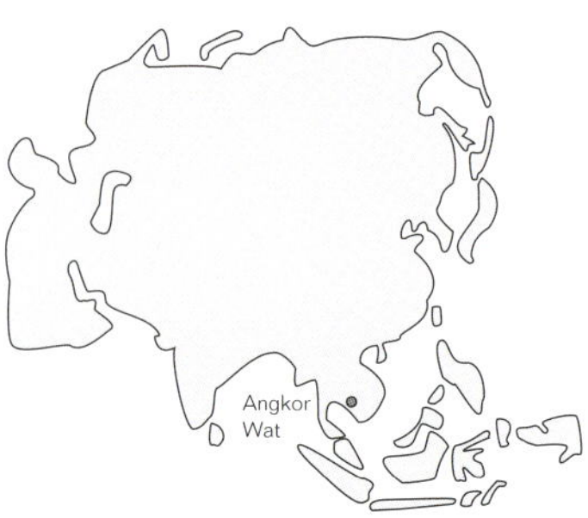

The Angkor complex was the spiritual centre of the Khmer Kingdom, and its main temple embodied a joining together of the worldly and spiritual principles of Khmer culture. Architecturally, the temple is the creative and aesthetic high point of the culture.

The heart of the temple complex, which is known as the Heavenly Palace, is ringed by a moat nearly 200 metres wide that symbolizes the primordial sea surrounding the inhabited Earth.

The central tower of the Angkor Wat temple rises 65 m above the complex.

DATES

✱ ***circa* 889/890:** King Yasovarman I took over what is today Cambodia, founding the capital city of Yasodharapura.

✱ **1002–50:** Reign of King Suryavarman I.

✱ **1113–50:** King Suryavarman II ordered the Angkor Wat temple complex built in the south-eastern quarter of the capital city.

✱ **1177–81:** Angkor was sacked and taken over by the Chams, the traditional enemies of the Khmer Kingdom.

✱ ***circa* 1200:** The "great royal city" of Angkor Thom was built nearby.

✱ **1353, 1393 and 1431:** The royal city of Angkor was sacked and plundered.

✱ **1907:** The French founded the society "Conservation d'Angkor" and began restoration.

✱ **1992:** Angkor was named a World Heritage Site by UNESCO.

✱ **1998:** International aid supported the preservation of Angkor.

In the centre of the moat, the "Wat" symbolizes the mountain of Meru, home of the Hindu gods and thereby the very universe itself. The ward of the sun god, the god-king Suryavarman II, commissioned the impressive, more than life-size statue of Vishnu in the gallery of its main entrance. Well aware of his responsibilities as a divine ruler, the statue is sculpted with Suryavarman II's own facial features.

The temple buildings themselves were constructed according to strict geometric principles in the form of three-stepped pyramids with five towers rising from the uppermost level. The central tower, an embodiment of the dead god-king's spirit, is in each case the highest of the five.

The most striking feature of Angkor Wat is the opulent decoration and sumptuous ornamentation covering every wall and surface. The dominating motif of the relief sculpture is that of the beautiful dancers of the heavens, Asparas and Devatas, who make ready – and supply – the joys of paradise to all the deities. Over 1,500 of these figures are found at Angkor Wat, all naked to the hips and wearing a low-slung, long skirt and a variety of fantastic hairstyles. Each figure is an individual masterpiece, and no figure is exactly the same as any other. As an inscription found in the temple reads: "Your slender, graceful, shining body, clothed in the most beautiful and luxurious cloth, outshines even the complete beauty of the god of the flowering arrow who is the god of love, delighting the earth like the crescent of the waxing moon."

The walls of the lowest level of each temple are decorated in bas-reliefs. The figural representations form a continuous chronology that relates a visual narrative of Hindu cosmology. The reliefs extend over 800 metres and cover a total area of 2,000 square metres.

Also common in many Angkor temples is the visual representation of a foam-bedecked ocean. This image is deeply tied into Hindu mythology, in which the Earth is perceived as a butter churn filled with foaming milk. The iconography was particularly appropriate to Ankgor Wat, which, for the Ancient Khmer, represented the physical and spiritual centre of an ever-changing universe.

Centre: Bas-relief sculpture depicting Asparas and Devatas, the beautiful dancers of the heavens, decorate many of the temple walls.

Bottom: The temple complex of Angkor Wat is, according to the *Guinness Book of World Records*, the largest religious complex in the world.

THAILAND

Ayutthaya

FOUNDED BY THE KHMER SOMETIME BEFORE THE MID-FOURTEENTH CENTURY, THE CITY OF AYUTTHAYA WAS KNOWN AS THE "SACRED CITY OF THE ANGELS AND KINGS" AFTER KING RAMATHIBODI I MADE AYUTTHAYA HIS ROYAL CAPITAL.

In Thailand, even today, the panorama of the medieval city of Ayutthaya brings to mind a stage set from "The King and I" with its magnificent temple complexes, massive Buddha statues and 'chedis' (temple towers) soaring as much as 80 metres high. For more than 400 years the kings of Ayutthaya – there were 35 of them in all – ruled the great land of Siam from its confines. The city grew into one of the largest and most prosperous in all of South-east Asia, with a population of around one million at its height. The glory days of the city of Ayutthaya came to an end in the eighteenth century, when it was invaded by Burmese troops. Around 65,000 people still live in what is today a small provincial capital.

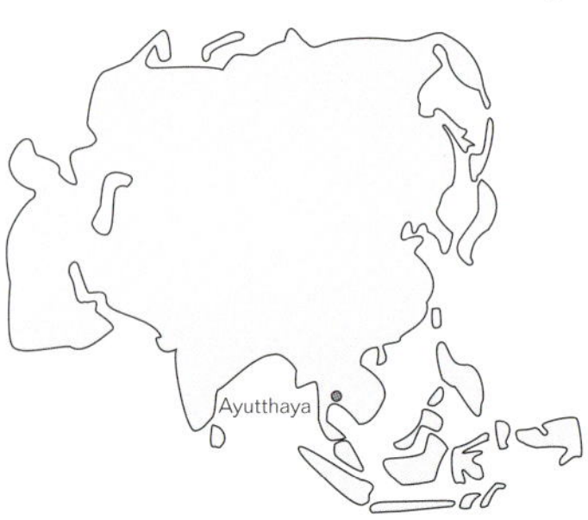

Ayutthaya rose in the fourteenth century, thanks to the decline of the previous capital, Sukothai. In 1351, Ramathibodi I moved his administrative offices and royal residence to the site of an older Khmer-founded city located on an island between the Maenam Chao Praya, Pasak and Lopburi rivers, today some 70 km north of modern Bangkok. The fertile river plains, rich harvests, and a highly efficient system of tax collection formed the basis of Ayutthaya's prosperity and wealth. Regular trade relationships with other lands were firmly in place:

Right: The ritual centre of the city was the temple of Wat Mahathat.

Below: The temple of Wat Phra Si Sanphet in Ayutthaya is one of the city's most beautiful sacred buildings.

business with China, Java, Malaysia, India, Ceylon, Japan and Persia flourished, as did trade with Portugal, France, Holland and England through their Far Eastern outposts. Temples, palaces and giant Buddha statues were erected, all made of the finest materials and elaborately decorated. The chedis were given particular attention, with the domes of the towers completely covered in gold leaf.

At the end of the seventeenth century, the city began to crumble as the kings of Ayutthaya involved themselves in a series of costly military conflicts with neighbouring Burma. The massive city wall, built of well-fired mud-brick in the sixteenth century, held off numerous sieges by Burmese troops. But, finally, on 7 April 1767, Ayutthaya fell. The Burmese breached the wall, plundered the temple treasuries and demolished most of the beautiful city. According to legend, the very eyes of the great Buddha statues flowed with tears as Ayutthaya was destroyed.

Ayutthaya lay in rubble and ashes, and all attempts at rebuilding came to nothing after King Rama I moved his court to the newly founded capital city of Bangkok.

Today, only a hint of Ayutthaya's former grandeur and glory remain among the ruins. The imposing, towering, bell-shaped chedis and ruins of temples and monasteries are mere reminders of the medieval past, when the chambers of these structures housed saintly relics alongside the mortal remains of the kings and members of the royal family. The tower of the temple of Wat Mahathat was once said to be the last resting place of the physical remains of the historical Buddha himself.

During its golden age, Ayutthaya boasted three royal palaces, 375 temples, 94 city gates and 29 forts. The most beautiful of these temples is without a doubt Wat Phra Si Sanphet, which was built in the fifteenth century with three soaring chedis. The ashes of King Ramathibodi II as well as those of his father, Ramathibodi I, the first two kings of Ayutthaya, were kept here in this most visible symbol of the city.

The ruins of Ayutthaya are a magnificent legacy of this once marvellous city and its tremendous cultural achievements. The aesthetic influences of the Khmer, India and Ceylon met here in a glorious celebration of form and richness of style. The world would never know anything like it again.

DATES

* **1350–1767:** Reign of the five dynasties of the Kingdom of Ayutthaya.
* **1350:** King Ramathibodi I founded the city as his royal residence and administrative capital.
* **1350–1488:** Golden age of Ayutthaya art.
* **1492–1532:** Construction of the chedis of Wat Phra Si Sanphet.
* **1569:** The 80-m-tall chedi of Phu Kao Thong was built.
* **1590–1605:** Reign of King Naresuan.
* **1656–1688:** Reign of King Narai.
* **7 April 1767:** Ayutthaya destroyed by the Burmese.
* **1956:** First attempts at restoring the city.
* **1958:** The artistic treasures of Wat Ratchaburana were rediscovered.
* **1979:** The restoration of Wat Putthai Sawan was completed.
* **1991:** Ayutthaya was named a World Heritage Site by UNESCO.

IRAQ

Babylon

LYING ALONG THE EUPHRATES RIVER SOME 90 KM SOUTH OF BAGHDAD, THE CITY OF BABYLON, LONG FAMED FOR ITS FANTASTIC BUILDINGS AND ELABORATELY DECORATED WALLS, WAS ONCE THE CAPITAL OF THE GLORIOUS BABYLONIAN EMPIRE.

The Hanging Gardens of Babylon were one of the Seven Wonders of the Ancient World. Described by Greek historians who may or may not have seen them in person, archaeologists and historians have yet to reach consensus on who built them and, how and indeed, whether or not they ever really existed. Who would be able to grow such a lush garden of trees and flowering plants in the middle of the desert's relentless heat? Their construction has long been associated with the reign of Nebuchadnezzar II (605–552 BCE,) because his rule marks the golden age of the Neo-Babylonian kingdom.

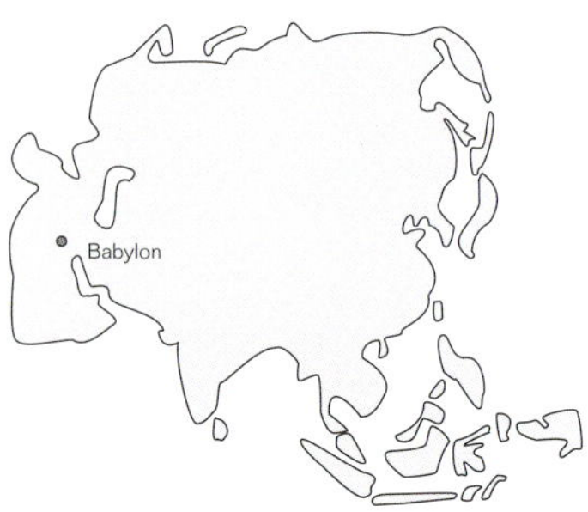

Experts believe the term "hanging gardens" can be traced back to a translation error: "overhanging" would perhaps be a better word. According to an account by the Greek historian Strabo, the gardens were built atop a vaulted foundation, rising to a series of rectilinear walls up to 120 metres long crowned by an enormous vaulted roof. This would have been an exceptionally large building with a vault far surpassing any others known from that time period. Needless to say, the dimensions supplied vary enormously depending on the source.

The masonry of the vault, described as being either sun-dried or fired mud-brick, would have to have been encased in airtight cladding in order to protect

FACTS

✱ Even today, there is no modern-day historical research or archaeological evidence providing clear and incontrovertible proof of the existence of the Hanging Gardens of Babylon. Scholars continue to research and archaeologists will dig on, until the hoped-for evidence of this second of the Seven Wonders of the Ancient World is found.

Did it really look like this? A historical illustration of the legendary Hanging Gardens of Babylon.

the bricks from moisture. It is likely that several layers of lead, pitch and glazed tile were employed towards this end. These measures were absolutely essential because of the damage moisture could wreak on load-bearing architectural elements, such as vaults and the walls that supported them. Moisture could bring about the quick collapse of any building constructed almost entirely of straw-tempered mud-brick. Under normal conditions, the desert environment of Mesopotamia lent itself to the use of this very common building material. But for an elaborate garden of non-native species in need of frequent watering, a structure made of mud would be a problem. **Once the layers of isolating materials** were in place and the mud-brick protected, what must have been a thick layer of soil was put down, because at the behest of the Babylonian king, trees were planted in the garden along with other plants. Nebuchadnezzar assigned his generals the task of bringing back samples of different plants from their campaigns and expeditions. Was this, then, the world's first botanical garden, founded in the middle of the desert? **Keeping the garden well watered** required immense effort. The hot, dry Mesopotamian desert climate would have led to rapid evaporation, and an enormous water supply would have been needed to ensure the plants' survival. The water would have to be drawn from the nearby Euphrates River, but how could it be brought to the garden? The simplest solution would have been a kind of conveyance system to carry pitchers to the top of the gardens, from where it could be distributed to the terraces below, via a network of drains or canals. Another theory has water brought to the site and distributed by means of a sophisticated irrigation system. Most likely, the "energy source" to run such a system would be the muscles of draft animals or slaves.

Above: The Processional Way was a stone-paved street where elaborately choreographed military parades and religious processions took place.

Left: Excavation has uncovered the foundations of Nebuchadnezzar II's palace. Many scholars believe that he may have been the king who built the Hanging Gardens.

MYANMAR

Bagan

WITH OVER 2,000 PRESERVED BRICK TEMPLES AND PAGODAS, THE HISTORIC ROYAL CITY OF BAGAN IN MYANMAR IS ONE OF THE MOST IMPORTANT AND IMPRESSIVE ARCHAEOLOGICAL SITES IN ALL OF SOUTH-EAST ASIA.

The former rulers of Bagan achieved their power through a subtle interplay of worldly and spiritual power. By the mid-ninth century, Bagan had already become the economic and political centre of Upper Burma, with its golden age unfolding between the years 1044 and 1112 during the reigns of King Anawratha and his son, Kyanzittha. Both regents made use of Buddhism to support their religious hegemony and as an instrument of power. In 1056, after his conversion to Buddhism by a wandering monk, Anawratha drove the priests of the competing snake cult out of the capital city of Bagan.

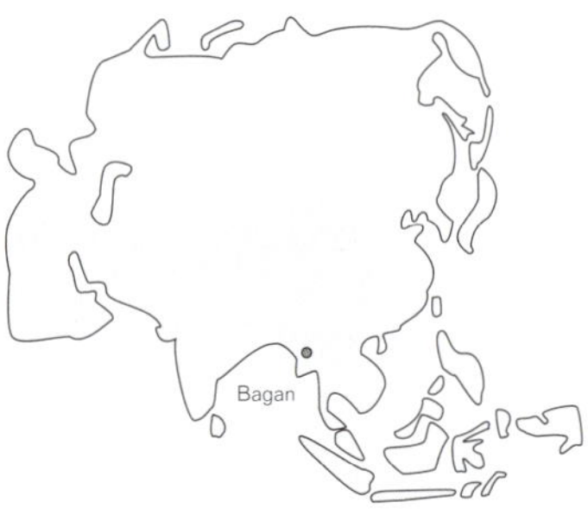

Bagan's power and influence grew during the reigns of the Kings Anawratha and Kyanzittha, growing in size until it covered an area of more than 40 km^2 at its greatest extent, making it the largest city in the medieval world, five times as large as contemporary London. And it was a peaceful city from the middle of the ninth through the twelfth centuries. This freedom from the direct effects of war and conflict allowed the city to grow and develop undisturbed. Within a period of 250 years the pious kings commissioned some 6,000 religious structures, of which perhaps some 2,000 temples and pagodas still survive. Unfortunately, a great many of the buildings were either destroyed completely or

The Dhamm-yan-gyi-Pahto, built in the 12th century, is the largest temple in Bagan.

DATES

* **9th century:** Bagan became the economic and political capital of Upper Burma.
* **1044–84:** Reign of King Anawratha.
* **1056:** Anawratha drove out the snake cult.
* **1084–1112:** Reign of King Kyanzittha.
* **1105:** Construction of the Ananda Temple began.
* **1287:** The Mongols under Kublai Khan occupied Bagan. The kingdom dissolved into numerous small states.
* **1975:** An earthquake destroyed a large part of Bagan.

suffered severe damage as the result of a catastrophic earthquake in 1975.

The glory years, the years of peace and prosperity, were followed by centuries of decline. The rulers had nearly emptied their treasuries to pay for their extensive building programmes and, at the same time, they had sharply reduced their income by extending tax-free status to all religious institutions within the kingdom, which included many prosperous temples and monasteries. The governors of provinces controlled by Bagan withdrew their support and stopped paying tributes, leading to a financial crisis that weakened the army and left Bagan's defences in tatters. Bagan finally fell to the much-feared Mongol ruler Kublai Khan in 1287, with the last Burmese king fleeing before him. With the mythos of Bagan destroyed, what was once a unified kingdom collapsed into numerous small states.

Today, some 700 years later, Bagan is considered to be the most important archaeological site in South-east Asia. In addition to the outstanding architectural monuments, the walls of Bagan are decorated with the oldest monumental paintings known from the region, dating to between the eleventh and thirteenth centuries.

One of the most beautiful monuments in Bagan is the Ananda Temple, now completely restored following its near levelling by the 1975 earthquake. King Kyanzittha commissioned the temple in 1105, the beginning of the so-called Middle Period at the site. Four enormous wooden statues of Buddha dominate the interior, two of them so cleverly carved as to give the impression that its facial expression changes as one approaches it. The largest temple in Bagan is the Dhamm-yan-gyi-Pahto, a pyramidal construction built in the twelfth century during the regency of Kalagya Min. Its bricks are set so close to one another that not even a pin can fit between them. It is said that masons who could not achieve this level of perfection had their hands amputated by order of the king.

The most famous of the 2,000 or so sacred buildings is without a doubt the Shwezigon Pagoda with its roof of shining gold. Begun under the reign of King Anawratha, it was completed in the twelfth century during the regency of his son, Kyanzittha. An emblem of the modern state of Myanmar, it retains its ancient lustre today.

Centre: The Shwezigon Pagoda, marking the northern boundary of the city, is probably the most famous of all of Bagan's temples.

Bottom: The Ananda Temple was completely restored after suffering severe damage in a 1975 earthquake.

PHILIPPINES

The Banaue Rice Terraces

THE WORLD-FAMOUS BANAUE RICE TERRACES ARE LOCATED ON THE NORTHERN FILIPINO ISLAND OF LUZON. IMMIGRANT INDONESIAN FARMERS BUILT THEM MORE THAN 2,000 YEARS AGO.

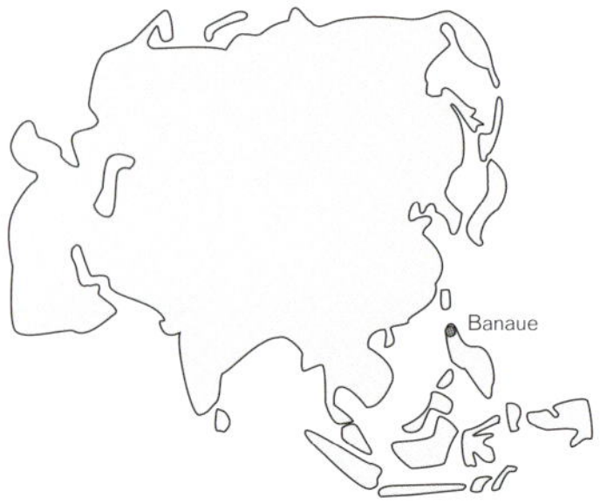

Rice fields stretch as far as the eye can see, in every direction. The awesome Banaue rice terraces rise from the valley floor, some as high as 1,500 metres, like stairways to heaven, with low walls retaining each one. They were built here in the northern part of Luzon, long ago, by the Ifugao, a tribal people thought to be an immigrant group originally from Indonesia. It is said that if every stone and mud wall supporting the terraces were laid end to end, they would reach halfway around the world. These rice fields are a unique cultural adaptation to the rough mountain terrain, a masterpiece of irrigation technology, and an exceptional architectural achievement.

According to Ifugao myth, there have been people living on the slopes of the Cordillera Mountains since before recorded time, but they were hunters, not farmers. One day, a man out on a hunt came across a plant he had never seen before. He planted its grains and watered them and, ever since, the people of the northern Philippines have enjoyed the blessings of the god Mah-Nongan. So says the legend, but the reality is quite different.

The Ifugao people built the stepped rice fields that climb up the Cordillera with nothing more than their bare hands and simple tools to help them,

FACTS

✱ **Location:** The Banaue Rice Terraces are located on the island of Luzon in the Philippines.

✱ **Age and size:** They are over 2,000 years old and cover an area of 250 m². They rise to heights of up to 1,500 m.

Rice farmers working in the Banaue rice fields. The work is extremely hard and yields little beyond basic sustenance.

mastering slopes of up to 70 per cent. The farmers' work was made more difficult by the exceptionally hard bedrock underneath, yet they kept on building, higher and higher. The highest terrace climbs 1,500 metres, with each individual terrace perfectly matched to the ins and outs of the rough terrain. Every accessible square metre of land – many of the terraces offer only a few square metres of arable surface – was exploited to wrest this indispensable staple grain from the barren ground.

Rice fields require a great deal of water. If the terraces were ever allowed to dry out, the already sparse harvest would fail entirely. To prevent this catastrophe, an extensive irrigation system was created to provide the Banaue rice terraces with the necessary moisture. The water flows down from the very top of the mountains through a network of canals, bamboo pipes and ditches to the terraces at the highest levels. Once they are flooded, the water cascades down to the next highest level. This ingenious method provided all the terraces, from the uppermost to the lowermost, with a constant flow of water.

Working in the rice fields is difficult and laboriously, and the harvest just barely meets the nutritional needs of the farmers and their immediate families. With their very survival dependent on the success of the rice harvest, the farmers view the enterprise as a partnership between the gods and men, one that has allowed the rice terraces to serve as the basis of life in the region for more than 2,000 years. Today, however, rice farming in the north Philippines is less attractive as the younger generation leaves the region for the economic promise of the big cities. More and more often, the rice fields lie fallow and terraces are allowed to collapse. The threat to their continued existence is acute.

Above: The humble homes of the rice farmers of Banaue.

Left: In 1995, the over 2,000-year-old rice terraces were declared a UNESCO World Heritage Site.

INDONESIA

The Temple of Borobudur

LYING IN THE MIDDLE OF THE JUNGLE ISLAND OF JAVA, THE TEMPLE OF BOROBUDUR IS THE LARGEST TEMPLE IN SOUTH-EAST ASIA. BUT IT IS A PUZZLING PLACE. WHY WAS SUCH A MAGNIFICENT BUDDHIST SANCTUARY BUILT IN THIS UTTERLY ISOLATED SPOT?

What purpose could this enormous temple serve in central Java, one of the most inaccessible regions in all of South-east Asia? Many questions remain unanswered. For centuries, the Temple of Borobudur slumbered in the jungle, like Sleeping Beauty, overgrown with trees and entangled in vines. Only rediscovered in the nineteenth century, the attractions of the Temple of Borobudur today draw Buddhist pilgrims and tourists alike. This holy Buddhist site radiates such a unique aura of peace and contentment that visitors believe they can almost sense the breath of Buddha.

The temple complex was presumably constructed during the Salilendra Dynasty (750–850), most likely around the year 800 CE. There are few records and precise information is lacking. Here the followers of Buddha erected the “Thousand Sculpture Mountain” on top of well-built foundations. But why was the Temple of Borobudur built at all? On this point even the experts disagree. We know for certain that its construction was completed in 830 and that it served as the centre of Buddhism on Java until 919, after which the sanctuary in the jungle was slowly forgotten. When a location like this is abandoned, its decline and decay is a forgone conclusion, and so it was for Borobudur. Volcanic eruptions badly damaged

Enormous stupas and colossal figures of Buddha are found everywhere on the step pyramid of the Temple of Borobudur.

FACTS

✻ UNESCO World Cultural Heritage List: Borobudur (also spelled Borobodur) was placed on the UNESCO World Cultural Heritage List in 1991.

✻ Buddha: The Enlightened One, a being who has achieved purity, completeness of spirit and limitless unfolding of his potential: perfect wisdom and endless empathy with the suffering of all living things.

✻ Stupa: A stupa is a semi-spherical hill erected over the remains of the dead. It symbolizes the perfect balance of energy within the universe.

✻ Sir Thomas Stamford Raffles (1781–1826): The British explorer and scientist who founded the city of Singapore and was named governor of Java in 1811. In 1814, he rediscovered the Buddhist temple complex of Borobudur while exploring the area for new plant species. Raffles Sea is named after him.

the structure and what remained after the natural disaster was quickly overgrown by the creeping green carpet of the jungle.

The temple hill in the jungle was rediscovered in 1814 in the course of an expedition led by the governor of Java, Sir Thomas Stamford Raffles, who put the temple on the map. The first part of the complex would only be cleared in 1835 as archaeologists and other experts, recognizing that a great treasure lay buried under the mounds of volcanic debris, trees and thick overgrowth, were increasingly drawn to the site. They campaigned for the complete exposure of the ruins and battled for their preservation. However, it was only in 1955, following years of ongoing diplomatic negotiation, that the government of Indonesia together with UNESCO came to an agreement permitting the temple's excavation and restoration. The work finally began in 1973. Upon its completion in 1983, Borobudur shone with all its ancient glory. The spirit of Buddha was once again present.

At first glance, Borobudur resembles a stepped pyramid. The structure itself consists of nine levels, in plan nearly square, with a total area of about 15,000 m^2. Atop these are six galleries, also nearly square, decreasing in size as they rise, followed by three circular terraces with 72 stupas. At the very top lies the main stupa, a pagoda with a diameter of nearly 11 metres. The six square galleries are decorated in figural reliefs depicting the life and work of Buddha. Their combined length is over 5 km.

The Temple of Borobudur represents the central, highest truth of Buddhism: the universe itself. Buddhist cosmology divides the universe into three parts. Kamadhatu, occupied by humans, is a world of wishes and desires. Rupadhatu is the transitional world in which people are freed from their physical form and attachments to worldly things. Finally, there is Arupadhatu, the world of the gods, a perfect world of complete enlightenment. Borobudur is built according to this vision of the world. Every part of the temple complex is dedicated to one of these three realms of existence.

Today, officials are making every effort to ensure that this holy Buddhist pilgrimage site can endure. Since 1995, a plan has been in place that sets limits on the enormous throngs of visitors in order to protect this cultural monument of immeasurable worth for another thousand years.

Centre: Over 500 Buddha statues adorn the temple.

Bottom: Bas reliefs decorate the walls that climb along the rising galleries. The total length of the reliefs is over 5 km.

JAPAN

Fujiyama

FUJIYAMA IS JAPAN'S MOST IMPORTANT SYMBOL. ITS SILHOUETTE APPEARS ON BANKNOTES AND STAMPS, AS WELL AS IN COUNTLESS PAINTINGS AND DRAWINGS. THE PRIMARY RESIDENCE OF THE SHINTO GODS, IT IS JAPAN'S SACRED MOUNTAIN.

Fujiyama, or *Fuji-San*, as it is known is Japanese, is one of the most famous volcanoes in the world and the highest mountain in Japan. Located in Fuji-Hako-ne-Izu National Park on the main island of Honshu, its remarkable, nearly symmetrical volcanic cone rises fully free-standing over the landscape. According to an Ancient Japanese legend, the massif rose from the plain during an earthquake all at once, in one night. In Japan, the mountain is holy, one of the Japanese people's most enduring visual references. **Fujiyama stands on the exact part** of the Earth's crust where the Eurasian, North American and Philippine tectonic plates meet. The mountain is a classical shield volcano, of which there are many around the Pacific "Ring of Fire". Vulcanologists categorize it as "active but with little risk of eruption", and indeed, since 781 there have only been six recorded eruptions. The most recent event took place some 300 years ago during the Edo period, when the mountain spewed volcanic fire from 24 November 1707 to 22 January 1708. The lava and smoke originated in a secondary crater halfway up the mountain. This second peak, called the Hoeizan Peak, is still easily recognized today. This eruption was extraordinarily violent, burying the streets and houses of Tokyo over 100 km away in a

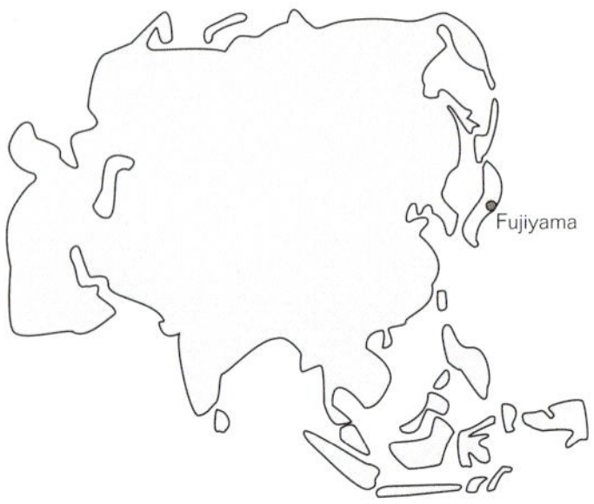

Right: Tradition meets the modern world: a Japanese bullet train zooms past Japan's holy mountain.

Below: Faithful Shinto pilgrims carry torches on their climb to the shrines that cover the slopes of Fujiyama.

thick layer of ash. Scientific and archaeological investigation shows that Fujiyama itself has been in existence for more than 10,000 years and has long been considered a holy mountain.

The volcano is a sacred mountain in the Shinto faith. For followers of this religion, which is practised nearly exclusively in Japan, Fujiyama is the primary residence of the gods. Ainu, the god of fire, is worshipped at the very top of the mountain and Fujiyama's slopes are peppered with countless temples and shrines. During the pilgrimage season in July and August, tens of thousands of believers journey there to pray.

An unknown monk was the first to ascend to the peak of Fujiyama in 663, and today mountain climbers are commonly found among the more than 2 million annual visitors, side by side with the pilgrims. Of these, perhaps 200,000 will make it all the way to the top to enjoy the breathtaking view into the 200-metre-deep mouth of the crater. With its exceptionally regular profile, Fujiyama is a relatively easy climb, although, according to an old Japanese proverb, "Only fools climb Fujiyama twice". There are three different routes leading to the volcanic peak. On beautiful summer days during the July and August pilgrimage season, up to 3,000 mountain climbers set out well before dawn in order to reach the summit in time to experience the sunrise over the Pacific from Japan's highest point. Women were forbidden to set foot on the peak before the Meiji Period (1868–1912), but are among the most frequent visitors today.

The volcanic cone's symmetrical form makes Fujiyama the most beautiful mountain in Japan and, indeed, the world. Its image is a favoured motif in Japanese art; no other natural feature has been photographed, printed, painted and drawn as often as this holy mountain. The most famous work of art devoted to Fujiyama is probably the print series "Thirty-Six Views of Mount Fuji", created by Katsushika Hokusai (1760–1849). His coloured woodcuts are masterpieces of Japanese printmaking, the art known as 'ukiyo-e'. In addition to the pictorial arts, literature and poetry have also invoked Fujiyama as a source of inspiration, where it is frequently the geographical backdrop to Japanese folk tales and novels, as well as a favourite theme of a large body of national poetry in this Land of the Rising Sun.

FACTS

✱ Size and location: Fujiyama (or *Fuji-san*) is 3,776 m tall and located on the island of Honshu, about 100 km west of Tokyo.

✱ Status: It is categorized as an active shield volcano with little risk of eruption.

✱ History: Fujiyama was formed some 100,000 years ago, achieving its current profile within the last 10,000 years.

✱ First to climb it: An unknown monk was the first to climb to the top of the mountain in 663.

✱ Eruptions: There have been six eruptions since 781, with the last occurring between 24 November 1707 and 22 January 1708.

CHINA

The Great Wall of China

THE GREAT WALL OF CHINA IS THE LARGEST STRUCTURE EVER BUILT BY HUMAN HANDS. IT IS SO ENORMOUS THAT, UNDER OPTIMAL CONDITIONS, IT CAN BE SEEN WITH THE NAKED EYE FROM OUTER SPACE.

The mysterious realm of China is called *Zhongguo* in Mandarin Chinese, the "Central Kingdom". Legends, myths and history have long been associated with this most populous country on Earth. The accomplishments of the Chinese people and the things they built are as famed as any of China's impressive cultural achievements. Filigree porcelains and the finest painted silks are found side by side with magnificent, grandiose palaces and monumental structures of all kinds. One of these – along with China's earthshaking inventions, including paper, gunpowder, wheelbarrows and the kite – can be considered one of the Central Kingdom's greatest achievements: the Great Wall of China. **China has always been a country** controlled by ruling dynasties; even today, Communist leader Mao Zedong's grandson is part of the government. It has also always been a land of contradictions: open to the world, yet insulated; progressive, yet traditional; diplomatic, but imperialistic; peaceful and warlike. When construction on the Great Wall began more than 2,200 years ago, it was designed as a fortification to keep out marauding nomads from the north, but also to cordon off and delineate China's own civilization and cultural sphere of influence.

FACTS

✻ Size:
The Great Wall of China is estimated to be between 6,000 and 6,500 km long, and is 6 m wide.

✻ Height of the towers:
The wall averages 8 m high with towers rising as high as 12 m.

✻ Number of towers:
There were between 20,000 and 25,000 towers along the wall.

✻ Building time:
The wall was built over a period of some 200 years.

The Great Wall winds over hills and through valleys into mountainous northern China. Its construction took 200 years and claimed the lives of hundreds of thousands of workers.

There is a long tradition of wall building in China. In early historic times, peasants were already building walls out of carefully worked stone to protect their fields and pastures against wild beasts and the winds that could blow away the precious topsoil. Chinese cities were always ringed by walls, with individual houses and gardens within the city encircled by walls of varying sizes. In the third century BCE, Chinese troops crossed the Yellow River into the south. The generals immediately ordered fortification walls to be raised in order to secure the newly conquered territories. Construction of the first unified system of defences along the northern border of the empire began sometime after 220 BCE at the behest of the first Chinese emperor, Qin Shi Huang Di (260–210 BCE), who feared that China would be overrun by marauding hordes of nomads from Mongolia.

Qin Shi Huang Di and his ministers feared the wild Huns most of all, and no gap that might let them in could be left in the defences. The emperor therefore ordered that all the fortification walls already in place be strengthened and then joined together to provide an impenetrable line of defence. A massive undertaking! Yet even this was not yet the Great Wall. This first construction phase took ten years, producing a composite wall with sections made of mud-brick, fieldstone and wooden palisades. In the following centuries, nearly every ruler would improve the wall and repair any damage – right up to the thirteenth century, when the wild horsemen of much-feared Mongol prince Ghengis Khan overran and levelled large parts of it. But the records of its continual construction are clear up to that point: in 446 CE, 300,000 forced labourers built a new section of the wall; in 555 Emperor Tian Bao set 1.8 million peasants to the task; and in 607 the Sui

Above: One of the 25,000 towers that once graced the wall. These signal and watch posts could house up to 50 soldiers.

Left: The Cloud Terrace at the Juyongguan Pass.

The towers of the Great Wall served as observation points and defensive positions.

Dynasty strengthened the fortifications, employing up to 2 million workers, half of whom died working on the enormous task.

The Great Wall owes its present appearance primarily to the Ming Dynasty (1368–1644) following their success in driving the Mongols back to the north. Thus, the Great Wall of China as we know it first came into being during the fourteenth-century period of the Ming Dynasty, when the bloody events of the recent past still cast a shadow on the dynasty's glory. The Ming emperors remembered well the invasion of Gengis Khan and recalled how he had overrun the still inadequately fortified wall, leading to the occupation of a large part of the country by the hated Mongols. They were determined that this would never happen again. The planned construction, which would take 200 years to complete, would be counted among the greatest of all time. For two centuries, thousands of commandeered soldiers, indentured labourers and peasants, forced into vassalage, worked on this enormous project.

Along its entire length, the Great Wall consists of two parallel masonry skins of carefully laid brick and fieldstone with a space of 6 or 7 metres between them. The fill between the retaining walls was a mixture of sand, stones and any trees that stood in the way of the Wall's progress. The corpses of the workers who died on the building site were also part of the fill. Hundreds of thousands perished during the Great Wall's construction.

The top of the wall was finished with three to four courses of brick coping, carefully laid, with the joints filled in with lime. An extensive drainage system was laid out to draw off rainwater. The end result was essentially a fortified, elevated street, well-suited to the movement of troops. Five or six horsemen or as many as ten foot soldiers could march next to one another along the 5- to 6-metre-wide expanse. Two-metre-high battlements protected them on the north side, with a shorter wall, 1 metre tall, along the south. The Ming emperors wanted to build much more than a fortification wall.

In addition to a strong defensive system, the wall was designed to serve as an effective means of communication over the vast expanses of China's northern border. Riders and foot soldiers were able to use the wall to move swiftly through the hilly landscape.

DATES

* *circa* 220 BCE: At the behest of the emperor Qin Shi Huang Di, who reigned from 221–210 BCE, construction was begun on the first closed system of defences against invaders from the north.
* **1345:** Buddhist monks built the Cloud Terrace, a gate tower with inscriptions in Sanskrit, Tibetan, Mongolian, Uighur, Chinese and Tangut.
* **1368–1644:** The construction of the most massive defensive system in the world took place under the Ming Dynasty.
* **1957:** Restoration of the Great Wall began with the section at Badaling.
* **1985:** Restoration of the over 10-m-high and 5-m-wide section of wall near Mutianyu was completed.
* **1987:** The Great Wall of China was named a World Heritage Site by UNESCO.

The wall is constructed of two parallel masonry skins made of brick and rubble set 6 to 7 metres apart along its entire length.

The Great Wall provided other means of communication as well. A huge number of towers, used for observation and as manned defensive positions, were built at regular intervals along the wall. They are up to 12 metres high, well above the wall's average height of 6–8 metres, so that flag and smoke signals can be easily passed from one tower to the next. Large enough to function as small, fortified bastions and able to house 50 soldiers, the towers follow the line of the wall, surrounded by as many as nine additional walls to strengthen the position.

Over the centuries, large portions of the Great Wall have suffered a great deal of damage. Some sections collapsed entirely, and others have been gutted by the impoverished rural population, who, in need of the valuable building material, used the Great Wall as a quarry.

What is certainly the oldest surviving section of the wall, called the Cloud Terrace, is located at the Juyongguan Pass not far from Beijing. Built by Buddhist monks during the Yuan Dynasty (1271–1368), the gate carries an inscription celebrating the peaceful coexistence of neighbouring cultures. Proverbs, teachings and prayers are engraved here as well, dedicating the Cloud Terrace to a god called "the King of Heaven" who would protect them.

The Great Wall of China was declared a World Heritage Site by UNESCO in 1987. Today, it extends approximately 5,900 km along the northern Chinese border. Specific measurement of its actual length is next to impossible because parts of the wall are not one wall, but several more or less parallel stretches of fortification with a great many junctions, twists and turns. Nevertheless, it is without a doubt the largest structure on Earth and the only feature visible with the naked eye, weather conditions permitting, from outer space.

Above: Wall, wall, wall, as far as the eye can see! Although its length cannot be calculated exactly, most estimates lie between 5,900 and 6,400 km.

Left: Troops could move very quickly along the "High Street", where up to ten foot soldiers or five horsemen could advance side by side.

CHINA

Karst Formations of Guilin

IN THE NORTHERN PART OF THE CHINESE PROVINCE OF GUANGXI, THE LI RIVER FLOWS LIKE A BAND OF BLUE SILK THROUGH THE PICTURESQUE LANDSCAPE SURROUNDING THE CITY OF GUILIN. FROM THE RIVER'S SHORES RISE THE FAMOUS DISTINCT ROCK FORMATIONS.

The city of Guilin, first mentioned some 2,100 years ago during the Qin Dynasty, can look back on a long and colourful history. Now as then, however, it is its natural features that attract the most attention. Guilin is located on the shores of the Li, a river that flows through a remarkable limestone landscape that came into being more than 200 million years ago. Tectonic shifts and a rising seabed emptied a primordial inland sea, leaving behind a fantastic vista of numerous prominent and bizarre pinnacles, known to geologists as 'karst formations'.

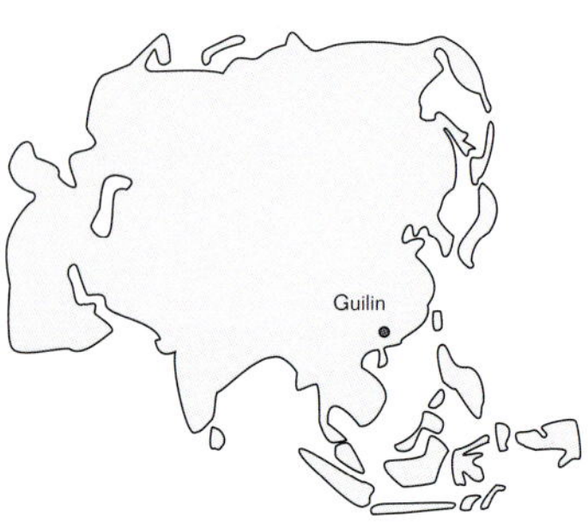

Karst landscapes are the product of erosion and are typically characterized by rugged cliffs, sinkholes and caves. The native stone is usually gypsum or limestone. Over a great length of time, the surface is slowly eroded, washed away by precipitation. As the water flows away over the cliffs and flanks of the hills and steep slopes, it leaves behind deep furrows and channels known as 'karren'. The water penetrates the porous bedrock, eating away the stone to form wide, branching tunnels and caves of all sizes, some with enormous, cathedral-like chambers. In subtropical and other warm, humid climates, like the conditions around Guilin, towers, cones and humps of limestone are common, many

Right: Stalactites and stalagmites in the Reed Flute Cave of Guilin.

Below: The Elephant Trunk Hill (Xiangbishang) resembles an elephant drinking from the river.

large enough to be visible from far away, rising from the landscape as distinct formations. While their appearance is a not uncommon result of extreme and intense erosion over a long period of time, the karst formations of Guilin are far and away the most beautiful examples of the type. For the Chinese, the Guilin region is the very epitome of natural beauty. As an ancient proverb says, "the landscape around Guilin is the most beautiful beneath the heavens".

The most recognizable feature of Guilin, called the Elephant Trunk Hill (Xiangbishan), rises from the blue confluence of the Yang and Li rivers. This is a natural arc of stone that resembles an elephant standing in the Li River sucking up water with its trunk. East of Guilin city lies the 40-hectare Seven Stars (Qixingyan) Park. As the name suggests, it includes seven of these fantastic limestone formations that, taken together, resemble the Big Dipper constellation. Also within its bounds are the Seven Star caves, Camel Hill, Guihai Stele Forest, the Longying Cliffs and other magnificent natural wonders. The largest and most impressive of all the karst formation caves is known as the Reed Flute Cave (Ludiyan), a unique stalactite cave deep within the Mountain of Light (Guangming) directly northwest of the city. This nearly 240-metre-deep cave contains a sea of stalactites and stalagmites. One chamber of the cave, the Crystal Palace of the Dragon King, is so large that 1,000 people could easily fit inside. The cave is called the Reed Flute Cave because of the lush growth of reeds at its entrance, reeds that are still used to make traditional flutes.

The very centre of the city of Guilin, which has a population of over a million, is the location of yet another magnificent formation rising over the roofs of the city: the Peak of Unique Beauty (Du Xiu Feng). More than 300 steps have been cut into its 152-metre-high cliff face. The Peak of Unique Beauty lies near the former palaces of the South Chinese kings, the Wangcheng. Very little remains of the palaces themselves, however, except for a pair of rundown fortifications and the ruins of four monumental gates.

The karst formation called Piled Silk Bundle (Die Cai Shan) resembles a pile of different coloured silk cloths stacked on top of one another. During the Ming Dynasty, four Chinese logograms were chiselled into the limestone proclaiming this and the surrounding region *Jiang Shan Hui Jing Chu* – "where the fantastic landscapes meet".

FACTS

*** Type of landscape:** The South Chinese Guilin landscape is described as a karst formation with conical and tower karsts.

*** Age:** Its geological age is ca. 200 million years old.

*** Attractions:** Local sights include the Reed Flute Cave, Elephant Trunk Hill, Peak of Unique Beauty, Wave Subduing Hill and Hill of the Seven Coloured Levels.

VIETNAM

Halong Bay

IN THE NORTH VIETNAMESE HALONG BAY, NATURE HAS PRODUCED ONE OF THE MOST EXTRAORDINARY KARST LANDSCAPES IN THE WORLD. THE BAY'S NEARLY 2,000 SMALL ISLANDS FORM A LANDSCAPE AS MAGNIFICENT AS IT IS BIZARRE.

The fifteenth-century Vietnamese king waxed poetic upon seeing the island world of Halong Bay near the Tonkin Gulf: "Hundreds of streams flow around the hills, the wide-strewn islands like the sea's chess board, rising up to meet the sky." The primal forces of nature created the most beautiful island landscape in the world in northern Vietnam. In an area of around 1,500 km², some 2,000 small rocky islands came into being about 300 million years ago. Consisting primarily of shelly limestone formed in a marine environment, each island is a labyrinth of caves, grottoes and winding tunnels.

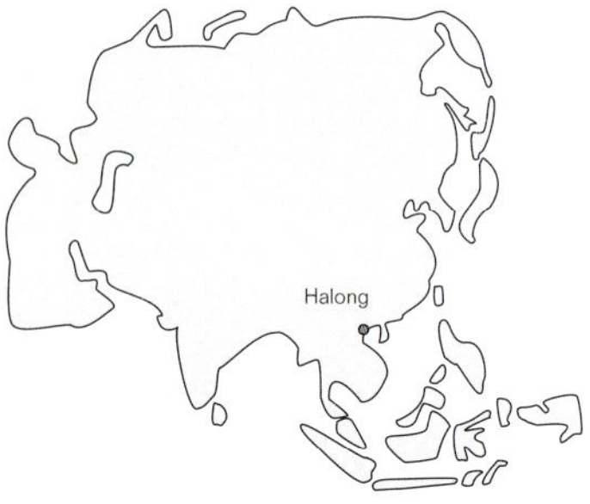

The legends about Ha Long, which means "descending dragon", tell of a dragon sent by the gods to defend the local inhabitants from enemies invading the region from the north. The dragon Ha Long drove the invaders back through the bay, striking at them with powerful blows of its tail, carving up any landmasses in its path into smaller and smaller islands. The enemies were driven out permanently; the islands and caves remained.
Out of gratitude, the local inhabitants named the bay after the dragon that saved them: Halong. Even today, it is said that the dragon lives somewhere in the bay, deep beneath the water's surface, where it continues to ensure the well-being of the bay people.

The cliff faces are hollowed out into enormous caves in numerous places, as can be seen here, in this view of a fishing boat from inside the Hang Trong Grotto.

FACTS

*** Location:** Halong Bay is located in the Tonkin Gulf, Vietnam.

*** Unique:** The bay contains over 2,000 rocky islands made of shelly limestone.

*** Area:** Its area is approximately 1,500 km^2.

*** History:** Its geological origins go back over 300 million years.

*** World Heritage:** Halong Bay was named a World Natural Heritage Site by UNESCO in 1994.

Today, the dragon protects the nearly 300 families that make their living by fishing on the bay. The fishing villages have no streets and no town square, but are villages that float on the water. Most live in small houseboats with bamboo roofs that serve both as housing and as a place to tie their fishing vessels. They will never leave "their" bay, and spend their entire lives on water. Many of these families have followed the ebb and flow of the tides for generations, going about their daily work sailing between the rocky islands.

For them, Halong Bay itself is home, giving them nourishment, housing and protection. If a storm rises up out of the South China Sea, the fishermen can easily take shelter in one of the many grottoes that dot the islets. Tunnels lead to protected waters inside the rock formations, which are themselves otherwise uninhabited. Over the course of millions of years the caves and grottoes have developed bizarre stalactite formations filling domelike chambers, while stalagmites ring the shoreline of cave seas.

Settlement among the islands of Halong Bay has been forbidden since 1994, with an exception made for the traditional fishermen and their families, who are officially tolerated because they clean up after the ever-increasing numbers of tourists visiting the bay. This has ensured that, up to now, the ecosystem of Halong Bay has remained intact. The flora and fauna that inhabit its waters are lush, with a particularly wide range of species present. The islands are also the much-visited hunting grounds of a variety of tropical birds and seabirds, from herons to eagles to parrots, some species of which have virtually taken over entire islands. The underwater environment is a veritable paradise for fish, crustaceans and corals. Over 150 species of coral and well over 1,000 species of fish have been identified thus far in Halong Bay, where they thrive on the nutrient-rich reefs. Lobsters, prawns and crabs hide themselves in the caves and fissures of the rugged underwater mountains.

Unfortunately, the natural paradise of Halong Bay is also under threat, mainly by the pollution that is the product of industrialization in nearby, highly productive coal mining regions. UNESCO has supported the efforts of the Vietnamese government to protect the country's number one tourist attraction and one the world's most endangered landscapes.

Centre: The Vietnamese fishermen are permitted to go about their daily work inside the nature preserve. In compensation, they clean up the 'legacy' (i.e. the refuse left behind by tourists).

Bottom: Over 300 families still live permanently in Halong Bay and make their living by fishing. They live on houseboats and houses set on floating rafts.

INDIA

Hawa Mahal

HAWA MAHAL, THE "PALACE OF THE WINDS", IS THE EMBLEM OF THE CITY OF JAIPUR ABOUT 300 KM SOUTH-WEST OF DELHI. ALTHOUGH LITTLE MORE THAN ITS FAÇADE SURVIVES, IT IS ONE OF THE MOST-PHOTOGRAPHED BUILDINGS OF THE SUBCONTINENT.

When the elaborately decorated five-storey façade of the Hawa Mahal reflects the red of the setting sun, all of Jaipur is enveloped in a reddish haze, radiating a soft pink light. The capital of the state of Rajasthan is often called the Pink City because of this peculiar effect. The city of Jaipur, first founded in 1727, is a jewel of Indian architecture. Even its most simple houses were built of red-brown brick, and its monumental buildings lead viewers back in time to an India of the far distant past. What marvellous tales these walls could tell of A Thousand and One Nights!

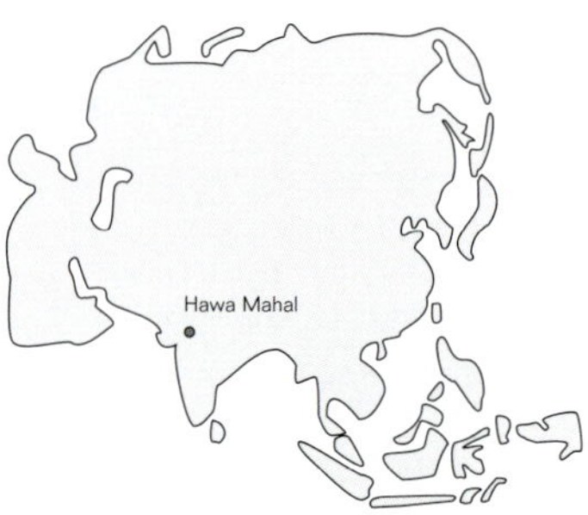

The "Palace of the Winds" is located in the heart of Jaipur's Old City. Consisting entirely of a single façade, Hawa Mahal is a masterpiece of architecture, a castle-in-the-air in every sense of the word.

In 1799, the ruler of Jaipur, Maharaja Pratap Singh II, commissioned the Hawa Mahal as the east wing of his already enormous fairy-tale palace. The five storeys, each just one room deep, were stacked like the cells of a beehive atop one another, with stone grilles over each window to allow breezes (*hawa*) to pass through and circulate throughout the building. It had over 950 windows and bays, giving the palace façade the air of an oversized, finely worked jewellery box or treasure chest. Indeed, the latter is

FACTS

*** Name:** The name Hawa Mahal means "Palace of the Winds".

*** Location:** It is located in the old city of Jaipur, capital of the Indian state of Rajasthan.

*** Construction:** It was commissioned by Maharaja Pratap Singh II, who hired Lad Chand Usta, an astrologer, as his architect in 1799.

*** Use:** The Hawa Mahal is part of the palace harem. It has 953 windows and bays on its façade, permitting the women who lived inside to look out without being seen.

The bays with their tiny windows resemble the cells of a beehive. The women of the harem could sit behind them, unnoticed, and observe the whirl of activity taking place on the streets below.

exactly what the palace was meant to be. The façade hid its very special treasures from the eyes of the common people, for the Hawa Mahal was built for the maharaja's harem.

It was Pratap Singh II who built the Hawa Mahal as an extension of his harem, the hidden quarters occupied by the women of the court. The Hawa Mahal with its many stone-grilled windows would permit the women to look out on the busy street life as well as the colourful festival processions of the maharaja himself, all without attracting a single curious stare from the general public. Designed as a fantastic façade blocking all access from the outside, the Hawa Mahal needed no gate or door and, in fact, it has no front entryway at all. It could only be entered from the rear, directly from the other parts of the maharaja's palace. The sheer number of windows, niches and bays – 953 in all – illustrate how lavish and over-the-top the lifestyle of the Jaipur rulers could be, as does the pomp and circumstance with which the maharaja celebrated his festivals.

A great many stories and legends swirl around the Palace of the Winds. One of these tells of the maharaja's crown jewel, the Sawai Jai Singh, one of the greatest treasures in all of India. According to tradition, it was built into the foundations of the Hawa Mahal. Maharaja Pratap Singh II employed his astrologer Lad Chand Usta as his architect, and it is said to have been on his advice that the jewel was buried in a subterranean chamber, again, according to legend, together with a poisonous snake to guard it from theft. The snake was so deadly that merely sniffing its breath would send any invader directly to the afterworld. These legends may be the reason why so many snake charmers congregate around the Hawa Mahal, practising their trade in the streets that lie in the shadow of the Palace of the Winds.

Above: Today, a group of apes occupy the former harem of the maharaja's palace in Jaipur.

Left: The Hawa Mahal is five storeys high. Over 950 windows and bays decorate its elaborate façade.

TURKEY

The Treasures of Istanbul

WHETHER IT IS CALLED BYZANTIUM, CONSTANTINOPLE OR ISTANBUL, AS IT IS NOW, THIS MAGNIFICENT CITY STRADDLING TWO CONTINENTS, AND THE CAPITAL OF THREE WORLD EMPIRES, HAS NEVER LOST ITS ABILITY TO FASCINATE.

Yet, at the same time, the city has changed. While the walls of Byzantium were home to a population of half a million, at least ten million people live in Istanbul today. Just as Byzantium was the famous capital city of the Byzantine Empire, inheritor of Rome's glory, Constantinople was the residence of the Ottoman Sultans, as well as the political capital and administrative centre of their wide-ranging empire. Modern Istanbul is the densely populated, world-renowned spiritual and cultural centre of the Republic of Turkey, the geographical interface between Orient and Occident. In this melting pot of cultures, the eastern and western hemispheres meet in a unique synthesis within this fascinating city where tradition and modernity live side by side.

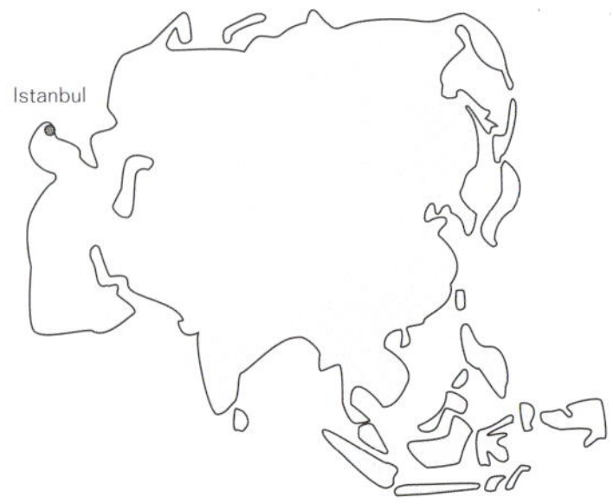

Asia and Europe meet here on the straits called the Bosphorus, with Istanbul extending along the coast on both sides, straddling two continents. While the two halves are physically held together only by the thin bands of its filigreed bridges, historically and culturally they have been inseparable for centuries.

It was the Delphic Oracle who told a Greek named Byzas, a native of Megara, to leave his homeland to found the city of Byzantium. Listening to the oracle, Byzas did just that, settling along the famous Bosphorus in 658 BCE. His colony, Byzantion, brought

Right: The Church of Holy Wisdom, the Hagia Sophia, is a monumental example of Byzantine architecture.

Below: A view of the nave, Hagia Sofia's enormous central space.

the world of the Mediterranean closer to the distant peoples of the Black Sea, making it an important trade centre. Its prime geographical location would give it international significance under the reign of the Romans, Byzantines and Ottomans.

In 333 CE, the Roman emperor Constantine I, a supporter of Christianity who nevertheless remained deeply rooted in Roman traditions, moved the capital of the Roman empire from Rome to the city on the Bosphorus, first renamed "Nova Roma" and later Constantinople after the emperor himself. Constantine would build his new Rome on the city's seven hills, but it would be Justinian I who would build the monumental patriarchal "Church of Holy Wisdom", the Hagia Sofia, over the ruins of a sixth-century temple. The very definition of the Byzantine style of architecture, this enormous, innovative and influential sacred structure was completed within a mere five years.

The year 1204, when a new Crusade was launched, was a dark year for the "Pearl on the Bosphorus". On their way to the Holy Land, Crusaders attacked the city, plundered its treasures, and slaughtered its inhabitants in a bloodbath that may have killed as many as 100,000 of its population of half a million. Artworks of immeasurable worth were destroyed or taken away; most would never be returned. After this devastating blow the city very slowly recovered, and by the fourteenth century it had regained much of its old glory. The streets pulsed with life, while art and architectural achievements reached new heights. Yet the Ottomans were soon on the scene, ending the Byzantine dream of an eternal city on the Bosphorus. Over the next 500 years, well into the twentieth century, the Ottoman Sultans remade Constantinople in their image, with the fate of the city inexorably linked to the fortunes of the empire.

Hagia Sophia, the Church of Holy Wisdom, is a uniquely monumental example of Byzantine architecture. This ecclesiastical masterpiece was built between 532 and 537 with no less a figure than Emperor Justinian I himself taking full responsibility from the very beginning as "Building Master in Charge". He visited the construction site daily to monitor its progress, bringing in the experienced architect Isidorius of Miletus to direct the design.

Despite the enormous difficulties encountered during its construction – its walls collapsed several times due to earthquakes and the accelerated pace of construction, which often did not allow enough time for the mortar between the bricks to dry before continuing ever upwards – the emperor and his architect

FACTS

✱ World Heritage:
The historical sections of Istanbul, including famous buildings, such as the Hagia Sofia, Blue Mosque and Topkapı Palace, were declared World Heritage Sites by UNESCO in 1985.

✱ Humble sultan:
Even the sultan bowed before entering an Islamic holy building. An iron chain hangs from the ceiling of the western gate to the courtyard of the Blue Mosque, positioned so as to force the sultan to bow his head as he rides into the sacred space, a symbolic act of humility and respect.

The magnificent Blue Mosque takes its name from the elaborate blue and white tiles decorating the dome and the upper registers of its walls.

achieved their goal of producing a magnificent building in record time. With a breadth of 31 metres and a height of 55 metres, the most outstanding feature of Hagia Sofia is its dome rising above the central space. The interior of the church is illuminated by light from windows at the base of the dome, giving it a sense of lightness that defies belief. Equally impressive are the mosaics, columns and galleries, as well as the four minarets added by the Ottoman rulers following their conquest of Constantinople in 1453. In that year, this centre of Orthodox Christianity was transformed into the city's primary mosque, a position it held until 1932. Atatürk, the father of the modern Turkish Republic, turned Hagia Sofia into a museum, and Christian insignia and furnishings were once again permitted in the building.

In the fifteenth century, the Ottomans built the sultan's palace – really a city within the city – at the very tip of the peninsula. The sultan and his administrators would reside and govern within the Topkapı Palace complex for the next 500 years. The sultan's personal living area, including a harem, was located at the centre of a series of courtyards, pavilions and gardens. At any given moment, as many as 40,000 people might live and work in Topkapı Palace. Its design and construction was entrusted to the most famous of all Ottoman architects, the master builder Mimar Sinan, who perfected the engineering and aesthetic qualities of the Byzantine dome. The palace represents the culmination of his superb artistry.

No other dynastic rulers' private quarters have attracted as much interest, much of it of an erotic nature, as the "forbidden place" of Topkapı Palace – its famous harem. Primarily the rooms where women and girls received instruction in music, dance and art, it was also the residence of the sultan's favoured wives, the ones who would bear him children. Within the harem, competition for this honour was intense, with the sultan himself making the final decisions. Up to 2,000 women and girls could live in the harem, guarded and watched over by an army of eunuchs.

The decor of Topkapı Palace reflects the immeasurable wealth of the Ottoman Empire. The interiors made use of only the finest building materials, the most expensive furnishings, the most luxurious carpets and most delicate tapestries. Extravagant quantities of gold were the material of choice for the opulently decorated spaces. Finely glazed Iznik tiles

Right: The sultan's harem was the home of up to 2,000 women and girls.

Below: Topkapı Palace enclosed an area of about 70 hectacres. As many as 40,000 people lived and worked here.

can be found throughout the palace, but especially in the harem, where the walls are covered in tiles decorated with entwining vegetation, the Tree of Life and the flowers of the heavenly garden.

The sultan commissioned the famous Blue Mosque at the beginning of the seventeenth century, selecting Mehmet Aga, a student of Mimar Sinan, as his architect. The new mosque, named for the blue and white registers of decorative stone and tile that adorn the dome and the upper parts of the wall, would stand directly opposite the Hagia Sofia. The tiles covering the lower parts of the wall are even more interesting because of their historical art value. These are the so-called "Iznik Fayence" tiles, identifiable by their red-brown pigment imported from eastern Turkey, each piece a masterpiece of the golden age of Ottoman decorative ceramics.

The six minarets of the Blue Mosque emphasize its importance within Islam, for none but the Great Mosque in Mecca, with seven, has more. According to court historians, the six minarets were built as the result of a misunderstanding between the sultan and his architect. The sultan had requested that the minarets be gilded, yet the budget did not permit the purchase of so much gold. In response, Mehmet Aga "misunderstood" the order, which in Turkish would have been for *altın* (gold) minarets, as an order for *altı* (six) minarets. Was the clever architect rewarded or punished for this mishap? The court chronicles do not say.

Constantinople was the lively and attractive centre of the Ottoman Empire until well into the nineteenth century, when the lack of a coherent political or economic policy on the part of the sultans began to have an effect. Industrialization, for example, was rejected outright by the sultans, and the empire suffered severe financial losses, bringing on its disintegration and ultimate collapse into bankruptcy. By 1923, Constantinople was no longer the capital city of Turkey. In a move designed to separate the new, post-imperial government as much as possible from that of the old Ottoman Empire, the capital was moved to Ankara. The sultanate and caliphate were abolished, with Arabic script replaced by the Latin alphabet. On 28 March 1930, the founder and president of the new Republic of Turkey, Kemal Atatürk, renamed the city – Constantinople would now be called Istanbul. The city on the Bosphorus between Asia and Europe retains its cultural and economic importance to this day. As the gateway to Europe, Istanbul is still hard at work, providing the impetus for Turkey's opening to the West.

DATES

* *circa* **658 BCE:** The colony of Byzantion was founded by Greeks.
* **196 CE:** The Roman emperor Septimus Severus conquered the city.
* **324:** Emperor Constantine entered the city. He renamed it Nova Roma, but on 11 May 440 it became Constantinople.
* **395:** Constantinople became the capital of the Eastern Roman Empire.
* **532:** Justinian I commissioned the Hagia Sophia, completed in 537.
* **1204:** Crusaders plundered the city, slaughtering many of its inhabitants.
* **1453:** Ottoman sultan Mehmet II conquered Constantinople after many years of siege.
* **1609–16:** The Sultan-Ahmet-Mosque, called the Blue Mosque, was built.
* **1923:** Turkey's capital was moved to Ankara.
* **1934–35:** Hagia Sophia became a museum.

JAPAN

The Itsukushima Shrine

SHINTO, THE "WAY OF THE GODS", IS THE PRIMORDIAL RELIGION OF JAPAN. ANYONE WHO DIES AUTOMATICALLY BECOMES A 'KAMI', OR SPIRIT, AND THEREBY PART OF THE DIVINE NATURE OF ALL THINGS. HONOURING KAMI IS THE FOCUS OF SHINTOISM.

While kami may reside in any tree, shrub, animal or, indeed, in an inanimate object, such as a rock or mountain, they are most properly worshipped in shrines. These are places where the kami gather – sacred, impenetrable places where they can reside undisturbed. Even the people who would like to honour them are forbidden to set foot where kami have taken up residence, which means that the intercession of priests is required to fulfil ceremonial duties. One such sacred place is the Shinto shrine on the island of Itsukushima, also known as Miyajima, located not far from Hiroshima. The island is understood to harbour a great many kami, and for many centuries was subject to a strict taboo: no one was allowed to set foot on its shores, not even a priest. As a result, when a shrine was erected to honour the kami by offering them prayers and gifts, it was built on pillars standing in the coastal waters, reachable only by boat at high tide.

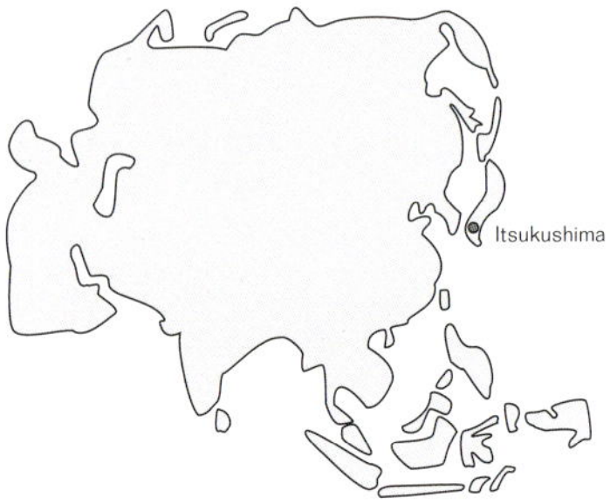

As one nears the filigree woodwork construction with its red columns and gilded decoration, the entire structure seems to float gently on the waves. Built on pilings sunk deep into the mud by believers who dared not break the taboo, the shrine itself sits just offshore, approached by an enormous gate ("torii") set in front of the shrine in the middle of

The 16-m-tall gate, called a 'torii', stands in the bay as the entrance to the shrine. It symbolizes the imaginary border between the profane and the sacred. The Itsukushima torii is one of the emblems of Japan.

DATES

*** 592–628** Empress Suiko's regency. It is thought that the first shrine on this site was built in 593.

*** 806:** The Buddhist monk Kukai climbed Mount Misen, the highest point of the island.

*** 881:** First documented evidence of the shrine.

*** 1118–81** The reign of the warlord, Taira no Kiyomori.

*** 1164:** He commissioned building of the main Shinto shrine buildings, at the same time donating 33 Buddhist Sutra scrolls to the monks on the island.

*** 1207 and 1223:** The complex was destroyed by fire.

*** 1325:** A typhoon heavily damaged the buildings.

*** 1571:** The complex reached its current form.

*** 1874–75:** The great torii was rebuilt.

*** 1996:** The shrine was named a World Cultural Monument by UNESCO.

the bay. The 16-metre-tall gate stands in water except for a short period at low tide, when visitors can approach it by foot through the surrounding mud. The torii of the Shinto shrine of Itsukushima is one of the most photographed sights in Japan.

The first shrine building was erected in the sixth century, reaching its present-day form around 1168 under the patronage of the famous Taira no Kiyomori, a much-feared warlord. While many bright red columns support the roof of the shrine, it is otherwise open to the elements on every side, and has no permanent walls. This leaves the interior of the shrine open to divine nature, permitting the kami to come and go freely with no restrictions.

What was forbidden in Shintoism was a challenge to the Buddhists, who were the first to break the taboo and step on Itsukushima Island. Zen Buddhism is the second largest religion in Japan, long in competition with the Shinto belief system. It was a Buddhist monk, Kukai, who in 866 first stepped on the island while on a journey to the ancient imperial city, Kyoto. This vigorous follower of Guatama Buddha, tying his pack tighter, climbed the island's highest peak, Mount Misen, in the process stomping on Shinto beliefs with his bare feet. But Kukai climbed Mount Misen with conviction; after all, from a Buddhist perspective, the physical world has no meaning. According to legend, Kukai then lit a fire on top of the mountain, pulled an iron pot from his pack and boiled water in it. Since that time, there has always been a Buddhist monk posted atop the mountain to make sure that Kukai's fire never goes out and that there is always enough water boiling in the pot.

It is possible that the fact that Kukai's actions went unpunished was enough to undermine Shintoism. Whether it was Guatama Buddha himself who called Kukai to this act of provocation, as tradition recounts, is unknown. We do know that Shintoists and Buddhists share the island in peaceful agreement, now and likely in both the recent and distant past, each practising their religious rituals side by side and even with each other. The atmosphere of the Shinto Shrine of Itsukushima is dominated by the emptiness of its space. A person who enters the shrine stands alone in the presence of their very self. In the Buddhist temple, in contrast, worshippers prostrate themselves, kneeling in humility before an image of the great Buddha.

Centre: At high tide, the filigree, open-sided Shinto shrine seems to float gently in the water.

Bottom: The shrine is supported by bright red columns, but is otherwise open to the air on all sides with no permanent walls.

ISRAEL

Jerusalem

JERUSALEM IS A RELIGIOUS FOCAL POINT FOR THE THREE GREAT FAITHS OF JUDAISM, ISLAM AND CHRISTIANITY; IT IS ALSO RECORDED IN EIGHTEENTH-CENTURY BCE LETTERS FROM THE REIGN OF PHARAOH ANKHENATON AS URUSHALAIM, CITY OF PEACE.

For Christians, the Old City of Jerusalem and its nearby environs are holy because this is the site of the passion, crucifixion and resurrection of Jesus Christ. For Jews, Jerusalem is the Holy City, the capital of the first kingdom of the Jews. And for Moslems, the city is holy because of its connection with the Prophet Mohammed's journey to heaven. He is understood to have ascended to heaven from what is today the Temple Mount, known as the "Noble Sanctuary", *al Haram al Sharif* in Arabic. Over the centuries the city has frequently been the focus of sectarian violence, war and other varieties of conflict between religions and governments. Indeed, over the course of its long history, Jerusalem, a city that means so much to so many people all over the world, has known few periods of peace, though "peace" is a part of its name: *shalom* in Hebrew and *salam* in Arabic.

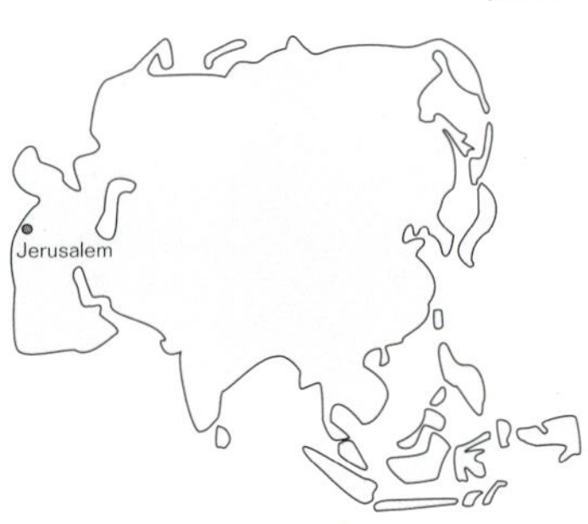

Jerusalem is one of the oldest urban settlements: the area has been continually occupied for at least 5,000 years. Egyptian sources mention the city in the eighteenth century BCE by the name Urushalaim, one translation of which is "city of peace". The legendary King David conquered Jerusalem in 997 BCE, making "the City of David" the centre of the Kingdom of Israel. Since then Jerusalem has served as the reli-

Right: The Church of the Holy Sepulchre is the holiest site of Christianity. Six Christian churches administer it.

Below: The Western Wall, or Wailing Wall of the Temple Mount.

gious and cultural centre of Judaism. It was David's successor, Solomon (969–930 BCE), who built the great Temple to Yahweh in the centre of the Old City. Over the following centuries it was repeatedly desecrated and destroyed. Herod the Great built the Second Temple on the site, which in turn was destroyed by the Roman Titus in 70 CE. The Arabs conquered Jerusalem in 637, leaving the Christian population in peace following the Orthodox patriarchs' voluntary handover of the city.

Crusaders rode into the city under the command of Gottfried von Bouillon in 1099, and in just three days proceeded to slaughter the civilian population, killing as many as 20,000 inhabitants. By 1187, Saladin, then sultan of Egypt, had succeeded in regaining control of Jerusalem. Between 1229 and 1244 it was once again the Crusaders, this time under Emperor Frederick II, who ruled the city. Thereafter, the city was ruled by the Ayyubids and Mamluks. By 1516, the city was only inhabited by about 10,000 people and was no longer important. Only Moslems were given citizenship and legal rights.

The Ottoman Turks took over rule of Jerusalem in 1516, leading to a period of expansion and progress. Sultan Suleyman I, the Magnificent, rebuilt the fortifications around the city, walls that still stand today, giving Jerusalem's Old City its characteristic appearance. Jews and Christians were considered second-class citizens in that period, a situation that continued into the middle of the nineteenth century, when the situation worsened. In the years following 1860, more and more Jews emigrated to Jerusalem, settling in new quarters outside the old city walls. Then came World War I, during which British troops occupied Jerusalem in 1917. The British mandate as well as growing Jewish immigration led to increased tensions and overt conflict between the Arabs, the Jews and the British.

In 1947, the United Nations adopted the Partition Plan for Palestine, ending the British mandate and dividing the country into two states: one Jewish and one Arab. The status of Jerusalem was to be international. The Jews accepted the plan and declared the State of Israel. The Arabs rejected the Partition Plan and declared war on Israel. Jerusalem was consequently divided, with its western part within Israel and its eastern part annexed to Jordan. In 1950, Israel declared Jerusalem its capital city. With a few exceptions, the international community refused to recognize Jerusalem as such.

In the Six Day War of June 1967, Israeli paratroopers occupied East Jerusalem, and by the end of

DATES

* ***circa* 1000 BCE:** The fortified city of Zion (Jerusalem) is founded.

* **587 BCE:** Nebuchadnezzar conquers Jerusalem and destroys the First Temple.

* **164 BCE:** The Temple Mount is recaptured by the Maccabis.

* **66 CE:** Year of the Jewish Revolt against Rome.

* **70:** Titus destroys the Second Temple.

* **135:** Jerusalem is destroyed again.

* **335:** The Church of the Holy Sepulchre is consecrated.

* **527–565:** Golden Age of Byzantine Jerusalem.

* **1187:** Saladin conquers Jerusalem.

* **1538–39:** The Ottoman rulers build the Jaffa Gate and restore the Lion Gate.

* **1887:** A new gate is built providing entry to the Christian quarter.

The al-Aqsa Mosque, the largest mosque in Jerusalem, rises on the Temple Mount, which Moslems call al-Haram al-Sharif. Built by Islamic rulers and considered an affront by many Jews and Christians, who feel its existence diminishes the significance of the site according to their faiths, the al-Aqsa mosque has often been the site of religious confrontation.

June, despite the United Nations' protest, Israel annexed East Jerusalem to Israel and declared it to be within the municipal boundaries of Jerusalem. The Israeli occupation of East Jerusalem remains a subject of controversy and is considered by many parties as one of the major hindrances to peace between Israelis and Palestinians.

Jerusalem is still a city of many religions and related movements and cults. Over the course of many centuries, the world religions of Judaism, Christianity and Islam have left the deepest impression. Magnificent buildings, fascinating ruins and stunning masterpieces sit side by side, making the city a religious and historical art centre of the highest rank. In this regard, as well as in the religious sense, Jerusalem has been truly blessed.

The Church of the Holy Sepulchre is located at the very heart of the Old City. Eastern Orthodox Christians call it the Church of the Resurrection, believing it to mark the place where Jesus was buried and where he rose again from the dead. The altar of the church lies directly over a hole in the bedrock, believed to be the very hole in which the cross of the crucifixion once stood. Scholars continue to debate whether this is indeed Golgotha, which the Bible says was outside the city, as would be expected according to what is known of Roman executions and Jewish burial practices. Although alternate sites for the crucifixion and burial of Christ have been proposed, belief that this is the place goes back at least to the time of Constantine the Great, and there is scholarship that suggests the church did lie outside the city walls at the time of the events in question.

The administration of this holy site is shared among the Greek Orthodox, Roman Catholic, Armenian, Syrian Orthodox, Coptic Christian and Ethiopian churches. The wide variations between their individual beliefs can lead to tension and territorial infighting at this most revered place in all of Christianity.

The Dome of the Rock sits high above the city on the Temple Mount, called Haram al-Sharif in Arabic. It is among the oldest Islamic religious buildings in the world (687–691). It is not a mosque, but literally a shrine honouring "the rock", a hollow in the bedrock where, according to tradition, the Prophet Mohammed stepped and left this print as he began his ascent to heaven. The Dome is one of

Right: The Dome of the Rock is one of the oldest Islamic monumental religious buildings in the world.

Below: The famous Mount of Olives stands outside the gates of Jerusalem.

the earliest examples of monumental Islamic architecture and one of the most recognizable symbols of the city of Jerusalem. The shrine, octagonal in plan, is 55 metres in diameter. The exterior of its magnificent dome is covered in sheets of pure gold, but the elaborate mosaics that adorn every surface of its interior are, if anything, an even greater wonder.

The Western Wall that Jews revere is a remnant of the original 400-metre-long terraced platform that supported the Second Temple, built by Herod the Great on this site and destroyed by the Romans in the year 70 CE. The Wailing Wall, as other religious communities call it, is the holiest Jewish site. Ever since the Six Day War ended in 1967, large numbers of pilgrims have journeyed here to pray. Many faithful insert small pieces of paper with prayers and special requests into the cracks between the stones. Most Jews view the Western Wall as a symbol of the covenant between God and the Jewish people.

The al-Aqsa Mosque also sits atop Haram al-Sharif, not far from the Dome of the Rock. The Haram, with its two important sacred buildings, is the third most important site in all of Islam, after the Kaaba in Mecca and the Mosque of the Prophet in Medina. The al-Aqsa Mosque was begun some 30 years later than the Dome of the Rock (705–715) on the site of the Christian church of St. Maria, atop which the Moslem ruler al-Walid set a dome in 711, declaring the once-Christian basilica a mosque in the process. This deep affront to the Christian community, along with the fact that both the al-Aqsa mosque and the Dome of the Rock sit on the Temple Mount, has led to tensions between the different religions that have spread far outside Jerusalem itself.

One modern site in Jerusalem is devoted to the most horrifying events of more recent history. Known unofficially outside Israel as the Holocaust Museum, its official designation is "Holocaust Martyrs' and Heroes' Remembrance Authority". Its Hebrew name, *Yad Vashem*, means "a memorial and a name", a reference to the biblical verse Isaiah 56:5, which states: "And to them will I give in my house and within my walls a memorial and a name, worth more than all my sons and daughters, an eternal name that shall not be wiped out." Both a memorial and a monument to the Jewish victims of the Nazis, an entire, cavernous hall of the museum is covered with small, engraved plates bearing their names. A visit to Yad Vashem leaves a deep impression, with exhibitions of the horrors of the holocaust designed not so much to reproach as to raise awareness and rouse visitors to action.

DATES

* **1926:** The Church of the Holy Sepulchre was badly damaged by an earthquake.
* **1947:** Jerusalem was declared an international zone.
* **1948:** The Jewish quarter was partially destroyed by a Jordanian attack.
* **1948–68:** The Kingdom of Jordan administered the Old City and East Jerusalem.
* **1967:** The State of Israel took over the Old City and East Jerusalem during the Six Day War, reuniting the municipality.
* **1981:** Jerusalem was named a World Cultural Monument by UNESCO.

TURKEY

Cappadocia

OVER MILLENNIA, LAVA, WIND AND WATER HAVE PLAYED THEIR PART IN CREATING THE BIZARRE ROCK FORMATIONS OF CAPPADOCIA. THESE FORCES ARE STILL AT WORK TODAY ON THIS MASTERPIECE OF NATURE'S ART IN THE CENTRAL ANATOLIAN HIGHLANDS.

Cappadocia's fantastic landscape of rocks and cliffs is one of a kind: there is no other like it in the world. On this spot, millions of years ago, the Earth heaved and boiled and the nearby volcanoes of Erciyes and Hasan filled the air with their sulphurous smoke. A thick layer of ash covered the landscape and rivers of hot, glowing lava ran through it. This liquid landscape hardened, only to be further subjected to the whims of wind and water.

Millennia of heavy rainfall smoothed the rugged surface, collecting in rivers and streams that wound their way deep into the soft sedimentary bedrock. Meanwhile, the firmer strata, such as those composed of the igneous rock formed by volcanic action, stood firm in the face of the erosive forces, forming pinnacles that rise over the landscape like mountains with hats on their peaks, or perhaps giant mushrooms in a fairy tale. The Turks call these bizarre formations the *peri bacalar*, or "fairy chimneys". This magnificent landscape sculpted by natural forces extends over an area of 95 km^2, resembling a sculpture park that is forever under construction, as each piece is continuously altered into something new. The erosive forces carry on with their artistic efforts as if they were not yet satisfied with the result.

DATES

* *circa* 7000 – 6500 BCE: First human settlement in Cappadocia.
* *circa* 1600 – 650 BCE: Hittites, Phrygians and Lydians settled here.
* 402 BCE: The Greek historian Xenophon described the underground cities for the first time.
* 13th century CE: The Byzantine author Skutariotes described the Cappadocian cave cities.
* 1923: Greek Orthodox Christians abandoned the region following the Turkish War of Independence.

The Turks call the Cappadocian rock formations the *peri bacalar*, or "fairy chimneys".

When people arrived in this wild landscape, they settled here, seemingly against all logic, for it is not clear what this rugged, barren landscape had to offer. Yet the first traces of human settlement reach back far into the Neolithic period, nearly 10,000 years ago. The settlers gave Cappadocia its identity; throughout antiquity the inhabitants of this barely arable landscape were known as a wild, rough people. Up to very recent times, Cappadocians have altered the landscape to suit their purposes. They have dug into the rock formations, hollowed them out as living spaces, and sunk new caverns into the bedrock. The local stone is easily worked with the simplest tools, permitting entire cities to be settled in artificially created, or enhanced, tuff stone caves. In some cases, these underground cities extended deep beneath the surface, protecting their inhabitants from invaders as well as from the depredations of wind and weather. The caves remain pleasantly cool even on the hottest days, yet the bedrock also retains enough heat during the cold winters to keep the air temperature inside steady at between 10°C and 16°C.

Hittites, Phrygians, Persians and Romans have all settled here briefly, leaving behind sparse remains. Historically, Cappadocia was one of the most important centres of early Christianity, falling under the rule of the Byzantine Empire in 1071. Many of the over 1,000 cave churches date from the time when Christianity was spreading throughout Central Anatolia. Cave churches and cities are still being discovered today, often with interiors brightly painted with colourful frescos decorating walls and domed ceilings. They were places where early Christians could practise their faith in peace and security. Protected and hidden by walls of underground rock, with only a few, well-disguised entrances, these mysterious underground cities continue to fascinate.

Above: The village of Uchisar surrounds a rock formation in which the carved entrances to underground houses and churches can still be seen.

Left: The forces of erosion are responsible for the bizarre rock landscape of Cappadocia.

INDIA

Khajuraho

WHEN ENTERING THE TEMPLE COMPLEX OF KHAJURAHO, VISITORS SHOULD TRY TO SHED THE RESTRAINTS OF WESTERN MORALITY AND CULTURE. KHAJURAHO OFFERS AN EXPERIENCE OF IMMERSION IN THE STRANGE AND FASCINATING WORLD OF HINDUISM.

In 1839, British officer T. S. Burt came upon the sculpture-decorated temple complex of Khajuraho, reporting back with great exuberance that he had discovered what was "probably the most beautiful array of temples in all of India". However, what he wrote next about the subject matter of all that beauty betrays his own Victorian morality: "some of the sculptures are exceedingly improper and provocative...they include the depiction of the most shameful and indecent acts, profaning this Hindu religious site." **The Temples of Khajuraho** bear the stylistic signature of a rather unique school of architecture, one propagated by the Chandela kings between 950 and 1150, the time in which Khajuraho was built. There were originally 85 large and small temples here; today, only 25 of them remain. Each temple was designed as the embodiment of the human form: the foundation represented legs; the small spires, called 'shikhara', are laid out on an east-west axis in order from lowest to highest, representing the head. A disk holding a 'kalash', a pot full of nectar, crowns each spire, symbolizing immortality. The main shihkara is situated directly over the inner sanctum, the residence of the Hindu god to whom the temple is dedicated. The majority of the temples were dedicated to the three main

Details of two figures carved on the outer wall of the Parshvanatha Temple at Khajuraho: the god Vishnu, on the left, embraces the goddess Laksimi, on the right.

DATES

* **9th century:** The Temple of the 64 Yoginis (Chausath Yogini) was built. It had 64 compartments, each housing a statue of a servant of the goddess Kali. This is the oldest temple at Khajuraho.

* **930–950:** Lakshmana Temple was built.

* **950–970:** The Parshvanatha Temple, the largest and most beautiful of the Jain temples at the site, was built.

* **1000–1025:** Bloodthirsty Kali received a new temple: the Jagadambi.

* ***circa* 1130:** The Kandariya-Mahadewa Temple was built.

* **1150:** The Dulado Temple, one of the latest at the site, was built.

* **1870:** The Jain Shantinatha Temple was renovated and largely rebuilt.

FACTS

* The main gods of the Hindu belief system are Brahma, the Creator and god of wisdom; Shiva, the Destroyer and god of fertility; and Vishnu, the Preserver of the Universe.

Hindu deities: Brahma, Shiva and Vishnu. Others are dedicated to their many incarnations, embellished by the sculptor's imaginative powers. Khajuraho even has a few temples dedicated to the pantheon of another Indian religion, that of the Jains.

The graphic depictions of sexual acts unsettled the highly Victorian Captain Burt to his very core. In an explosion of creativity, the sculptors employed by the Chandela kings produced a unique interpretation of effervescent life: one that was opulent, sensual and, in part, involved a riot of passionate interaction between the sacred and profane worlds. In the context of Hindu mythology, of which we can be certain the honourable T. S. Burt had no knowledge whatsoever, these depictions of erotic acts are easily interpreted. According to Hindu belief, the act of love was not merely the uniting of man and woman, but of the male and female principles, abstract and eternal. Therefore, sexual intercourse symbolizes the creative act of the all-powerful deities that brought forth the entire universe. This melding of many into one universal entity is emphasized by the absolute equality accorded the male and female figures throughout the complex. The stylization and varieties of sexual congress depicted give spiritual weight to the act of love, portrayed with a self-awareness that negates any implication of vulgarity.

It is still not clear why the Chandela kings built the Khajuraho temples, which rank among the most magnificent architectural and artistic achievements of the Hindu world, where life is elevated from the realm of the base and vulgar to be understood instead as an aspect of the divine absolute.

The largest temple at Khajuraho is Kandariya Mahadewa. Dedicated to the god Shiva, its central spire is 31 metres tall. Over 800 figures carved from Kaimur sandstone decorate its walls and granite rosettes adorn its ceilings. Its impressive gateway, carved out of a single block of sandstone, consists of four elaborately sculpted arches resting on the heads of mythological crocodiles. As with all the Khajuraho temples, the erotic reliefs are concentrated on the exterior, on the sides of the building – never inside, never in the inner sanctum and never on the exterior near the main entrance. In fact, in Khajuraho as a whole, only about 10 per cent of all the relief sculptures fall into the erotic category that so shocked the early Victorians who rediscovered them.

Centre: Erotic figural groups from the outer façade of the Kanariya Mahadewa Temple.

Bottom: The Khajuraho temples bear the signature of a specific school of architecture that came into being during the years 950–1150 under the influence of the Chandela kings.

MALDIVES

The Maldives

ISLANDS IN THE SUN: NO OTHER COUNTRY IN THE WORLD FITS THIS DESCRIPTION AS WELL AS THIS GROUP OF 2,000 SMALL ISLANDS AND 20 CORAL ATOLLS IN THE INDIAN OCEAN OFF THE COAST OF SRI LANKA KNOWN TODAY AS THE REPUBLIC OF MALDIVES.

The Maldives are situated more or less in the middle of the Indian Ocean, some 450 km west of the southern tip of the Indian subcontinent and 700 km south-west of Sri Lanka. The island republic consists of 20 major coral atolls, extending over 800 km from north to south like a string of pearls, with the southernmost island lying just north of the equator. Of the 2,000 islets scattered among the atolls, around 200 are permanently inhabited and 87 others are reserved entirely for the use of tourists. Magnificent beaches and wondrous underwater nature preserves have led the Maldives to draw scuba divers, swimmers, sun worshippers, windsurfers and kayakers from all over the world like a magnet.

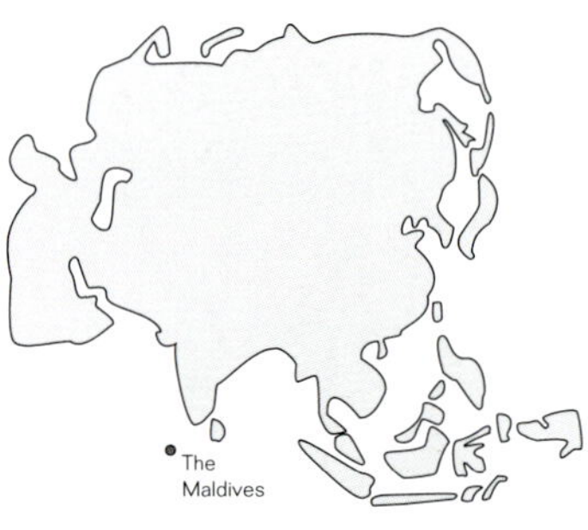

Their endless white sand beaches, crystal clear coastal waters, azure skies and non-stop sunshine have landed the Maldives on the cover of many a glossy travel magazine, making them a favourite destination for travel agents and holiday-makers alike. In fact, the Maldives are the genuine natural paradise they appear to be, particularly underwater. Divers exploring the species-rich waters of the coral reefs encounter nearly every life form that could possibly inhabit a tropical sea. The water temperature rarely falls below 27°C, with the air temperature

Right: A whale shark makes its way through one of the most magnificent marine animal preserves in the world.

Below: White sand beaches, crystal clear water and sunshine make the Maldives a tourist paradise.

ranging between the mid-20s during the monsoon months – which runs from November to March in the north-east, and from June through August in the south-west – to over 30°C. The natural beauty and tourist attractions, however, have somewhat obscured the fascinating historical background and present-day problems of the island republic.

The Maldives were first settled by Buddhist fishermen from India and Ceylon (today's Sri Lanka) in the fifth century BCE. Arab merchants and traders reached the islands in the twelfth century, establishing a sultanate and promoting Islam as the national religion. In the sixteenth century Portugal tried, and failed, to establish a colony there, defeated in a bloody war of rebellion by the local inhabitants. In the seventeenth century, the Dutch took over the government, ceding administration to the British in 1796. The Maldives were a British protectorate from 1887 to 1965. A republic was established in 1953, only to be struck down when the inhabitants voted to reinstate the sultanate under the leadership of Mohammed Farid Didi.

On 26 July 1965, the Maldives gained their independence, conditional on the sultanate being transformed into a republic. The president is the head of the government with unlimited executive powers. There are no political parties in the Western sense of the word and no religious freedom: the adherence of any citizen to a religion other than Sunni Islam is constitutionally banned. Human rights organizations have documented numerous rights violations and crimes and, despite the booming tourist industry, the inhabitants of the Maldives are among the poorest people in the world. Due to a lack of access to education and the fact that the strict variety of Islam promoted on the islands prohibits any contact with alcohol, foreigners are imported for most of the jobs related to tourism, with the majority of the bartenders, chefs and hotel workers coming from Sri Lanka, Indonesia, India and other non-Moslem countries.

In addition to all this, the islands of the Maldives are sitting on an ecological time bomb. If greenhouse gases in the atmosphere continue to increase, the resulting worldwide climatic disaster will hit these low-lying islands first, and most catastrophically. If global warming and the concurrent rise in sea level cannot be brought under control, the atolls and islets of the Republic of the Maldives will soon disappear under the waves, like many a legendary paradise.

FACTS

* **Name:** The official name of the islands is the Republic of the Maldives
* **Location and size:** The islands consist of 20 coral atolls and over 2,000 islets, of which 200 are permanently occupied and 87 are dedicated solely to tourism.
* **Area:** The islands have a total land area of about 300 km².
* **Inhabitants:** The population is approximately 350,000.
* **Capital:** The capital city is Malé, with 77,000 inhabitants.
* **Form of government:** The government is officially a republic with a strong executive branch led by the president.
* **State religion:** The state religion is Sunni Islam.
* **Main economy:** Tourism is the economic backbone of the country.

SAUDI ARABIA

The Sacred Mosque of Mecca

MECCA: THE VERY MENTION OF THE NAME FILLS THE HEARTS OF MOSLEMS EVERYWHERE WITH EMOTION AND LONGING. EVERY YEAR, MILLIONS OF PILGRIMS JOURNEY TO THE CITY THAT IS THE BIRTHPLACE OF THE PROPHET MOHAMMMED.

Mecca, also known as al Makka, is located in a desert-like depression between the coastal plain and the highlands of the interior of the Arabian Peninsula. Each year, millions of pilgrims from all over the world journey to Islam's holiest site to pray at the birthplace of the Prophet Mohammed. Born in Mecca *circa* 570, he brought the words of Allah to the Arabs and founded the religion of Islam. The Hajj, which is the Moslem word for 'pilgrimage', brings huge crowds of believers to Mecca's sacred mosque, al-Masjid al-Haram, one of the largest Islamic sacred buildings in the world.

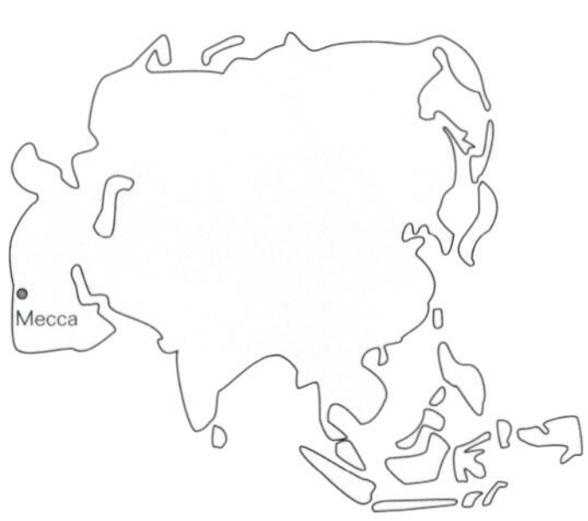

For Moslems, a pilgrimage to Mecca, called the Hajj, is one of the Five Pillars of Faith. That means every able-bodied Moslem with the means to afford the journey is required to make the Hajj at least once. The pilgrims' ultimate goal is the Kaaba, Islam's central sanctuary. The name means "cube", a reference to its shape, but devout Moslems call it *Bayt Allah*, the House of God. Its dimensions are 12 x 10 x 15 metres (w x l x h); it is located in the enormous interior courtyard of the Sacred Mosque. The Kaaba is completely covered by a thick, black tapestry called the 'Kisba'. Pieces of the so-called "black stone" (*al-Hajar al-Aswad*) are built into its south-east corner. According to tradition, these are

FACTS

✻ **Name:** The city is known as Mecca, or in a more accurate transliteration, *al-Makka*.

✻ **Sanctuary:** The central shrine is the Kaaba in the interior courtyard of the Sacred Mosque, the largest Islamic religious building in the world.

✻ **Function:** Mecca functions primarily as the most important Islamic pilgrimage site.

✻ **Inhabitants of Mecca:** The city has a population of 1.2 million that can swell to over 3 million during the Hajj season.

✻ **Unique:** Mecca is the birthplace of the Prophet Mohammed (*circa* 570), the founder of Islam.

Moslem pilgrims pray at the gate leading to the interior of the Kaaba. The shrine is completely covered with heavy brocade inscribed with verses from the Koran.

the stones Abraham received from the Archangel Gabriel to help build the Kaaba. Scientists believe that these are fragments of a meteorite, although this remains an assumption. The stones have never been subjected to scientific analysis.

During the Hajj, pilgrims circle the Kaaba seven times in a clockwise direction, praising Allah as they do so, a procession known as the 'tawaf'. With each revolution the pilgrim attempts to touch or kiss the black stone that, along with the Kaaba itself, defines the direction (*qibla*) that Moslems face during daily prayers, no matter where they are in the world.

Tradition says that the Kaaba was the world's first sacred building, erected by Adam himself, only to be forgotten for many centuries before Abraham and his son Ismail were led there by God and told to rebuild it. The Kaaba has been an Islamic sanctuary since 632 CE, when it was the focus of violent civil conflict between Moslems and non-believing Meccans, as well as the focus of disputes among the Moslems themselves. As late as 931, the black stone was stolen and taken to Bahrain, only to be returned to Mecca 20 years later after lengthly diplomatic negotiation. Mecca was conquered by Egypt in the thirteenth century and was controlled by the Ottoman Turks from the sixteenth century onwards. In 1630, Sultan Murad IV commissioned the rebuilding of the Sacred Mosque. Sheik Hussein ibn Ali, the sultan of Mecca, was finally able to free the city from Turkish control in 1916. He also made the city into the religious centre of Saudi Arabia and the entire Moslem world that it is today. A genuine metropolis, with 1.2 million year-round inhabitants, that number can swell to 3 million in the pilgrimage season. Although non-Moslems are not permitted to enter Mecca, the word has entered many languages as a universal metaphor for the goal of any purposeful journey.

Above: This historical depiction of the Kaaba and Sacred Mosque dates to the middle of the 19th century.

Left: The minarets of the Sacred Mosque are less familiar than the inner courtyard of this largest mosque in the world, where the Kaaba is located.

NEPAL

Mount Everest

MOUNT EVEREST SOARS 8,848 METRES INTO THE SKY ALONG THE BORDER BETWEEN TIBET AND NEPAL. MANY LEGENDS AND TRADITIONS ARE ASSOCIATED WITH THIS, THE HIGHEST MOUNTAIN ON EARTH, WHICH HAS SEEN BOTH TRIUMPH AND TRAGEDY.

The "Holy Mountain" is named after the British engineer George Everest, who was commissioned by the British crown in the mid-nineteenth century to conduct a survey of India and the Himalayas. It was he who identified the mountain the locals called Chomolungma as the highest in the world. The summit was not reached until 29 May 1953, when New Zealander Edmund Hillary made it to the top with his friend, Sherpa Tenzing Norgay. The summit continues to fascinate, drawing experienced and amateur climbers alike from all over the world. Every year, thousands of them expend their best effort in attempts to summit the "Mother of the Universe".

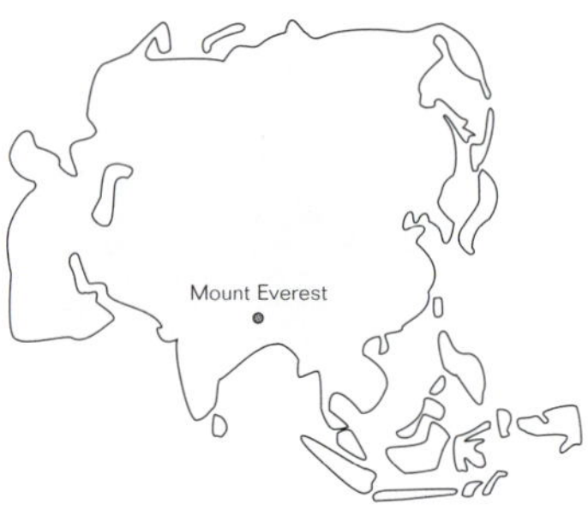

Long ago, before it received its English name, the mountain played a central role in the teachings of the Buddhist religion. Five fairy-like goddesses, the "Five Sisters of Long Life", are worshipped in the Himalayas; they are said to live at the tops of the highest mountains. Chomolungma, which means "Mother of the Universe" in the Tibetan and Sherpa languages, is the home of the goddesses Chomo Miyo Langsangma and Tashi Tserignma. As long as they are properly honoured, they will keep the evil spirits of the mountain at bay. For this reason, every Everest expedition begins with a sacrificial ceremony called

Chomolungma and its smaller brothers, Nuptse I (7,879 m) and Lhotse (8,501 m).

DATES

* **1924:** British climbers Mallory and Irvine attempted to reach the summit. Both died on the descent; whether or not they reached the top is a matter of debate.
* **1953:** Hillary and Tenzing were the first to reach the summit.
* **1960:** A Chinese expedition reached the summit via the northern route.
* **1978:** Messner and Habeler were the first to reach the summit without supplementary oxygen.
* **1980:** Messner reached the top on a solo expedition, again without the use of supplementary oxygen.
* **1980:** A Polish expedition was the first to reach the summit during the winter using the south saddle route.
* **1996:** Disaster struck a number of expeditions, leaving 15 dead.
* **2004:** The Sherpa Pemba Dorje broke the record for the fastest climb to the summit when he made it to the top from base camp in just over eight hours.

the 'Puja'. Only those who offer their sacrifices humbly will conquer the mountain and return safely. Many religious symbols and offering sites line the path to the base camp at 5,400 metres above sea level, including mani stones, a stupa covered with prayer flags, and a cemetery with 200 or so "stone men" set up as piles of rocks in memory of the dead.

As Edmund Hillary and Tenzing Norgay stood on the top of the world in 1953, they had no idea of the avalanche of publicity that would follow in the wake of their achievement. Everest was the last challenge on the earth – its conquest had been called "the third pole" – and now it, too, had been mastered. News of the first summit climb spread like wildfire around the world. Mountaineers and climbers of all nationalities began organizing expeditions. Although for many years the unstable political situation in the region would make receiving a permit to climb Everest dependent on complex diplomatic negotiations at the highest levels of government, the run on the mountain had officially begun.

Only seven years later, a Chinese expedition reached the summit from the northern, Tibetan side of the mountain. The first American team made it to the top in 1963, and in 1975 a British expedition pioneered a route up the south-west wall, one of the most treacherous climbs. In May 1978, Reinhold Messner and Petzer Habeler were the first to reach the top without the use of supplementary oxygen, and in 1979 a Yugoslavian expedition was the first to to reach the summit from the western ridge, the most difficult of the ridge routes. Polish climbers claimed the first winter summit across the south saddle route in 1980.

"Everest tourism" began in earnest in the 1980s. More or less experienced climbers with widely varying levels of preparation could buy their way into an Everest adventure – an adventure with a very uncertain outcome. Many underestimated the mountain while overestimating their own strength and ability. The lack of oxygen and extreme weather conditions above 7,500 metres in combination with the physical strain of the climb have led to the deaths of one in twenty of those who start out from base camp, and of one in ten for those who have passed through the "death zone" and made it to the summit. Because of the difficulty of transporting the dead, many of those who lost their lives in the effort are still there, in the arms of the "Mother of the Universe".

Centre: An unobstructed view of the summit of the world's tallest mountain is a rare event.

Bottom: The summit of Mount Everest is the highest point on Earth at 8,848 m.

TURKEY

Nemrud Dag

LOCATED DEEP IN THE TAURUS MOUNTAINS IN SOUTH-EAST TURKEY, THE CONICAL PEAK OF NEMRUD DAG IS VISIBLE OVER A GREAT DISTANCE. THE PLATEAU SURROUNDING THE PEAK IS THE SITE OF LONG-HIDDEN TREASURES OF ANCIENT ART AND ARCHITECTURE.

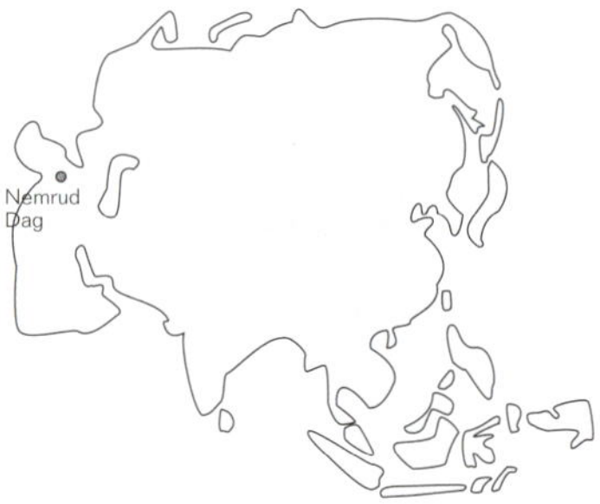

With an elevation of 2,150 metres, Nemrud Dag is one of the tallest mountains in northern Mesopotamia. For many years this prominent topographical feature hid ancient secrets that would only be uncovered in the late nineteenth century by a German engineer named Karl Sester. During the intervening centuries, what the mountain concealed was a secret known only to King Antiochus Theos of Commagene, who built a combination tomb and temple beneath the rubble-strewn slope beginning shortly after his accession to the throne in the first century BCE. This monumental grave-sanctuary was declared a World Cultural Heritage Site by UNESCO in 1987.

The tumulus grave near the peak of Nemrud Dag is the burial place of the kings of Commagene, a region of south-eastern Anatolia on the banks of the Euphrates. Antiochus I (69–36 BCE), who took the name "Theos" (god) shortly after he was crowned, commissioned a gigantic grave monument. It was to be a sanctuary dedicated to various gods, but also to himself and to the new religion he had founded, which he saw as a unification of Persian and Greek customs and beliefs. He chose the Nemrud Dag as the building site for the grave his architects and masons would erect here – near to the gods.

FACTS

✻ Commagene: In the 9th and 8th centuries BCE, Commagene, also known as Kummuch, was an independent principality. After 708 BCE it was an Assyrian province, and later a part of the Hellenistic territory of East Armenia. Antiochus I (69–36 BCE) was its greatest king. After the death of Antiochus III in 17 CE, Commagene was absorbed into the Roman Empire.

This is the colossal head of the statue of King Antiochus I Theos, the ruler who commissioned the grave monument. The location and monumental scale of the complex was designed to emphasize his close relationship with the gods.

Antiochus' building masters set to work. First they had to level a large area near the summit, large enough for a tumulus and a sanctuary. In the end, they cut away 200,000 m^3 of rock to create the artificial plateau on top of which the tumulus would sit, itself built from the debris from the levelling operation. The tumulus, with terraces on its northern, western and eastern sides, was over 50 metres tall and 150 metres in diameter.

The northern terrace is where pilgrims assembled. Here they were divided according to nationality and social class, and sent on either to the western or eastern terrace, accordingly. The western terrace supported a 9-metre-tall statue of Antiochus I, Theos, a god-king seated in the midst of his fellow deities Tyche, Zeus, Apollo and Heracles. Somehow, over the course of many centuries and numerous strong earthquakes, all these statues lost their heads. Torn away from their torsos, the divine heads now rest in a confused tumble near the statues' feet. Colossal statues were also a feature of the eastern terrace, distinguished by its finely laid, white stone pavement. One of these figures is probably King Mithradates I Kallinikos (108–69 BCE), who was Antiochus' father. A large altar for burnt sacrifices stood in front of it.

Another remarkable feature is the so-called Lion Head Horoscope, found on both the western and eastern terraces. The oldest known astrological chart in the world, the 2 x 2.5-metre relief slabs show the arrangement of planets and other celestial bodies on 7 July 62 BCE. According to two different interpretations, this represents either the day Mithradates or Antiochus inherited the throne or, as the most recent archaeological excavation has concluded, the day that construction of the combined grave monument-sanctuary atop Nemrud Dag began.

Left and Above: The heads of the statues of the gods and god-kings are thought to have become detached from the torsos as a result of many strong earthquakes in the region over the course of the past two millennia.

TURKEY

Hierapolis-Pamukkale

THE SNOW-WHITE TERRACES OF PAMUKKALE WERE FORMED AND ARE CONTINUALLY RE-SCULPTED BY WARM SUBTERRANEAN SPRINGS THAT SEEP THROUGH THE SURFACE. EVAPORATION LEAVES BEHIND MINERALS THAT HARDEN INTO A CHALKLIKE SINTER.

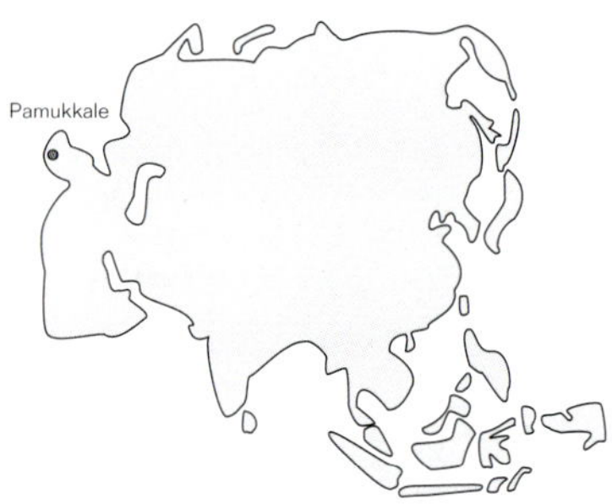

The city of Pamukkale, formerly Hieropolis ("Holy City"), was founded because of the warm springs found there. It was the centre of the cult of Cybele, an earth goddess worshipped as the Great Mother. It is estimated that around 100,000 people lived here during the city's golden age, when its inhabitants were famous for their wealth and prosperity. The enormous nymphaeum, a fountain house for collecting and distributing the healing warm waters, bears witness to the city's ambition, as does its gigantic theatre, which was large enough to seat 15,000 people.

The thermal springs bubbled up to the surface due to Pamukkale's location along a tectonic fault line. The water temperature hovers around 36°C and is enriched by a number of different minerals. When the minerals react with the oxygen in the air, carbon dioxide and calcium carbonate (chalk) are formed. The chalk accumulates everywhere, covering every surface, stone and rocky slope. It never ends! Layer upon layer, the landscape around the thermal springs has whitened and hardened as the minerals transformed the topography. From a distance, the thermal areas around the modern town of Denizli resemble fields of cotton. Indeed, the name Pamukkale in Turkish means "Cotton Castle", because with a little

Right: The chalk terraces of Pamukkale glow in the light of the setting sun.

Below: The ruins of Hierapolis mark it as the location of one of antiquity's most important baths and spas.

imagination, the frozen terraces could almost be part of an ancient fortification.

It is fairly certain that Hierapolis was founded here because of the springs. Little else is known about either its history or its origins. The inhabitants of the city were aware of the healing powers of its waters, as shown by the enormous nymphaeum they built to exploit their potential. The Roman Empire and the bathhouse culture that accompanied it were also factors in the success of Asia Minor cities like Hierapolis that had access to natural sources of hot water.

Archaeologists have spent over 100 years uncovering the remains of the baths and spas. Parts of the buildings themselves were covered with a 5-metre-thick accumulation of chalk, slowing down the progress of the investigation. What we know about the city's significance remains general and undefined. We know that it was a Hellenistic sanctuary, the centre of a cult of Cybele, and that during the second century BCE it became well-known throughout Asia Minor for its baths and healing waters.

The remains of the nymphaeum and theatre are located in the centre of the city. The theatre, dedicated to the goddess Artemis, is exceptionally well-preserved. With seating for at least 15,000, it had a two-storey stage that separated the performers from the orchestra. The stage is decorated with magnificently sculpted reliefs of mythological scenes related to Artemis, and on the columns on either side, to her brother, the god Apollo.

Hierapolis seems to have been a busy economic centre into the fourth century CE, famous in particular for its dyed wool products. The mineral content of the warm springs was well-suited to bring out different colours during the dying process, while making the wool easier to card and spin. Rome was the largest market for these goods, attracting merchants to Hierapolis from all over the empire. This gave the city a cosmopolitan outlook; people of a wide variety of cultural backgrounds and beliefs lived here.

But during the fourth century it all began to fall apart. The city of Byzantium put an end to the trade with Rome, and also to the Roman baths, which were transformed into churches. The evidence at Pamukkale for this period of decline includes the Church of the Apostle St. Philip, who according to tradition had been crucified in Hieropolis in the year 87 CE. Its presence attracted those who wished to be buried near the saint. As the many sarcophagi and graves scattered throughout the immediate area show, what had been one of Asia Minor's most attractive cities became, during the Byzantine era, its largest cemetery.

DATES

* **188 – 50 BCE:** Hieropolis was part of the territory controlled by the kings of Pergamon, one of whom, Eumenes II, was said to have built the first baths there in 190 BCE.
* **133 BCE:** Attalos III died, willing the Kingdom of Pergamon to Rome. Hieropolis was part of the Roman province of Asia.
* **60 CE:** Hieropolis was destroyed by an earthquake.
* **87:** According to legend, the Apostle St Philip was crucified here.
* **193–217:** The support of emperors Septimus Severus and Caracalla led to a period of prosperity.
* ***circa* 900:** Hieropolis is mentioned briefly in a letter of Pope Leo and described as the seat of a bishop.
* **1887:** Excavation at the site by German archaeologists began. Since 1957, Italian archaeologists have been in charge.
* **1988:** Pamukkale was named a World Cultural Heritage Site by UNESCO.

JORDAN

Petra

THE MYSTERIOUS ROCK-CUT CITY OF PETRA IS LOCATED DEEP IN THE JORDANIAN DESERT. ONCE A PROSPEROUS CITY, THE SITE BEARS WITNESS TO THE TIME WHEN THE NABATEANS WERE THE MOST POWERFUL TRIBE IN ALL OF THE NEAR EAST.

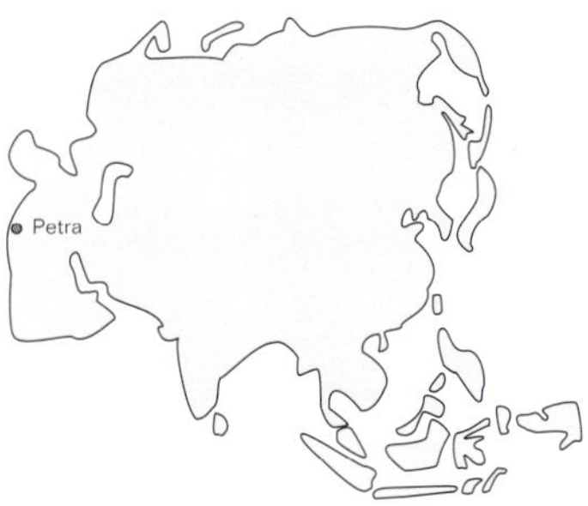

Located at the crossroads of a number of important caravan trails connecting Egypt, Syria and southern Arabia with Mediterranean economic centres and markets, from the fifth through third centuries CE Petra was one of the most important trade centres in the Near East. Every variety of luxury goods passed through the rock-cut city. The local topography played a role in keeping the city hidden, and thereby secure. Even today, Petra can only be approached overland through a narrow ravine: the *Siq* (Arabic for "shaft"). Traversing the narrow gorge of the Siq still presents challenges. In many places it is barely 2 metres wide, with sheer walls of rock on each side rising up to 100 metres, more or less perpendicular from the valley floor. The topography shields the path from light, making the way through the gorge dark and claustrophobic. **But once a trade caravan** made it through this gorge, it was richly rewarded for its efforts. Stepping through a narrow crack, travellers found themselves directly in front of a most amazing sight: the 40-metre-tall chiselled façade of the *Hazne al-Fir'un*, or "Pharaoh's Treasury". In fact, the terraces, columns and gabled roofs cut out of the rock have nothing to do with the Egyptian pharaohs. This is the façade of a tomb, with simple grave chambers.

The rock city of Petra can only be reached through the gorge called the Siq. When travelling through it, take the advice of an old Bedouin guide: "Start early along your way, for the path through the gorge is long and difficult, and the wonder of the treasury is best experienced in the morning light...."

DATES

* 312 BCE: Alexander the Great's general Antigonos I led an unsuccessful campaign against the Nabateans at Petra.
* *circa* 169 BCE: King Aretas I reigned.
* *circa* 120–96 BCE: Reign of King Aretas II.
* 87–62 BCE: Reign of King Aretas III, who expanded his "caravan state" by conquering Damascus.
* 62 BCE: Nabatea became a vassal of Rome.
* 106 CE: Emperor Trajan incorporated the territory into the Roman province of Arabia Petraea, naming Bosra its capital city.
* 1170–1188: The Crusaders occupied and fortified parts of Petra during the First Crusade in the early 12th century, but abandoned the fortifications in 1189.
* 1217: Last mention of Petra in a Western source.
* 1812: J. L. Burckhardt rediscovered Petra.
* 1985: Petra was named a World Cultural Heritage Site by UNESCO.

The city carved out of rock experienced its golden age between the first century BCE and the first century CE after the Nabatean king, Aretas III Philhellenos (87–62 BCE), conquered Damascus and besieged Jerusalem, setting the stage for conflict with Rome. While Petra did become something comparable to a Roman vassal after the king's death, its prosperity continued unhindered, with its temples and palaces becoming more and more monumental. During the first half of the first century CE, Aretas IV commissioned the main temple located in the centre of the city. At this time as many as 40,000 people lived in the rock-cut of Petra.

Soon thereafter, however, the conflict with Rome became more intense. After the Romans took control of the caravans, Petra's prosperity came to an end. The Roman emperor Trajan crushed the Nabateans in the year 106. Their kingdom was absorbed into the Roman Empire and the legendary city of Petra lost its importance. When the Arabs arrived in the area in 663, the last inhabitants of the city, most of them Christians, fled before them. Over the following centuries the desert reclaimed the temples and palaces. Petra fell into ruin and was soon forgotten, except in legends, which – outside of the local area – were widely considered too fantastic to be true.

In August 1812, a Swiss adventurer named Johann Ludwig Burckhardt heard about the hidden rock city and, disguising himself as a Moslem, let it be known that he was looking for a guide to lead him to the "Grave of Aaron", which regional tradition placed at the site, so that he might go there and pray. A local Bedouin guide led "Sheik Ibrahim" through the gorge to Petra, where, he told his client, Moses had struck his staff on the rock, bringing forth water as he led the Jewish people out of their Egyptian prison to the promised land.

The Hazne al-Fir'un, the treasury that is really a rock-cut tomb, is now restored to its former glory, as is the first century CE Roman theatre that could seat 5,000 spectators. Also under restoration is the funerary temple of al-Deir, one of the most impressive monuments in Petra. It is a round temple so large that the urn that rests on top of its pointed roof is 9 metres tall. Based on its size alone, al-Deir surely represents the apogee of the architectural skill of the Nabateans – but the city surrounding it is perhaps their true memorial.

Centre: The funerary temple of al-Deir is the largest structure in Petra.

Bottom: The facade of Hazne al-Fir'un, called the "Treasury of the Pharaoh", is 40 m tall.

MALAYSIA

Petronas Twin Towers

AT 452 METRES HIGH, THE PETRONAS TWIN TOWERS IN KUALA LUMPUR WERE THE TALLEST BUILDINGS IN THE WORLD FROM 1998 TO 2004. THE TWIN GIANTS ARE THE MAIN OFFICE OF MALAYSIA'S NATIONALIZED OIL INDUSTRY.

The Petronas Twin Towers were the project of Malaysia's ambitious premier, Mahathir Mohammad. The buildings were designed to serve as a new Malaysian symbol, showcasing the country's unmistakable traditional, Islam-influenced building style and the high-tech engineering emblematic of the modern nation state. The architect Cesar Pelli designed buildings with a ground plan in the form of an eight-pointed star, an Islamic symbol of order and harmony. He then increased the area of the footprint, and thereby the amount of usable space, by placing cruciform bays within the angles. This efficient, structurally integrated plan gave the engineer, Charlie Thornton, the opportunity to build two very tall buildings of unique stability. It was a combination of Pelli's ground plan and Thornton's structural engineering that made the Petronas Twin Towers the tallest buildings in the world.

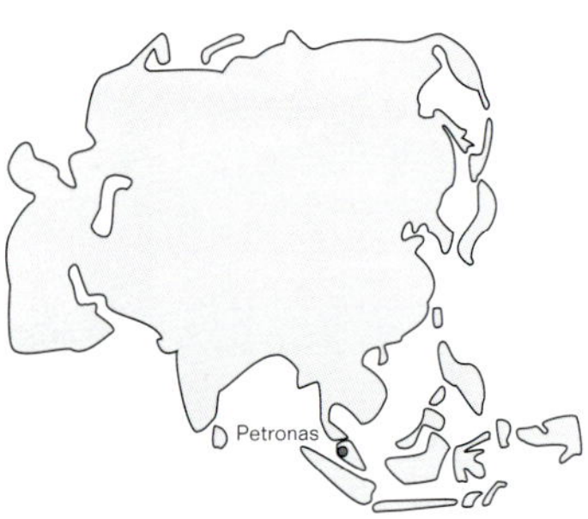

In the early days, predictions regarding the construction were largely negative. It became clear in 1992, shortly before the cornerstone was laid, that the building site was unsuitable. The bedrock was determined not to be strong enough to bear the towers' weight, and all construction came to a halt. Thornton made the bold decision to move the complex 60 metres away, where the bedrock lay much

FACTS

✻ Location: The Petronas Twin Towers are located in the capital city of Kuala Lumpur, Malaysia.

✻ Construction: They were designed by Cesar Pelli and built 1992–1997.

✻ Size: The towers are 452 m high with 88 occupied floors.

✻ Area: Each tower weighs around 300,000 tons and consists of 160,000 m^3 of concrete.

✻ Exterior: The surface area of the windows is 77,000 m^2, and the steel exterior cladding covers 65,000 m^2.

✻ Costs: The construction costs were over $800 million.

✻ Use: Tower 1 is the head office of the Malaysian nationalized oil industry, Petronas. Other tenants include the Kuala Lumpur city centre shopping mall and hotel complex, an art gallery and a concert hall that can seat 840.

The lobbies of the Petronas Towers house the Suria Shopping Centre, a luxury hotel and a concert hall that can seat 840 people.

deeper. The gigantic skyscrapers had to be supported on a massive concrete foundation set on piers sunk 120 metres into the ground in order to reach bedrock far below. These are still the world's deepest concrete foundations. Specially prepared super-high-strength concrete was poured into the foundation trench by a fleet of mixing trucks arriving every 2 minutes for 52 hours. Because the towers' primary structural element is reinforced concrete, they are twice as heavy as a comparable steel-framed structure. The foundation of each tower bears almost 300,000 tons.

A construction period of six years was planned, with every day beyond that term costing the company $700,000 in penalties. Construction workers – up to 2,000 per day, seven days a week – laboured under intense pressure, particularly since making the deadline required that each of the 88 storeys be completed within four days. This sped construction along to the extent that the building was completed ahead of schedule, with several building industry world records set along the way. One team, for example, succeeded in pumping concrete from ground level to an elevation of circa 335 metres using specially designed equipment. It was also one of the first building projects to employ GPS technology in place of more traditional surveying techniques.

A 400-ton bridge joins the two glass and concrete towers at their 41st and 42nd floors, some 171 metres above ground. Although this "sky bridge" was initially designed as an aesthetic detail and practical feature facilitating stability and circulation, Thornton emphasized its potential as an "emergency exit" following the destruction of the World Trade Center in New York on 11 September 2001.

The Petronas Towers were opened, on time, in 1997. At 452 metres, they were – until 2003 – the tallest buildings on Earth.

Above: Architect Cesar Pelli successfully integrated traditional Malaysian building techniques and Islamic stylistic elements into a modern skyscraper.

Left: The sky bridge joins the towers at the 41st and 42nd floors.

CHINA / TIBET

Potala Palace

HIGH ABOVE THE CAPITAL OF TIBET, LHASA, THE POTALA PALACE COMPLEX SITS ON TOP OF MAR-PO-RI: THE 'RED HILL'. FOR CENTURIES, UNTIL THE CHINESE OCCUPATION OF TIBET IN 1959, IT WAS THE GOVERNMENT SEAT AND RESIDENCE OF THE DALAI LAMA.

The Dalai Lama fled from his seat of government in the Potala Palace in 1959 following a massive onslaught by invading Chinese troops. With or without the Dalai Lama's presence, the Potala Palace remains the most sacred site in Tibetan Buddhism. According to ancient tradition, the palace is the residence of the Bodhisattva known as "Avalokitesvara in the land of pure enlightenment". According to Tibetan Buddhist belief, the reigning Dalai Lama is the reincarnation of Avalokitesvara. This gives the physically enormous Potala Palace a comparably immense religious and spiritual dimension within Tibet and among believers all over the world. Since the occupation of Tibet by the Chinese, the Potala Palace has been neglected, all the while remaining an important pilgrimage site drawing Buddhists from across the globe. Its official function today is as a museum.

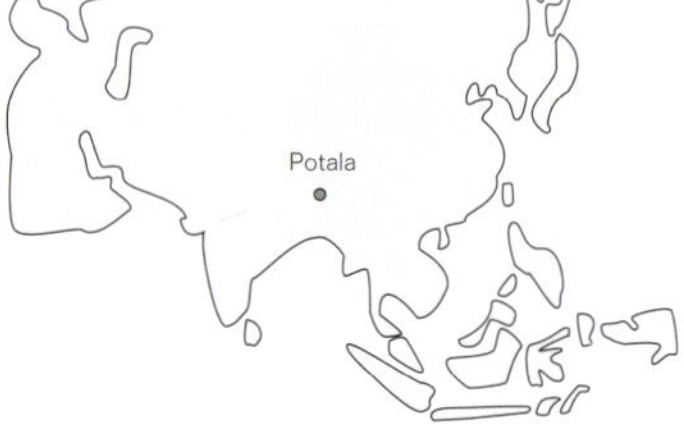

Although the earliest parts of the Potala Palace date to the year 637 CE, the large complex we recognize today, began with the construction of the Potrang Karpo (White Palace) in the seventeenth century, with work completed in 1648. The fifth Dalai Lama is said to have been its architect. The Potrang Marpo (Red Palace) was completed in 1694, after his death. The palace remained essentially unchanged into the

Right: The Potala Palace was placed on the UNESCO list of World Cultural Heritage Sites in 1994.

Below: The grandiose Potala Palace is reflected by the Lhasa River.

twentieth century, until 1922, when the thirteenth Dalai Lama renovated the red palace, adding two additional floors. Since the eighteenth century, when the so-called Summer Palace of Norbulingka was built within the city walls of Lhasa, Potala had also been known as the Winter Palace because it was used exclusively during the winter months.

The Potala Palace survived China's Cultural Revolution with relatively little damage, which is surprising considering the great harm done to other cultural monuments by marauding troops during this period. In 1994, Potala (the Summer Palace of Norbulingka) and the nearby Jokhang Temple were placed on the UNESCO list of World Cultural Heritage Sites, preserving Lhasa as an important destination for Buddhist pilgrims.

The damage to the palaces that did occur during the 1959 invasion has been repaired in the meantime, with the entire palace restored to its original condition. Potala today stands 13 storeys high, covers an area of 300 x 330 metres (10 hectares) and has no fewer than 999 rooms.

The upper two floors of the Red Palace house the private apartments of Tibet's now exiled political and spiritual leader, the Dalai Lama. In addition to meditation halls, ceremonial rooms and many smaller chapels, the Potala Palace also encloses the burial stupas of the Dalai Lama's previous incarnations. Eight of them are buried here, beginning with the fifth, whose grave is by far the largest and most elaborate. The construction and decoration of the nearly three-storey-tall stupa incorporates almost 3.7 tons of gold.

The present Dalai Lama was driven from his land by invading Chinese troops in 1959. Since then, the country known as the "Autonomous Region of Tibet" has been politically fully incorporated into the Peoples' Republic of China. The degree of compulsion involved in Tibet's allegiance to China, as well as the abuse of the rights of its people to self-determination, have long been a matter of some discussion, both inside and outside the country. Politically, the international community regards Tibet as a state under the control of China, refusing to recognize the government in exile, which is headed by the current Dalai Lama from a monastery in northern India. As a result, any relationship or negotiations with the Dalai Lama must take place in a religious context, with his status as a spiritual leader the only aspect that can be openly acknowledged. For many Tibetan Buddhists, however, the two roles remain inseparable.

FACTS

* **Dalai-Lama:** The Dalai Lama is the title of the highest-ranking secular and spiritual leader in Tibetan Buddhism. The current Dalai Lama, the fourteenth, is the monk born as Tenzin Gyatso.

* **Chörten:** The stupa as a Buddhist cult structure is characterized by its whitewashed main dome, usually somewhat bell-shaped, set atop a base with multiple steps. Its form varies geographically, resembling a pagoda in some locations and a simple conical hill in others.

* **Lhasa:** Lhasa is the capital city of the Tibetan Autonomous Region of the Peoples' Republic of China. It lies at an altitude of 3,600 m above sea level on the northern border of the Himalayas.
In 1950, it supported a population of 50,000, nearly all of native Tibetan ancestry. Today, its population has swelled to nearly ten times that much, mostly due to immigration from other parts of China.

TAIWAN

Taipei 101

HIGHEST, FASTEST AND SAFEST – THESE ARE PROBABLY THE WORDS THAT BEST DESCRIBE THE UNIQUE SKYSCRAPER LOCATED IN THE HEART OF THE TAIWANESE CAPITAL OF TAIPEI. IN EVERY WAY, TAIPEI 101 IS A BUILDING OF SUPERLATIVES.

Highest: Taipei 101, at 508 metres, is currently the tallest building in the world. Fastest: its turbo-lifts are the fastest in the world. Safest: the Taipei 101 Mega-Tower is considered the safest skyscraper ever built.

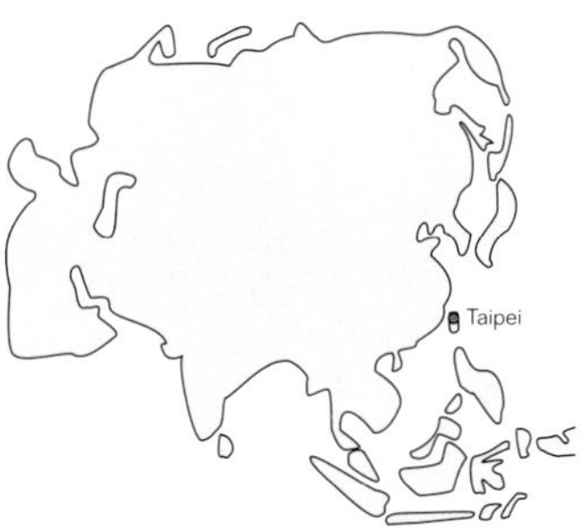

Taipei 101 stands in one of the most geologically unstable areas in the world, which is also subject to some of the most severe storm conditions known anywhere. The Philippine and Eurasian tectonic plates meet directly beneath Taiwan, causing earthquakes of varying magnitude almost daily, with as many as 1,000 recorded per year. Another annual event is the typhoon season, producing swirling winds of up to 240 km per hour. Finally, there is the matter of the subsurface supporting the giant building: Taipei and its surroundings are really just an enormous, partially drained swamp. Bedrock lies as much as 60 metres below the surface, meaning the foundations of any large building must be anchored at that depth.

The design of Tapei 101 is based on the strong and elastic bamboo stem. To ensure its stability, 557 steel pilings were driven well into the bedrock, supporting 9,000 tons of steel plating. Each corner of the gigantic building is further supported by two mega-pylons running through the entire building, all the way up to the 62nd floor, which serve as Taipei 101's primary

FACTS

✻ History: The cornerstone for Taipei 101 was laid in January 1998. It was officially opened on the last day of December 2004.

✻ Costs: The building costs totalled over $2.5 billion.

✻ Height: It is the tallest building in the world, its 510 m surpassing the Petronas Towers, the previous record-holder.

✻ Lifts: Taipei 101 has 63 lifts, 34 of them double-decker. At up to 65 km per hour, these are the fastest lifts in the world.

✻ Floors: The building has 101 floors and 5 basement levels. The lobby is on the 4th floor, a garage on the four lowest basement levels and a shopping mall on the first three floors and uppermost basement level. The 5th floor is a conference centre. Floors 6–85 are office space, with a viewing platform and restaurants occupying the 87th–90th floors. The building's mass damper structure extends through the 87th to 91st floors. The uppermost floors are devoted to service equipment.

Tapei 101's gigantic shopping mall extends over three floors and one basement level. In addition to an array of shops, there are numerous bars, restaurants and other entertainment venues within the complex.

weight-bearing elements. Each pylon of high-strength concrete – 65,000 tons were poured – has a diameter of 3 metres, with the steel plate supporting each floor a mere 8 cm thick. This is what gives the building its stability. For protection against fire, each column, pillar and pylon were sprayed with inflammable foam.

The giant steel elements needed to complete the building were manufactured in southern Taiwan and transported on special vehicles to the building site. This required the development of a new system of logistics. The steel beams and plates were so large that they could not be stored at the site; every piece transported in had to be set in its final location immediately. This was particularly problematic during construction of the tower above the occupied floors, requiring the development of a special crane for quick positioning of steel elements weighing up to 90 tons. This crane was permanently anchored to the steel frame deep inside the building, permitting it to rise along with the skyscraper, floor by floor.

In spite of its steel and concrete construction, Taipei 101, like other huge skyscrapers, can pitch from side to side in heavy winds, such as those of a typhoon. Experts predicted pitch of up to 2.5 metres, measured from the top of the building to its base.

To lessen the damage to the building during extreme conditions, a mass-oscillation damper was installed on the 88th floor, capable of reducing the building's movements by 40 per cent. The device is essentially a large steel ball with a diameter of 5.5 metres and weighing 660 tons, suspended between 16 thin steel trusses reaching from the 87th through 91st floors. It works like a pendulum, compensating for any tilt of Tapei 101 by rolling along the scaffolding in the opposite direction. This permits the building to react to the elements like bamboo in the wind, always returning to the vertical, strong and elastic at once.

Above: The architect C.Y. Lee with his masterpiece, Taipei 101, in the distance.

Left: Sixty-three lifts convey employees and visitors to their businesses and offices.

INDIA

The Taj Mahal

THE TAJ MAHAL, A BEWITCHING MARBLE GRAVE MONUMENT IN THE NORTH INDIAN CITY OF AGRA, IS A TESTAMENT TO THE UNDYING LOVE OF MOGUL SHAH JAHAN FOR HIS WIFE MUMTAZ. BETWEEN 1631 AND 1648, HE BUILT THIS WONDER IN MEMORY OF HER.

The Taj Mahal is widely considered to be one of the most beautiful buildings in the world, a masterpiece of Indo-Islamic architecture. The Mogul ruler Shah Jahan had material for his building brought to Agra from all over Asia, transported by over 1,000 draught elephants. The Shah spared neither effort nor expense in creating a magnificent, everlasting monument to his great love.

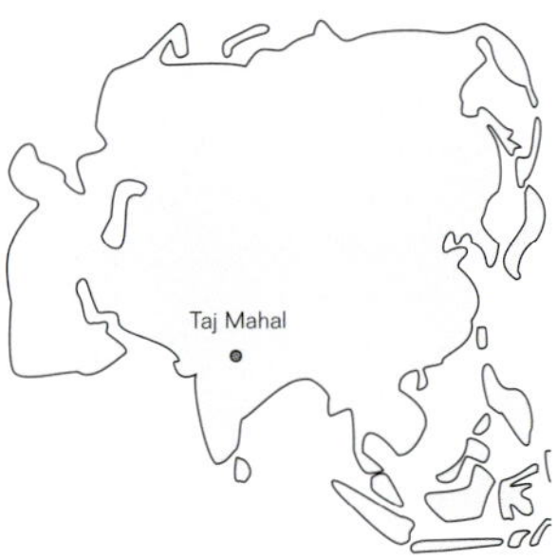

Passing through the main gate, itself an impressive monument with 22 domes, one enters an earthly paradise. The entire complex, including the gardens, covers eight hectares. The monument itself, with its four gently tapering minarets, is in sublime architectural harmony with its guesthouse and mosque. Over 20,000 workers and artisans contributed to its completion.

The Taj Mahal is a masterpiece, both in terms of architecture and aesthetics. The enormous dome soars to a height of 59 metres, its corners flanked by four 40-metre-tall minarets carefully positioned so as not to fall on the main building in case of an earthquake. Even more complex, from an engineering point of view, is the building's substructure, designed to bear the weight of the dome by distributing it throughout the entire building. A series of domes resting on smaller domes, each supporting another,

Anyone passing though the beautiful gate into the Taj Mahal complex encounters a perfect, harmonious architectural universe.

FACTS

✱ Strange: An oft-repeated though never verified tale holds that in the early 19th century a British colonial leader planned to disassemble the Taj Mahal and bring it back to England, where pieces of it were to be auctioned off.

✱ Uncertain: No one is quite sure when the Taj Mahal was finished. The date is usually given as 1654, but Shah Jahan's court chronicles record the building period as beginning one year after Mumtaz' death (1631) and continuing for 12 years, which dates its completion to 1643. Meanwhile, the inscription over the main gate claims it was finished in 1648. In 1652, Prince Aurangzeb remarked in a letter that the Taj Mahal was already in need of repairs.

as well as a clever system to regulate the level of groundwater below the surface, ensure that the Taj Mahal does not sink into the ground.

For the decorative elements, which cover every surface of the building, Shah Jahan employed the Venetian Geronimo Veroneo and the Frenchman Austin de Bordeaux. They supervised the intricate inlaid and mosaic decoration, which makes use of no fewer than 60 different kinds of precious and semi-precious stones. The artisans fitted the inlaid pieces so precisely that the gaps and edges between the motifs and the surrounding stone cannot be seen with the naked eye; a powerful magnifying glass is required to do so. Other spaces within the tomb are decorated with equally opulent floral relief sculpture in marble, meander patterns and verses from the Koran.

While the Taj Mahal was under construction, Shah Jahan codified his artistic tastes, making them into law. While his obsessive mourning led him to create this monument of overpowering beauty, it also led him to lose all focus and perspective. With state bankruptcy threatening because of the immense costs incurred by the Taj Mahal, a situation likely to be worsened by the construction of a second mausoleum of black marble planned for Jahan himself, the shah found himself usurped by his own son, Aurangzeb, who kept his father under house arrest for the rest of his life. Jahan spent his final eight years living in the Red Fort in Agra, from which he had an unobstructed view of the Taj Mahal. After his death in 1666, Jahan was buried there at the side of his beloved Mumtaz.

The reputation of the magnificent monument in Agra spread quickly throughout the world, making the Taj Mahal a pilgrimage site from its very earliest days onwards. Many who come here do so to marvel at the treasures and opulence. Others are fascinated by the architectural harmony. Still others see the tomb as a religious sanctuary, for Mumtaz died while giving birth to her fifteenth child, and in Islamic tradition, a woman who dies in childbirth is to be honoured as a martyr. The Indian poet Rbndranath Tagore may have expressed it best when he described the Taj Mahal as “a tear on the cheek of the world”.

Centre: The richly decorated marble of the Taj Mahal is actually only its exterior cladding. The walls themselves are constructed of flat bricks.

Bottom: The Taj Mahal is an architectural masterpiece – pure Indian exotica with Persian and Central Asian influences. The central dome is 59 metres tall.

CHINA

Tiananmen Square

LOCATED IN THE HEART OF BEIJING, TIANANMEN SQUARE – THE "PLACE OF HEAVENLY PEACE" – IS THE LARGEST ENCLOSED OPEN SPACE IN THE WORLD. IT WAS FIRST OPENED TO THE PUBLIC IN 1911 AFTER THE COLLAPSE OF THE CHINESE MONARCHY.

Tiananmen Square is a creation of modern China. For the hundreds of years of the Central Kingdom's existence, large, public assembly places did not exist. It was only in 1911, after the collapse of the imperial monarchy, that China's new leaders began building large squares and plazas for the people. The Place of Heavenly Peace lies in the very heart of Beijing, with its northern side defined by the Gate of Heavenly Peace, the main entrance to the Forbidden City. Before 1911, Tiananmen was the name for the large area just outside the imperial palace gates, where administrators and ministers had their offices. It was in front of the gate that Mao Zedong announced the creation of the Peoples' Republic of China on 1 October 1949.

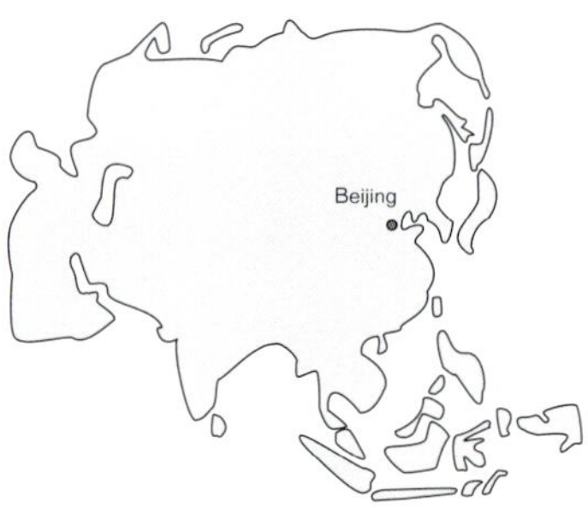

Today, the mausoleum where Mao's mummified corpse is on display lies near that same gate. A history and revolution museum was built along the plaza's eastern flank in 1959, with the Great Hall of the People along the west. The Monument to the People's Heroes, a 40-metre-tall quadratic stone stele inscribed with the words of Mao Zedong and Zhou En Lai, dominates the centre of the plaza. The area enclosed by the plaza is more than 40 hectares, making it the largest enclosed plaza in the world.

Right: Tiananmen Square is the largest enclosed plaza in the world, with an area of over 40 hectares.

Below: The Great Hall of the People is located on the western side of the square.

The residents of Beijing call Tiananmen Square "the place of the incidents". Ever since the most recent incidents took place, the Plaza of Heavenly Peace has been closed off to general use, for fear of further incidents and the worldwide uproar they might cause.

The first great demonstration in Tiananmen Square took place on 4 May 1919, incited by the Treaty of Versailles, which had ignored China's claims to territory seized by Japan on behalf of Germany. Students and intellectuals took to the square demanding democratization of the domestic political process and a greater role for China with respect to the West. This "Fourth May Movement" was a strong influence on later political developments in China.

On 1 October 1949, Mao Zedong, who had taken the title of "Great Chairman", stood in the square to declare the founding of the Peoples' Republic of China and its government by the communist party.

The next incident took place on 4 April 1976, the traditional Chinese "Day of the Dead". Thousands of mourners gathered in Tiananmen Square with wreaths and flowers for their beloved, recently deceased President Zhou Enlai. During the night, however, opposing political forces cleared away the flowers by order of the government. Over the following days thousands of people gathered at the square to demonstrate against this act. The police and army reacted with brutal violence and mass arrests.

The most recent incident occurred during the night of 3 June 1989, when the army, using tanks and other weapons, broke up a peaceful demonstration for greater democracy that had occupied Tiananmen Square since the previous April. According to accounts assembled by international organizations, the Peoples' Army killed as many as 3,000 demonstrators. To this day, the Chinese government views the use of military force against the demonstrators as justifiable, in strong contrast to how most of the rest of the world viewed the incident.

As a result, demonstrations in Tiananmen Square are strictly forbidden today. The square is only opened for official purposes, such as mass marches or military displays. The leaders of China celebrated the fiftieth anniversary of the Peoples' Republic there on 1 October 1999 with a giant military parade and organized mass procession. Over a million people were ordered to the Place of Heavenly Peace, where they were instructed to "rejoice" for the benefit of the world media.

FACTS

* **Name:** Tiananmen Square translates as "Place of Heavenly Peace". It has a total area of 40 hectares, making it the largest enclosed space in the world.

DATES

* **1911:** The square was opened to the public.
* **4 May 1919:** Student protests leading to the formation of the 4th of May movement broke out on that day in 1919.
* **1 October 1949:** The "Great Chairman" Mao Zedong declared the People's Republic of China from Tiananmen Square.
* **4 April 1976:** The police broke up a demonstration following actions taken on the Day of the Dead.
* **3/4 June 1989:** The Peoples' Army attacked student protesters, killing as many as 3,000.
* **1 October 1999:** China celebrated its 50th anniversary with processions and military parades in Tiananmen Square.

CHINA

The Forbidden City

IN THE HEART OF BEIJING LIES THE MOST ENDURING SYMBOL OF CHINESE IMPERIAL POWER: THE FORBIDDEN CITY, A PHYSICAL MANIFESTATION OF THE SUPERIORITY OF A CHINESE CULTURE AND HISTORY THAT EXTEND MORE THAN 5,000 YEARS INTO THE PAST.

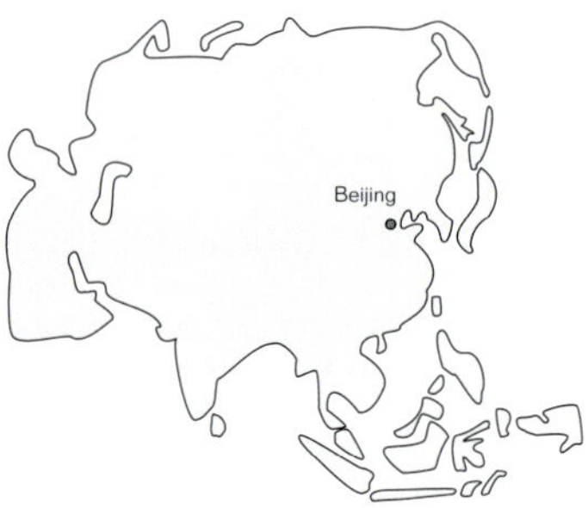

Before 1924, this gigantic complex, the largest palace in the world, could only be entered by a small circle of carefully chosen people with strong connections to the rulers. For hundreds of years the Forbidden City was its own universe, cordoned off from the rest of society. From here the emperors, the "sons of heaven", ruled over the Central Kingdom and decided the fate of the empire. **In 1402, Yong Le** rose to the head of the Ming Dynasty and declared himself emperor. He moved the capital to Beijing for a period of peaceful, prosperous reign. By 1406, Yong Le required a residence fitting his status, leading to the first plans for the palatial city. It would be called Zi Jin Cheng, the Heavenly Forbidden City, centre of the universe, and all other palaces would stand in its shadow. **Over one million workers** were relocated here to build the complex. The emperor commandeered an additional 100,000 of the finest craftsmen and artisans for the decorative work. At a kiln site located some 15,500 km away, a cohort of workers fired over 20 million bricks, which were trimmed to size and transported to Beijing. Thousands of heavy blocks of stone were brought to the capital over similar distances, requiring a tremendous outlay of workers, draught animals and engineers to build the necessary

FACTS

*** Location and size:** The Forbidden City is located in Beijing, China. It includes an area of 72 hectares, 4.6 of which are occupied by buildings.

*** Palaces:** The complex includes 890 palaces with nearly 9,000 rooms.

*** Foritfications:** Its wall is 10 m high and 3.4 km long, with 4 towers and 4 gates.

DATES

*** 1368–1644:** Rule of the Ming Dynasty.

*** 1723–26:** Some buildings inside the Forbidden City are the Palace of the Heart's Desire (1723–26) and the Palace of Continence and Moderation (1731)

*** 1900:** The Boxer Rebellion briefly gave freedom fighters control of Beijing.

*** 1924:** The Republican army of Chiang Kai Shek drove Emperor Pu Yi out of the Forbidden City.

*** 1987:** The Forbidden City was listed as a World Cultural Heritage Site by UNESCO.

Gilded sculptures of lions, symbolic of the power and strength of the emperor of China, are everywhere to be seen in the Forbidden City.

roads along the way. Even the wood had to be brought in from tropical forests far to the south.

The skill and creativity of the building masters, craftsmen and their assistants were proven by the result. After a construction period of only three years, this monument to the power of the emperor in the heart of the capital was complete.

At Yong Le's behest, an unprecedented array of palaces, pavilions, plazas, gates, bronze and stone sculptures, waterways and bridges covering 72 hectares had been built. The palace was said to have 9,999 rooms, because tradition held that only a heavenly palace could have 10,000, leaving the Son of Heaven to content himself with one less. A more accurate survey counted 8,600 rooms currently in existence. The sturdy, cannon-proof fortification wall around the Forbidden City, 10 metres high, is more than 3.4 km long, each of its four corners distinguished by a castle-like tower. Despite the wall's length and the size of the complex, there are only four gates. To provide further security, the exterior wall is surrounded by a 52-metre-wide moat. Inside the walls are two courtyards, around which cluster palaces, halls and gates, such as the Palace of Heavenly Purity, the Palace where Heaven and Earth Meet, the Palace of Earthly Peace and the Hall of Supreme Harmony.

The Chinese emperor ruled from the Forbidden City until 1912, when Pu Yi, the last emperor, was confined by Republican guards to an inner pavilion of the palace under house arrest. Shortly thereafter, the monarchy was officially dissolved; Republican troops led by Chiang Kai Shek drove the imperial family out of the palace in 1924. Today, the Forbidden City is referred to by the generic term 'Gugong' (former palace). It has been open to the public as a museum since 1924. Many of its treasures are on display in the National Palace Museum in Taipei, Taiwan.

Above: The magnificent grand staircases, galleries and water features are part of the distinctive decoration of the Forbidden City.

Left: Like most of the buildings in the Forbidden City, the Hall of Supreme Harmony is constructed almost entirely out of rare tropical wood.

CHINA

Terracotta Army of Xi'an

THE FIRST CHINESE EMPEROR, QIN SHI HUANG DI, WISHED TO BE ACCOMPANIED INTO THE AFTERWORLD BY AN ARMY OF HEAVILY ARMED WARRIORS, BATTLE HORSES AND CHARIOTS. THE FAMOUS XI'AN TERRACOTTA ARMY WAS CREATED TO FULFIL HIS DESIRE.

Many archaeologists consider the clay army to be the eighth Wonder of the World. Discovered in 1974, its excavation has been long and complicated, requiring painstaking attention to detail. Around 8,000 figures of soldiers and horses have been uncovered thus far. Experts estimate that this may represent one-quarter of the number buried.

Qin Shi Huang Di ascended to the throne of the Kingdom of Qin at the age of 13. At that time, China was a mosaic of small to medium-sized principalities and kingdoms that were more or less related to one another as friends or enemies. Qin Shi Huang Di began by conquering all the lands that bordered his own kingdom, Qin, joining them together into a single empire in what would today be the greater part of eastern China. This was the original Chinese Empire, making Qin Shi Huang Di the first emperor of China, which he ruled from 221–210 BCE. Despite intense effort, his scientists and scholars were unable to discover an elixir to give him eternal life. Out of fear of what would happen after death, Qin Shi Huang Di began building his burial complex shortly after taking the throne. It would take an army, he thought, to protect him in the afterworld, and so the manufacture of the terracotta army began. Over 700,000 people worked at the task.

The soldiers were meant to accompany and guard the emperor on his journey into the unknown of the afterlife. For this purpose, they are outfitted with all the gear and weapons required for battle.

FACTS

* **Emperor Qin Shi Huang Di** reigned over China from 221 to 210 BCE. He is considered the founder of the nation. In addition to the tomb at Xi'an, he was responsible for construction of the oldest sections of the Great Wall of China.

* **Xi'an** is the capital of the Chinese province of Saanxi, the starting point of the famous Silk Road. Today, Xi'an has a population of more than 7 million. There are a number of historical sights in the city in addition to the terracotta army, including the enormous Wild Goose Pagoda and the Great Mosque, the latter one of the four best-known Islamic religious buildings in China.

In 1974, a group of Chinese peasants drilling a well came across part of the long-buried terracotta army. Archaeologists and conservation experts have excavated over 8,000 individual figures so far, including warriors, horses and chariots. But this is probably only a fraction of what remains to be found. It seems likely that the emperor would want a full complement of armed soldiers at his side, which in the period in question would number about 30,000. **These guardians were placed,** standing, into three pits near the tumulus of their dead emperor. Remarkably, they were arrayed in a battle formation. The first three rows consist of 204 archers, defining the first line of attack. The rest of the army follows, with units set off on each side to protect the flanks and a rear guard at the back. **Equally impressive is the care** given to the precise finishing of each figure, be it a soldier or a horse. The smallest details of their hair, uniforms, facial expressions and armour were included in the representations, down to the contemporary features indicating their rank within the "pinyin", or cavalry. Each figure is a unique clay model. No two are alike in any detail, even in regard to their pose or expression. The weapons they carried are also originals, illustrating the masterful level of skill and attention to detail the emperor's artists and craftsmen brought to the task. **Since 1974, three chambers** of terracotta figures have been uncovered, but also one other, found completely empty. Is it possible that the terracotta army of Qin Shi Huang Di was never completed? Was one of the chambers discovered and plundered long ago, with its contents completely destroyed in the process? That the immense project was never completed as planned seems the most plausible interpretation. Qin Shi Huang Di died suddenly, and his newly formed empire suffered through a long period of unrest, peasant revolt and bloodshed. According to the later historian Sima Qian, the tomb contained not only an army, but also a scale replica of the universe, complete with gem-covered ceilings representing the cosmos, and flowing mercury representing the great earthly bodies of water. Recent scientific work at the site has shown high levels of mercury in the soil, further confirmation of what were long thought to have been semi-legendary accounts of the first emperor of China, who certainly did not enter the afterlife unattended.

Centre: A look at the faces of the soldiers shows that each one is unique.

Bottom: According to historical sources, Qin Shi Huang Di would have had an army of 30,000 armed men, horses and chariots at his side.

Art and architecture have been at the forefront in Europe for many centuries. Its extraordinary buildings and other man-made wonders dating from classical times to the present day, be they castles, towers, palaces, sacred buildings or bridges, are famous the world over. Equally fascinating are Europe's diverse natural wonders, often unique and, too often, fast disappearing.

EUROPE

GREECE

The Athenian Acropolis

EVEN TODAY, ANCIENT ATHENS IS FREQUENTLY DESCRIBED AS THE CRADLE OF WESTERN CIVILIZATION. WELL BEFORE THE DAWN OF THE COMMON ERA, THE CITY WAS ALREADY THE HIGHLY DEVELOPED CENTRE OF A UNIQUELY ACCOMPLISHED PEOPLE.

The ancient city of Athens was famous for its poets, philosophers, politicians, architects, artists and musicians. A prime mover within this society was Pericles, so much so that the fifth century BCE golden age of the city is often referred to as "the age of Pericles". Having made his name as a politician, it was his will and organizational ability that led to the building of the prominent temple complex of the Athenian Acropolis, a sanctuary deliberately designed to stand as a symbol of democracy and freedom. These monuments have come to symbolize humanity and civilization for all people.

The Athenian Acropolis is easily the most recognizable fortified citadel in the world. After the Persians destroyed the city in 470 BCE, Pericles first decided to maintain the ruins on top of the Acropolis as a memorial to the war dead. Soon afterwards, however, as Athens began to enjoy its new role as leader of the Greek world, he changed his mind and decided to rebuild the monuments instead. Under the direction of the famous sculptor Phidias, the architects Iktinos, Kallikrates and Mnesikles designed the temple complexes and other buildings for the newly conceived Sanctuary of Athena Athenaios on the Acropolis. Between 467 and 406 BCE they completed the Propylaon, Erechtheion, Nike Temple and Parthenon.

FACTS

*** Athens:** The city was named in honour of Athena, the Greek goddess of wisdom. The city is today the capital of Greece, and with over 750,000 inhabitants, the largest city in Greece. According to tradition, King Kekrops founded the city in the distant past. Archaeological excavation shows that Athens has been continuously occupied for at least 5,000 years, making it one of the oldest settlements in Europe. In 1985 it was awarded the title "cultural capital of Europe". In 1987, the Athenian Acropolis was named a World Heritage Site by UNESCO.

The Temple of Athena Nike, begun around 420 BCE, is an outstanding example of Greek architecture.

Pericles wanted Athens to become a new centre of the Greek realm, which required visible symbols and an inspired citizenry. Thus, the Parthenon, his temple on the Acropolis dedicated to Athena, had to be a showpiece. Pericles commissioned the best architects and gave the task of directing the building and sculptural programmes to Phidias, the most famous sculptor of classical antiquity. Together with the architects Iktinos and Kallikrates, Phidias completely reorganized the plan of the temples. The Propylaon, a monumental gateway designed by Mnesikles, was located at the top of the entrance ramp. Upon passing through the Propylaon, visitors were confronted by the Parthenon, standing tall on a terrace built out of the debris of the old Athena Temple to the north. It housed a colossal gold and ivory statue of Athena, the work of Phidias himself.

The main altar of the sanctuary lay over the east end of the original Temple to Athena, the one destroyed by the Persians. The sacrifices associated with the Panathenaia, Athens' most significant festival, were celebrated here, in the open air. The Erechtheion, the third-largest building on the Acropolis, stood nearby. This temple was dedicated to several deities, rather than just one. It encloses a further altar to Athena at its eastern end. To the south, at a slightly lower level, was an altar for Poseidon, god of the sea, defeated by Athena in a competition to determine who would be Athen's patron deity. In a gesture commemorating this event, which the Greeks viewed as historical rather than mythological, Poseidon was worshipped on the Acropolis. In a crypt under the Caryatid, or *kore* (maiden) porch, lie the remains of the city's ancestral kings, Erechtheus and Kekrops I. The priest-hero Butes was also honoured here.

The Nike Temple lies on a northern spur of the citadel near the Propylaon. Kallikrates is named as

Above: The classical colonnade of the Parthenon.

Left: The Parthenon is one of the greatest temples of all antiquity and the high point of classical Greek style.

The Caryatid, or maiden porch of the Erechtheion on the Athenian Acropolis.

the architect of this smallest, most delicate of all the Acropolis temples. Erected late in his life, it seems to have been built against Pericles' wishes. In the course of the Panathenaia festival a temporary stage and backdrop would be erected on the Acropolis. A long line of Greeks from all over the Mediterranean gathered in a great procession, entering Athens through the Dipylon gate, marching through the Agora, the central marketplace, and continuing up a series of broad ramps to the main altar on the Acropolis.

The Parthenon was completed in 438 BCE. At one time, nearly every surface of this extravagant building was decorated with sculptures by Phidias. With its classical proportions, the Parthenon is an almost perfect building, the zenith of Ancient Greek architecture. Pericles used it as a means of awakening a new sense of self-awareness in the citizens of Athens. As the Parthenon was to Athens, so should Athens be to the rest of the world: a focal point and source of continual inspiration. Pericles was not universally praised for his masterpiece. In fact, he was sharply criticized because of the costs involved. Contemporaries often referred to him as a spendthrift, dressing up the city "like a prostitute".

Despite all criticism, Pericles continued to build. The Propylaon (437–432 BCE) was his monumental gateway, designed to make the maximum impression on guests coming to the city, including many diplomats and kings. The wings of the gateway held dining rooms where they could be properly entertained.

In the end, even Pericles himself had to make concessions to reality. Criticism of the aesthetic inappropriateness of the work continued and, given the financial crisis of the times, the amount of labour and materials consumed could not be justified. Pericles the statesman and politician had to compromise to save the project from being completely abandoned. If he had had his way, every square metre of the Acropolis would have been covered with large, monumental buildings. In this sense, the distinctly non-monumental proportions of one of the later Acropolis buildings, the small temple dedicated to 'victory' (*Nike* in Greek), were a kind of defeat. When his contemporaries saw the scaled-down plans for the Nike Temple, they knew that Pericles' power and influence were no longer absolute.

Although his design for the Nike sanctuary was executed on a somewhat smaller scale than Pericles

FACTS

✻ Pericles:
Pericles (493–429 BCE), son of Xanthippos and Agariste, was a member of the most ancient family of Athens. As a statesman and politician, Pericles, along with some of his contemporaries, is considered one of the founders of modern democracy. As an architect and city planner he is responsible for the famous Odeion, Propylaon and Parthenon as well as the Athenian Acropolis in general. He died of plague in 429 BCE.

The architects of the Athenian Acropolis produced masterpieces epitomizing the classical style, such as this Ionic capital from the Parthenon.

originally wanted, visitors to the Acropolis would agree that the overall, triumphant effect of the Western world's greatest sanctuary is in no way diminished. Sadly, the great visionary would not live to see either the Nike Temple or the Erechtheion completed. In 430 BCE, Athens was struck by a great plague. Pericles fell sick and died the next year.

With the Acropolis, Pericles wanted to communicate a single message: Athens should become more conscious of the glory of its origins and the valour of its heroic past. As could be seen in Phidias' Parthenon sculptures, monstrous creatures had threatened the early Greeks, among them centaurs and other gruesome barbarians from foreign parts of the world. The gods had stood by Athens then as they would continue to against powerful opponents like the Spartans and Persians. By the time of Pericles' death, however, an era had come to an end, and the golden age of Athens was over. Athens would nonetheless remain the archetypical Greek city, and the Acropolis its symbol.

For many centuries the temples on the Acropolis remained in reasonably good condition. Then, in 1687, it was attacked and besieged by the Venetians, who had discovered that the Turks were using the Parthenon as their gunpowder magazine. It was hit by a bomb and exploded. From this point onwards, the wheels of time, further destruction and relentless vandalism did great damage to the buildings on the Acropolis. Yet some pieces survive relatively unharmed, "thanks" to the efforts of British Lord Elgin. In 1800, he was commissioned to go to Athens and catalogue the sculptures of the Parthenon pediment and frieze. As he became aware of French interest in acquiring the sculptures, he had the marble figures sawn off and brought to London, where they still can be admired in the British Museum.

Above: The relief sculpture of the east frieze of the Parthenon showing Poseidon, Apollo and Artemis.

Left: The ruins of the Parthenon.

SWITZERLAND

Aletsch Glacier

THE ALETSCH GLACIER IS THE LARGEST AND LONGEST ALPINE GLACIER. FOR MORE THAN 10,000 YEARS, IT HAS COVERED THE SOUTHERN FLANK OF THE BERNESE ALPS IN THE CANTON OF WALLIS, BUT ITS SURVIVAL IS THREATENED BY GLOBAL WARMING.

The icy giant winds its way like a frozen river over a distance of more than 22 km, from the high altitudes of the Jungfrau at 3,800 metres above sea level down to the Rhône Valley. Arcing through the mountains, it currently terminates at an elevation of around 1,560 metres, below the tree line. The sight of the Aletsch Glacier is fascinating, but also frightening. The mighty forces that drive it through the valley are threatening and destructive, despite the fragility and impermanence of the glacier itself.

The Aletsch glacier feeds off three powerful moving icefields – 'firns' – that meet at Konkordiaplatz, an irregular, gently sloping ice field covering 6 km^2 located just below the Jungfrau massif. From the west comes the Aletsch firn, running along the northern foot of the Aletsch and Dreieck horns. From the north-west comes the Jungfrau firn, the shortest of the three tributaries. Some 7 km long, it originates on the southern flank of the Mönch, at the Jungfaujoch and along the eastern Jungfrau slopes. From the north comes the 8-km-long firn known as Ewigschneefeld ("eternal snowfield") that begins at the Mönch and makes a wide arc to Konkordiaplatz.

Beneath the Konkordiaplatz, the Aletsch Glacier, the product of these three icefields, emerges as an

Right: The Aletsch Glacier is the largest glacier in Europe.

Below: Scientists stationed at the Jungfrau have recorded the glacier's movements over the course of several years.

enormous river of ice 1.5 km wide on average, pushing its way through the landscape at a pace of up to 200 metres per year, or 60 cm per day. The Glacier moves south-east down the valley towards the Rhône River. By the time it has reached its lowest elevation, the Aletsch is practically covered by mounds of rock and other debris picked up along the way, called a 'moraine'. At its terminus, at an altitude of 1,560 metres, it transforms into the Massa stream, which empties into the Rhône just above the town of Brig.

Two distinctive dark lines can be seen along the entire length of the glacier, from Konkordiaplatz to its end at the Massa. These are its deposits of middle moraine, rocks brought down from the Kranzberg and Trugberg mountains, kept separated into distinct lines because of the glacier's three feeders.

The Aletsch glacier is nourished upon snow that falls at an elevation of around 4,000 metres, and Glacier ice is really nothing more than compressed snow. Layer by layer, a dense snow pack forms in the high altitude regions, where the constant pressure and weight of accumulated snow leads to the formation of a firn, which itself will eventually turn into moving glacial ice, a process that can take up to ten years. The mass will only begin to move once the pressure has become great enough to force it forwards.

Up close, the glacier resembles a kind of garden, with streams, trenches, furrows and deep crevasses. Its surface is covered by fine, grey-brown dust formed when the glacier rubs against the rock walls of the valley, loosening rocks and gravel that will accompany it on the long journey down into the valley.

People have lived near the glacier for thousands of years, yet even those who do so today and are accustomed to its presence consider it something out of the ordinary. Folk tales surround the glacier known locally as the "white giant". The progress of the ice mass can still rouse fear and terror in the hearts of the inhabitants of Wallis, especially at night, when the uncanny creaks and booms made by the moving glacier are amplified by the surrounding deep silence of the high Alps. Since ghost stories are created to explain otherwise inexplicable natural phenomena, it is not surprising that locals believe that whenever a new glacial fissure cracks open in the Aletsch ice with a sound like the clashing of swords, moans can be heard coming from deep within the glacial mass. An old Walesian legend says that those who have the gift of second sight can see the poor souls frozen fast in the ice, trapped to be set free only when their sins are forgiven. For them, the glistening crevasses are gateways to the frozen bonfires of hell.

FACTS

* **Location:** The Aletsch Glacier is located in the Bernese Alps in the canton of Wallis, Switzerland.

* **Size:** Its average width is around 1.5 km. It covers an area of 87 km² and weighs around 27 billion tons.

* **Elevation:** Its highest elevation is over 3,800 m. Its lowest elevation is 1,560 m.

* **Travelling speed:** The glacier travels up to 200 m per year, or 60 cm per day.

* **Thickness of the ice:** The ice is thickest at Konkordiaplatz, where it is over 900 m deep. The ice is thinnest near its terminus below the tree line, where it is around 150 m thick.

* **World Heritage site:** The Aletsch Glacier was named a UNESCO World Cultural Heritage Site in 2001.

SPAIN

The Alhambra

THE MIGHTY, IMPOSING ALHAMBRA IS LOCATED ON A HILL RISING ABOVE THE ANDALUSIAN CITY OF GRANADA. THE MOORISH-STYLE FORTIFIED CITADEL IS BOTH THE OLDEST AND MOST IMPRESSIVE ARAB PALACE IN THE IBERIAN PENINSULA.

Early in 1492, the 700-year reign of the Arab kingdoms in Spain came to an end when the Spanish Christian kings deposed the Nasirid rulers of Granada, who had controlled the city and its environs for nearly 250 years. The Nasirids were forced to abandon their famous palace, the magnificent Alhambra. This "red citadel", actually an extraordinarily impressive architectural ensemble rather than an individual building, only divulges the treasures hidden behind its mighty walls on closer inspection.

The Alhambra is one of the most beautiful fortified palatial cities ever built. The complex conforms to the archetype of a medieval castle, which consisted of fortified upper storeys for the nobles, military and citizens and a lower, walled citadel for the merchants and artisans. In the year 1241, Ibn al-Ahmed founded the Nasirid Dynasty in Granada, calling himself Mohammed I. The Nasirids reigned until 1492. It was Mohammed I who commissioned the Alhambra citadel.

The first part of the enormous fortified complex, the Alcazaba (Upper City) was completed in the late thirteenth or early fourteenth century. The Mexuar, or Court of Justice, including the elaborately decorated Quarto Dorado (Golden Room), was the office of the sultan himself. Here he pronounced on legal

The world famous Patio de los Leones (the Lion Courtyard), the magnificent inner court of Mohammed V's palace, is lined with 124 marble columns.

DATES

* 1090: Beginning of the Almoravid Dynasty.
* 1238: The residence of Beni Nasr was built.
* 13th–15th centuries: The Alhambra was built.
* 1491: The Alhambra was besieged by the army of the Catholic Kings as part of the Reconquista.
* 2 January 1492: The city surrendered, bringing the Granada sultanate to an end.
* 1542: Granada University was founded.
* 1890: The Sala de la Barca was damaged by fire.
* 1936: The Church of San Salvador was burned to the ground during the Spanish Civil War.
* 1965: The Sala de la Barca was restored.
* 1984: The Alhambra was named a Cultural Monument by UNESCO.

matters, assisted by his officials. The walls of the Golden Room were adorned with the inscription: "Enter and do not fear asking for justice; you will receive it."

The Comares Palace, which housed the sultans' officials and administrators, is the masterpiece of the Alhambra complex. The Ambassadors' Room has a cedar-wood ceiling representing the seven heavens of the Koran, richly decorated with intaglio of ivory and mother-of-pearl. The personal attendants of Sultan Mohammed V (1354–91) gathered in the Lion Courtyard, a high point of Arabic architecture in Iberia and of Islamic art in general. The walls and ornamentation are decorated with red, green, gold and blue tiles. The courtyard, lined with 124 marble columns, owes its name to the fountain in its centre, which is supported by twelve marble statues of lions.

The most elaborately decorated room is the Two Sisters Room (Sala de las dos hermanas). Its dome is decorated in Moorish stalactite vaulting, with the interior surface divided into more than 4,000 glittering cells. On the walls are verses and poems in precious materials, such as gold and blue lapis lazuli.

The sound of water can be heard everywhere in the Alhambra. The citadel was designed to incorporate many wells. Sultan Mohammed I decreed that water would be the dominant element within his palace. His architects repeatedly incorporated water into the citadel plan as a decorative element. Filigree fountains blended perfectly with the artful play of glazed brick, marble floors and multicoloured tiles, known as '*azulejos*', which resemble relief sculpture.

On 2 January 1492, the Moors were driven out of Spain. During the reconquest of the Arab-ruled parts of the peninsula, the Catholic kings took possession of the Alhambra. Despite many wars and conflicts between Christians and Moors along the way, the period of Arab rule had been defined by a relatively high degree of tolerance and progress. For 700 years, Arab culture in Iberia had influenced art, architecture, philosophy, the natural sciences, astronomy and medicine in ways that had an enormous impact on Europe. The rediscovery of classical antiquity, one of many factors that led to the Renaissance, would not have been conceivable without the libraries of the Moors full of ancient texts and the resident scholars who could read them. The Alhambra's significance thus cannot be overestimated.

Centre: The Patio de los Arrayanes in the Comares Palace.

Bottom: Over 4,000 stalactites decorate the domed ceiling of the Sala de las dos ermanas.

GREECE

Mount Athos

HAGIO OROS IS THE GREEK NAME OF THE MONASTIC STATE OF MOUNT ATHOS. FOR OVER 1,000 YEARS, ORTHODOX MONKS HAVE LIVED RELIGIOUS LIVES HERE IN 20 LARGE MONASTERIES, WITHDRAWN FROM THE WORLD, YET RETAINING THEIR SOVEREIGNTY.

Athos, the holy mountain, rises 2,033 metres above sea level on the tip of the Chalcidice Peninsula. According to traditional legend, there was once a battle between the Olympian gods and the giants in which a giants, named Athos heaved a great stone at his opponent, Poseidon. The stone missed its target, falling instead into the sea, where it became the mountainous peninsula. More than 1,000 years ago, the Orthodox Autonomous Monastic State of Athos was founded on the slopes and hillsides of the holy mountain. Byzantine monks built the oldest monastery, Megisti Lavra, in the year 963. As early as 972, as part of a unique agreement, Athos was recognized as an autonomous theocratic state by the Byzantine Empire, with its sovereignty and protection guaranteed by the emperor himself. This made Athos the political and religious centre of Greek, Balkan and Russian Orthodox Christianity. During the fourteenth century, the golden age of the state, more than 40,000 monks lived in its 20 great monasteries and smaller "*skiti*", which are abbeys that resemble small villages.

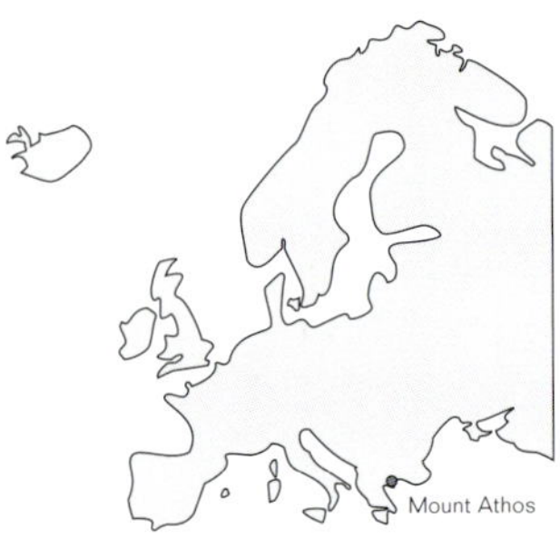

Although the population of the monastic state of Athos is technically subject to Greece, its autonomous status has continued to today, with the most

FACTS

* **Name:** The official name of Mount Athos is the Autonomous Monastic Orthodox State of Athos.
* **Location:** It is located in Macedonian northern Greece. Athos is the easternmost of the three Chalcidician peninsulas.
* **Capital:** Its capital is Karyes, with a population of 300.
* **Parliament:** The Holy Assembly (*Hiera Synaxis*) serves as its parliamentary body.
* **Population:** The population consists of 1,700 Orthodox monks.
* **Unique:** Monks and all males may enter the monastic state, but women, and most female animals, are forbidden any access.
* **Attractions:** The 20 large Orthodox monasteries with their world-famous frescos and magnificent collections of icons are among the most fascinating places to visit on the peninsula.

Founded in 1366, the Dionysiou Cloister is located directly on the coast of the Athos Peninsula. Its precious wall paintings are internationally renowned.

recent contract reaffirming its sovereignty written and signed in 1912. Decisions affecting its internal affairs are the responsibility of the monastic state's government, which is made up of the abbots of the 20 largest monasteries, who control all legislative and judicial affairs. A parliament of monks sits in the capital city off Karyes, as does their leader, the Protos (Elder Monk), who embodies the executive branch of government. The position rotates yearly between the abbots. The representatives of Greece in Athos are given the status of governors representing the Greek foreign office. Along with some other officials and the police, the governor of Athos is responsible for maintaining the contract with the monastic state as well as keeping the peninsula secure and orderly.

The lives of the monks play out in the "Garden of the Virgin Mary", as Athos is also known, according to the traditions of the Byzantine period when the monastic state was founded. Now as then, women and most female domestic animals as well, are forbidden to set foot within its borders. According to the monks, this ban is based on a Biblical tradition stating that the Virgin Mary chose Mount Athos as her own garden so that she could enjoy restful peace far from the company of any other female creatures. This form of gender discrimination has led to controversy within the European Union more than once, and has yet to be resolved. A few other curiosities strain the relationship between the monastic state and the EU as well, such as the fact that Athos pays no taxes to the EU because of its autonomous status.

Currently, some 1,700 monks live in the main monasteries in Athos. The opening of the Iron Curtain led to growth, as Orthodox believers from formerly Communist countries were able to join the monasteries or at least support them financially. As a result, the future of the state of Athos appears secure.

Above: Magnificent frescos adorn the walls and ceilings of the monasteries.

Left: The Cloister of Simonos Petras was founded in the 14th century.

BELGIUM

The Atomium

BRUSSELS IS MORE THAN JUST THE LOCATION OF MANY INSTITUTIONS AND AGENCIES OF THE EUROPEAN UNION. THE CAPITAL OF BELGIUM IS ONE OF THE MOST BEAUTIFUL CITIES IN EUROPE, WHERE TRADITION AND MODERNITY MEET IN A HARMONIC SYMBIOSIS.

The Belgian metropolis shows its modern face with a giant "sculpture", the world-famous Atomium in Heysel Park, a symbol of Brussels from the 1958 World's Fair. The architect André Waterkeyn designed the Atomium as a structure symbolizing the Atomic Age and the peaceful use of the products of nuclear fission. He reinforced these ideas by taking the very smallest physical unit, the atom, and enlarging it into an enormous pavilion where exhibitions could be held in the "nuclei".

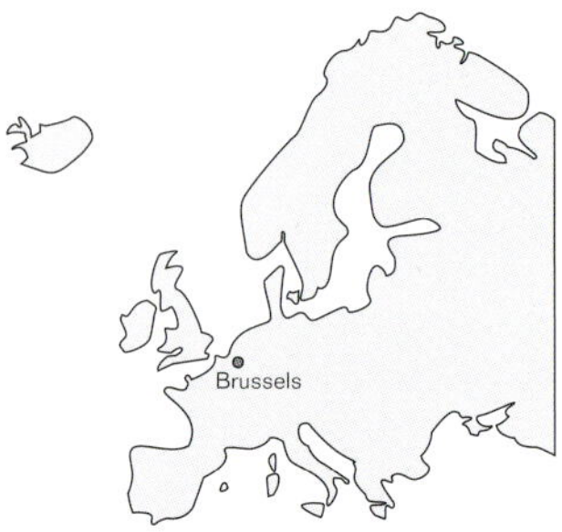

The futuristic Atomium is an oversized, three-dimensional model of an iron crystal consisting of nine atoms arranged around a cubic space – enlarged 165,000,000,000 times! The atomic model is 102 metres tall and consists of nine spheres. Around a central sphere, eight additional two-storey spheres, each 18 metres in diameter, are arranged in a basic cubic formation. They are connected to each other by means of tubes 3.3 metres wide and 22–29 metres long that contain escalators and walkways. Six of the nine spheres can still be entered; three have been closed for safety reasons.

Waterkeyn's original plan envisioned that the 2,400-ton construction could be anchored to the sculpture's central tube, which would itself be set in a concrete foundation. Statistical and simulation

Right: Restoration of the famous Atomium took place in 2005 and 2006.

Below: Escalators run within the tubes between the spheres.

studies, however, suggested that this method would not provide adequate support for the enormous weight of the structure. For technical and safety reasons, additional, less optically appealing support girders were added to secure three of the most vulnerable spheres.

In just under 25 seconds, a lift running up the central tunnel of the Atomium brings visitors to the uppermost sphere, where there is a restaurant and scenic view. From there, visitors can see not only the entire exhibition space of Heysel Park, but also enjoy a magnificent panorama of the rest of the capital, by day and night.

Three of the Atomium's upper spheres are empty, but the sphere at the base and four of the others housed international exhibitions on the peaceful uses of atomic energy during the 1958 World's Fair. At that time, the original budget of around $5.5 million for construction of the unique building-sculpture had to be doubled in order to ensure its completion. The escalation of the cost was primarily due to the expensive materials required to improve the structure aesthetically. In order to make the Atomium more visually appealing, the spheres were clad in a skin of aluminium so highly polished that it reflects the surrounding landscape on sunny days. At night, the exteriors of the tubes connecting the atoms are strung with lights that illuminate in a wave pattern, producing the effect of electrons that are bouncing between the nuclei of the reflecting spheres.

While the choice of an iron molecule for the scale enlargement made the Atomium a prestige object within the Belgian metal industry, its unique monumentality has impressed the importance of atomic energy research upon generations of visitors. Today, the Atomium, open to the public again since early 2006, is one of the biggest tourist attractions in Brussels. In 2005 and 2006, it was completely restored, and its aluminium cladding was replaced with a special coating to protect it against weathering. Now as then, the exhibitions inside the spheres teach visitors about atomic energy, space travel, astronomy, meteorology and – as was part of its original conception – about the need to use nuclear technology for peaceful ends.

FACTS

* **Name:** The Atomium is located in Heysel Park, Brussels, where it is used as an exhibition hall.
* **Opening:** The Atomium was part of the 1958 World's Fair exhibition in Brussels.
* **Construction:** The Atomium is a three-dimensional steel-framed structure. Its engineer/architect was André Waterkeyn.
* **Height:** It is 102 m high with spheres that are 18 m in diameter. It weighs around 2,400 tons.

GREECE

Delphi

THE LEGENDARY SANCTUARY OF APOLLO AT DELPHI LIES NORTH OF THE GULF OF CORINTH AT THE FOOT OF MOUNT PARNASSOS. AT "THE NAVEL OF THE WORLD", KINGS AS WELL AS PEASANTS VISITED DELPHI TO ASK ADVICE FROM ITS FAMOUS ORACLE.

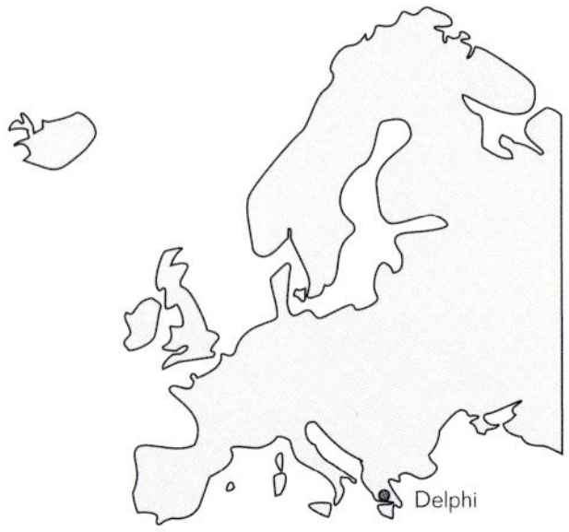

Delphi has been an important site of worship since the second millennium BCE, when it was originally dedicated to the Earth goddess Gaia. In the eighth century BCE, the cult of Apollo and its oracle became more influential. With the construction of the temple in 548 BCE, the conjunction of the worship of Apollo with the increasing popularity of his oracle made Delphi the centre of the ancient world, where fates and events – mythological, historical, or matters of daily life – were advised upon and interpreted.

Zeus, the father of the gods, was responsible for Delphi's advancement to the highest ranks of sacred sites. Far back in the mists of the primordial past, Zeus had desired that the entire earth be measured. He released eagles at each of its ends, and told them to land at the place where one met the other. This place at the foot of Mount Parnassos was declared the centre of the world – its *omphalos*, or navel. Here the city of Delphi was built.

Over the course of the following centuries, Delphi was destroyed several times by natural catastrophes and war. Its temples and houses were always quickly rebuilt because there was always funding available to do so. Offerings and oracle fees made Delphi an exceptionally lucrative cult site, and it

The round Tholos Temple in the Sanctuary of Athena Proanaia dates to the 4th century BCE. Three of its original 20 Doric columns have been re-erected.

DATES

* **8th century BCE:** Apollo was worshipped in the sanctuary.
* **548 BCE:** The Apollo Temple was built.
* **373 BCE:** The temple was destroyed by an earthquake.
* **330 BCE:** Alexander the Great completed reconstruction of the temple.
* **191 BCE:** Delphi was conquered by the Romans.
* **394 CE:** The ban of Theodosius closed all pagan sanctuaries, including Delphi.
* **1893:** Excavation of Delphi by French archaeologists began, clearing the site for the first time since antiquity.
* **1938–41:** The Apollo Temple was partially restored.
* **1987:** Delphi was declared a World Heritage Site by UNESCO.

would remain so well into the Roman period.

Apollo founded the Delphic oracle. According to legend, he stole Delphi from the Earth goddess Gaia. In the course of this struggle, he killed one of her children, a giant winged snake named Python whose blood pooled underground, giving off fumes that gave prophetic visions to anyone who inhaled them. Delphi's seers were always women, called Pythia, and set under Apollo's protection. The current Pythia was the only woman who was permitted to set foot in the Apollo Temple. Once inside, she inhaled the gases that entered the temple through fissures in the underlying rock. These put her in a trance, during which she would answer questions while pronouncing on events already underway and prophesy their outcome. Her prophesies could often be interpreted in more than one way, usually requiring some clarification by the corps of priests who stood nearby writing down every word. Over time, the oracle gained more and more influence over political events in Greece. Help was sought before important decisions were made, involving Delphi in nearly every politically significant event in the classical world. Not until 394CE, when the Christian emperor Theodosius banned all pagan cults, did the Oracle of Delphi come to an end.

Beginning around the time of the temple's founding in 586 BCE, the Pythian Games were held at Delphi every four years in honour of Apollo. These were the second-most important contests, after the Olympics in honour of Zeus. The Pythian Games began as music contests honouring the best composer for the kithara, an instrument similar to a lyre. More musical and athletic contests were added, along with chariot-racing and horse-racing. An enormous theatre that seated 5,000 was built, as well as a massive stadium for athletic events. These games continued every four years until the ban of Theodosius shut them down forever in 394CE.

From that point on, Delphi fell into a deep slumber. Its slopes were first cleared of centuries of overgrowth in 1894, when French archaeologists excavated at the site. Only six of the original 38 Doric columns of the Apollo temple still stand, but the theatre and great stadium have survived in good condition, just a little further up the slope. Near the excavation site, three columns belonging to a round structure dedicated to Athena Pronaia have been re-erected not far from the Castalia Fountain. Legend has it that whoever drinks from it receives the gift of poetry.

Centre: The great theatre could seat up to 5,000 people.

Bottom: The Pythian Games were celebrated with musical and athletic contests held in the stadium at Delphi.

FRANCE

The Eiffel Tower

THE DISTINCTIVE SILHOUETTE OF THE EIFFEL TOWER IS PROBABLY PARIS'S BEST-KNOWN SYMBOL. ORIGINALLY SLATED FOR DEMOLITION IN 1909, IT IS NOW IMPOSSIBLE TO IMAGINE THE SKYLINE OF PARIS WITHOUT IT.

The monument more emblematic of Paris than any other is named after the man who built it, the engineer Gustave Eiffel. The tower was erected between 1887 and 1889 as part of the Paris Exhibition, a World Fair that coincided with the celebration of the 100th anniversary of the French Revolution.

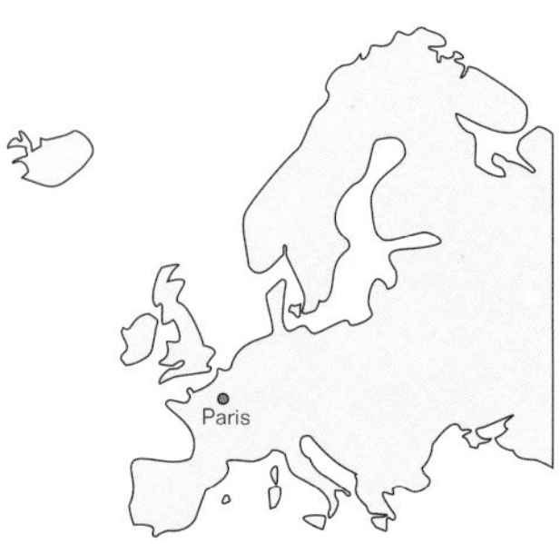

The famed tower stands exactly 300.65 metres high, just over 324 metres including the antennae that were added at a later date. At the time of its dedication during the Paris Exhibition, the Eiffel Tower was the tallest freestanding structure in the world. With its four pillars bedded in a massive concrete foundation, the tower itself is built entirely of iron that was smelted using a unique process that accounts for its extraordinary durability and resistance. The iron was forged piece by piece in the foundry of Gustave Eiffel and Co., from where it was transported to the Champs de Mars in Paris for assembly.

The Eiffel Tower is made of 18,038 individual iron modules, attached by means of 2.5 million rivets pounded in by workmen during a construction period of just 26 months. As a construction method, Eiffel's modular system was revolutionary. The structure is essentially the same as that of a half-timbered building, but with iron substituted for the classic

FACTS

✱ Function: The Eiffel Tower is both the emblem of Paris and a functioning radio tower.

✱ Building time: It was built between 1887 and 1889.

✱ Architect: Its architect was Stephen Sauvestre, but its builder/engineer, Gustave Eiffel (1832–1923) is better known. Among his other works are the Pont Maria Pio Garabit Viaduct and the iron armature for the Statue of Liberty.

✱ Structure: The tower is a free-standing steel-framed building.

✱ Size: The Eiffel Tower is 300.65 m tall, 324 m with its antennae, and weighs 7,300 tons. Including its concrete foundations, its weight is 10,100 tons.

✱ Platforms: There are three, at approximately 57 m, 115 m and 276 m.

✱ Steps: 1,665 steps lead to the top.

The Eiffel Tower illuminated by night is a truly fantastic sight emblematic of the French metropolis.

wooden frame. At the opening of the exhibition, the Eiffel Tower was a sensation, praised as an engineering masterpiece, the perfect combination of age-old frame and modern modular construction.

The original plan was for the tower to stand until 1909 and then be demolished. However, around that time, improvements in the practical applications of radio waves gave the Eiffel Tower a new purpose. Its height enabled transatlantic radio communication, a technology that would dominate the new century. It was therefore decided to let it stand.

The Eiffel Tower receives a new coat of paint every seven years to protect its surface (over 20 hectares!) from the elements. A crew of 25 painters works for 15 months to apply around 60 tons of paint, using 1,500 paintbrushes and 5,000 sanding disks. To ensure their safety at such dizzying heights, over 50 km of guide ropes and 20,000 square metres of netting are strung to protect them from falling. All these extras mean that a complete coat of new paint costs around $4 million. The colour of the paint varies from level to level, although the basic undertone is always bronze. The lowest level is the darkest; the higher levels are painted a lighter shade.

Gustave Eiffel called it the "300-metre-tower", but his critics associated his own name with the structure. A great many reacted to the tower harshly, publicly protesting its purported lack of aesthetic character in the strongest possible terms. Over time, however, both the tower and the name of the man who built it have withstood the critics and overcome all fears.

It was the people of Paris, having long since embraced the "iron lady" in their hearts, who silenced the critics. Since 1889, over 200 million people have visited the Eiffel Tower. The citizens of Paris knew what the critics did not – it is impossible to envision Paris without the Eiffel Tower.

Above: A poster advertising the Paris Exhibition of 1889.

Left: The Eiffel Tower is constructed from 18,038 iron modular components.

NORTHERN IRELAND

The Giant's Causeway

MORE THAN 60 MILLION YEARS AGO, IMMENSE FORCES RISING FROM THE INTERIOR OF THE EARTH IN NORTH-EAST IRELAND FORMED ONE OF THE MOST FAMOUS NATURAL WONDERS OF EUROPE: THE 400 BASALT COLUMNS KNOWN AS THE GIANT'S CAUSEWAY.

If one believes in the Ancient Irish tradition, it's the legendary giant Finn MacCumhaill who built the Giant's Causeway after falling head over heels in love with the beautiful daughter of a giant who lived on the Island of Staffa across the sea in Scotland. So that he could journey to the homeland of his beloved over land, he heaved gigantic blocks into the sea to form a path. He then carried her off, fleeing back to his home in Antrim. The giant Benandonner, who opposed the relationship because he himself wanted to marry the giant's daughter, followed the pair over the causeway to revenge himself on Finn. But Finn deceived him. He dressed himself up as an infant, lying down in the cradle of his own newborn child. When Benandonner arrived, the beautiful giantess presented the "baby" as her son by Finn MacCumhaill. Benandonner shrank away in fear – what kind of a giant must this MacCumhaill be if this giant baby was his son? He turned on his heels and fled in a panic back over the Giant's Causeway to Scotland, demolishing the path as he went. What remained of the causeway after his retreat is what we see there today, bearing mute witness to the domestic drama of giants. As romantic as the story may be, it's rather dull in comparison to the geological explanation of how the Giant's Causeway came into existence.

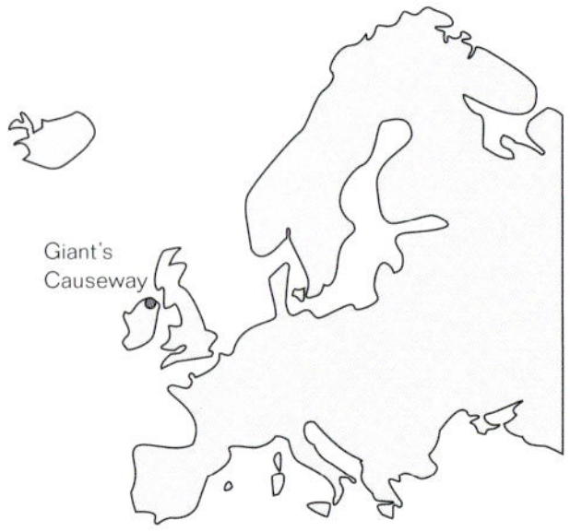

Right: The giant Benandonner fled over this causeway.

Below: The geometric organization of the basalt columns comes from lava cooling over an extended period of time.

More than 60 million years ago, as the North American and European tectonic plates began to drift apart, northern Europe was beset by a period of strong volcanic activity. In several places along the fault line running from western Scotland to the north-east of Ireland, the earth's crust was shattered by the forces of the tectonic shift and tension pulling the plates in every direction. Deep fissures formed, through which liquid magma flowed onto the Earth's surface, forming pools of lava that seeped through the limestone bedrock, where it cooled and hardened.

This process of cooling down took a very long time, causing the lava to harden not into rolling layers of stone, as is usually the case, but into regularly sized and shaped columns of basalt standing straight up, perpendicular to the surface. Over the course of two million years of cooling, the result was a plateau of basalt formations that covers the majority of the Antrim coast today. Over 40,000 perpendicular basalt columns are arrayed along a 5-km stretch of coastline, beginning in Antrim and ending in the sea. Most of the columns are hexagonal in section, although there are some with five, seven or eight angles. The tallest column is 12 metres high and some are up to 25 metres thick. Their association with the legend of Finn and Benandonner has led to fanciful names for some features. Thus, one set of basalt columns is known collectively as the Chimney Tops, because they tower among those around them. The ones called the Giant's Organ and Giant's Harp bring to mind oversized musical instruments. Other evocative features are the Giant's Boot, the stairlike Shepherd's Steps and the "hive" of the Honeycomb.

Once the flow of magma ceased, north-eastern Ireland enjoyed an extended period of subtropical climate. Wind and water continued to work on the landscape. The forces of erosion exposed a rust-red stone called 'laterite', the product of smaller eruptions that left behind canals, valleys and rounded lakes of lava, a group of which are called the Giant's Eyes.

The rugged landscape is home to a wide array of seabirds that took over the rock formation as a nesting place. Huge colonies of puffins, rock pigeons, fulmars, petrels, cormorants, redshanks, guillemots and razorbills inhabit the area. In addition, rare plants, including orchids exclusive to the region, grow between the basalt columns. The range of local plant and bird species expands the definition of the natural wonder of the Giant's Causeway beyond its geological magnificence. UNESCO recognized it as a World Heritage Site in 1986, and the government of Northern Ireland declared it a National Nature Preserve in 1987.

FACTS

* **Time of formation:** The Giant's Causeway formed some 60 million years ago.
* **Number of basalt columns:** The formation consists of over 40,000 basalt columns.
* **Height and size:** The tallest column is 12 m high, and the broadest is 25 m wide.
* **Famous attractions:** Among the most famous sights are the Chimney Tops, the Giant's Organ and the Giant's Boot.

PORTUGAL

Hieronymites Monastery

AFTER VIEWING THE CLOISTER OF THE FAMOUS MONASTERY OF THE HIERONYMITES, PORTUGUESE POET FERNANDO PESSOA EXCLAIMED RAPTUROUSLY: "IT IS A MASTERPIECE IN STONE THAT EVERYONE SHOULD SEE AND NEVER BE ABLE TO FORGET."

The poet was right. A visit to the monastery complex in Lisbon is a unique experience. The monastery was built because of a promise made by Manuel I. If Vasco da Gama returned safely from India, he would erect a monastery on to the site of an earlier hermitage built by da Gama's first patron, Henry the Navigator. To help the famous explorer find his way back, Manuel built an equally impressive, comparably enormous tower and lighthouse in the nearest harbour at the mouth of the Tagus River. Both the monastery and tower have been named World Heritage Sites by UNESCO.

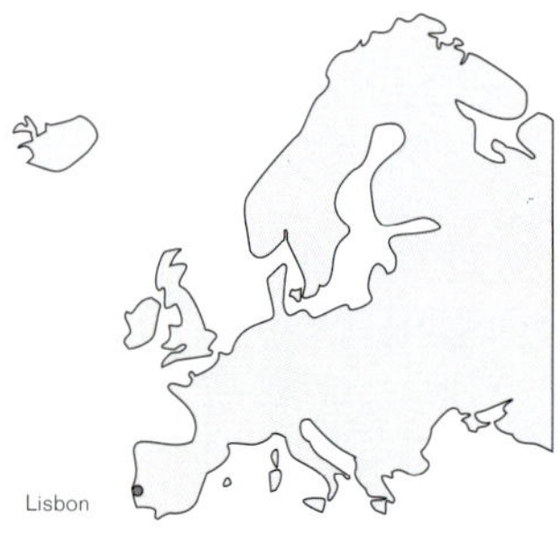

At the beginning of the sixteenth century, the golden age of exploration, Portugal was at the height of its power. Explorers like Vasco da Gama and Pedro Alvares Cabral were sailing the oceans. Lisbon, the city at the mouth of the Tagus, was the gateway to the New World, a world ruled by King Manuel I the Fortunate. Not much of a diplomat, he was nonetheless obsessed by power and glory. His dream of a world ruled by Portugal and his interest in maintaining its reputation as a great power made him one of the most productive builders in all of Europe.
In 1516, he completed the Torre de Belem, or Belem Tower, a fortified lighthouse at the mouth of the Tagus River. From the harbour of Lisbon his

The cloister of the Hieronymites Monastery is considered one of the most beautiful in the world.

DATES

* **1502:** Construction of the monastery begun by order of Manuel I.
* **1515–21:** The Torre de Belem was erected.
* **1517:** The monumental west portal with its statue of a kneeling Manuel I was completed.
* **1894:** A grave monument to Vasco da Gama, who is buried somewhere in the grounds, was erected in the monastery in the Almeida-da-Garrett Chapel.
* **21 December 1918:** Following his assassination, Portuguese president Dr Sidonio Pais was interred near the da Gama grave monument.

navigators went out into the world, returning to that same harbour from their highly successful journeys with ships full of exotic goods and treasures, guided by the lighthouse built for them by their king. Because it was fortified, Belem Tower also served as a guard tower and defensive bastion protecting the Portuguese capital. As Portugal's power and wealth increased so, too, did the need to defend the harbour against pirates seeking to steal these riches.

For the design of the tower, Manuel I called upon his chief architect and building master, a well-travelled master mason who understood the requirements of military installations as well as his patron's taste for delicate architectural details and elaborate ornamentation. The strong lines of the practical military structure are perfectly melded with decorative elements borrowed from other lands all over the world.

The Hieronymites Monastery, also known as the Mosteiro dos Jerónimos, is one of the most exciting architectural wonders in the world. For Vasco da Gama did indeed return from his Indian adventure, his ship laden with precious spices and other exotic goods. Manuel I immediately commissioned the Hieronymites Monastery. The construction was funded by the sale of the spices that da Gama had brought to his king from India.

Manuel I's architect, inspired by his own travels in oriental lands, built and chiselled a true masterpiece in stone in a style that became known as Manueline, a style that is found in Portugal and nowhere else in the world. The magic of the Manueline style is most directly expressed in the monastery's cloister, which has been signalled out as one of the world's most beautiful. As German author Reinhold Schneider (1903–53) wrote: "Fantasy plays out between the arches underneath the great dome resting on its massive pillars. Here, in the space in between, a tall, fragile-looking capitol sits atop a delicate column that seems to sway rather than stand. Every surface is covered with ornamentation of unfathomable richness in a harmony of excess. Gothic beasts, wreathes of vegetation, Indian plant varieties and intertwined Moorish motifs compete for space within borders consisting of the symbols of the sea and the sea journeys that evoke these wonders." Vasco da Gama's return brought Portugal, its king and the world great treasures – of which the Hieronymites Monastery is arguably the most precious.

Centre: The Hieronymites Monastery is emblematic of Portugal and the golden age of exploration.

Bottom: The inner courtyard and cloister of the monastery.

GERMANY

Cologne Cathedral

THE CATHEDRAL IS THE SYMBOL OF COLOGNE, AND MOST EVERYTHING IN THE CITY REVOLVES AROUND IT. LIKE A GUARDIAN TURNED TO STONE, THE WORLD'S THIRD-LARGEST GOTHIC CATHEDRAL STANDS IN THE MIDST OF THE CITY AND ITS INHABITANTS.

The official name of this imposing edifice is the "High Cathedral Church of Sts. Peter and Maria", but it is known simply as the Cologne Cathedral, a masterpiece of Gothic architecture. Of all the great churches in the world, no other incorporates the very essence of the High Gothic style quite like this one. At 157 metres, Cologne Cathedral is the second tallest church in Germany and the third highest in the world. Between 1880 and 1890, the beloved "Kölner Dom" was actually the tallest freestanding building in the world. The entire structure, including the imposing west wing with its two prominent towers, encompasses an area of more than 7,000 square metres, which remains a world record for religious buildings.

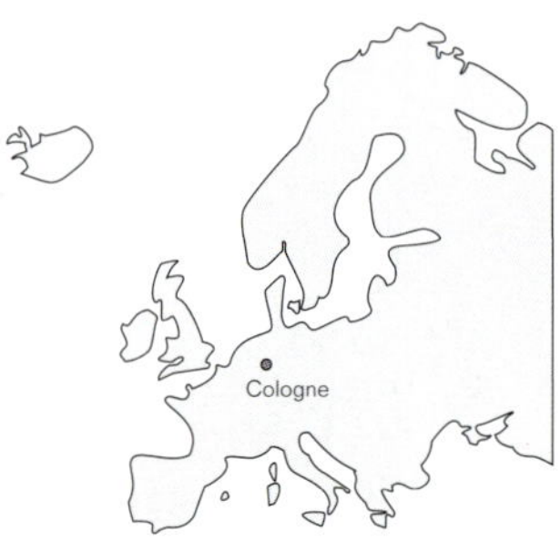

The plaza on which the Cologne Cathedral stands has been a gathering place for Christians since the late Roman period. This is where early Christians erected their first church, called the "oldest cathedral", some time after the fourth century CE. In the early ninth century, construction on the old Carolingian cathedral began. The building was completed in 873 and stood until the thirteenth century.

In 1164, the newly named archbishop, Rainald von Dassal, brought the relics of the magi to Cologne. Seized from Milan Cathedral by Emperor Frederick

FACTS

*** Size:** Cologne Cathedral is 144.5 m long and 86 m wide. The west end measures 61.5 m across. The east (transept) façade is 40 m wide.

*** Nave:** The nave is 45 m wide. Its height along the central axis is 43.35 m, sloping down to 19.8 m in the side aisles.

*** Towers:** The south tower is 157.3 m high; the north tower is just a few cm higher. 509 steps lead up to the top.

*** Roof:** The roof is between 61 and 109 m high, with the height of the east (transept) façade measured at 70 m.

*** Windows:** The windows cover an area of approximately 10,000 m^2.

*** Volume:** The total volume of the building, not counting buttresses, is 407,000 m^3. Its total weight approaches 300,000 tons.

*** Bells:** There are 12 bells, one of which, the "Petersglocke", is the world's largest free-swinging bell.

The nave of Cologne Cathedral is 43.35 m high.

Barbarossa, these most sacred holy bones needed to be housed in a shrine of worthy glory. Towards this end, Rainald von Dassel commissioned the most spectacular reliquary in all of Europe.

It was this shrine that drew pilgrims from all over the world to Cologne. The onslaught of the faithful soon had the old cathedral bursting at the seams. Plans for a new, larger, more magnificent building were finalized in 1225, and the cornerstone for a Gothic cathedral was laid in 1248. But by 1288, construction had already slowed to a virtual halt. The choir was only completed in 1322, and the south tower stood only two storeys high as late as 1410. In 1530, a lack of finances, as well general disinterest, stopped construction altogether. The cathedral remained an assemblage of incomplete structural fragments for the next 300 years. But worse was yet to come. In 1794, the French Revolutionary army invaded, causing the archbishop to flee, along with the cathedral treasury. The soldiers who occupied Cologne had no love for the trappings of organized religion. To illustrate this point, they used the cathedral as a horse stable and storage area. Cologne Cathedral would not be reconsecrated until 1801.

A blue enamel plaque located next to the cathedral's main entrance survives as a remnant of the resoundingly secular French occupation. It reads "Domkloster 4", the Cathedral's street address; it is the only church in the world that has one. Before the French took over, there were no house numbers anywhere in Cologne, making the unfamiliar streets difficult to govern. Thus, every building received a number and proper street address. Not even the cathedral was spared. Its official address is 2583½, Domkloster 4, Cologne – "½" identified it as a public building, which meant it was free from taxes. In this respect, at least, the cathedral received some relief.

Above: The two towers of the west wing.

Left: The golden shrine containing the relics of the magi is near the altar.

The cornerstone for the beautifully decorated main gatehouse was laid in 1842 in the presence of King Friedrich Wilhelm IV.

Sometime between 1814 and 1816, the long-lost original plans for the cathedral were found in two different locations: Darmstadt and Paris. At the same time, Gothic architecture was enjoying a period of renewed appreciation and enthusiastic revival. This led to the idea of completing the cathedral as planned, according to the original Gothic model. The Prussian king Friedrich Wilhelm IV stepped forward as the project's chief patron and political supporter. With Archbishop Johannes von Geissel supporting the project in the name of the Vatican, construction on the unfinished cathedral began anew on 4 September 1842, with the Prussian king himself present at the groundbreaking ceremony for the new gatehouse. He expressed his enthusiasm for the project in near poetic terms: "Here, where the cornerstone lies, the most beautiful portals in the world will rise, much like the two towers behind them."

The Prussian state put up one-third of the finance, but it was a civic organization called the Dombau-Verein (Cathedral Construction Group) made up of interested, ordinary citizens that raised the rest of the money through donations. The tremendous enthusiasm of the people of Cologne, and Germans generally, spurred the project along. Everyone was ready to give a little to help the cathedral.

Finally, on 15 October 1880, the cathedral's 600-year construction period came to an end. When the original plans were discovered, the nineteenth century architects decided to remain true to the medieval conception of the anonymous building master who drew up the plans in 1280. Thus, despite the fact that modern nineteenth-century technology played a role in the construction – the roof beams are made of iron instead of wood, for example – the result resembles an original Gothic building in every way. The roof beams proved their worth during World War II, when the cathedral was badly damaged by aerial bombardment. Despite sustaining 14 direct hits that destroyed most of the interior, the roof withstood the attacks and remained standing.

Cologne Cathedral, the seat of the Archbishop of Cologne, has one of the most beautiful exteriors of any Christian religious building in the world. But it is not only an impressive architectural wonder from the outside. Its interior is also of note, an outstanding example of the Gothic style. The late medieval choir stall, which could seat 104, is the largest in Germany.

DATES

✱ **1164:** The relics of the magi were brought to Cologne.

✱ **1180–1230:** The Three Kings Shrine was built.

✱ **15 August 1248:** The cornerstone of the Gothic cathedral was laid.

✱ ***circa* 1311:** The largest choir stall in Germany, with 104 seats, including two reserved for the emperor and the pope, was built.

✱ **1322:** The choir was consecrated.

✱ ***circa* 1355:** Tower construction began.

✱ **1814:** The first set of original plans for the west end were rediscovered.

✱ **1816:** The second set of original plans was found.

✱ **1842:** Construction of the cathedral began anew after over 300 years.

✱ **15 October 1880:** The cathedral was completed. From start to finish, it had taken 632 years to build.

✱ **1939–45:** The cathedral was damaged during World War II.

✱ **1996:** Cologne Cathedral was named a World Cultural Heritage Site by UNESCO.

The roof of the Ludwig Museum, devoted to modern art, stands in stark contrast to the Cologne Cathedral in the background.

Among its unique features are the two seats that are left empty, reserved for the pope and the emperor.

A golden sarcophagus, the Three Kings Shrine, houses the bones of the three magi from the east who brought gifts to the infant Christ in Bethlehem. It is still one of the most important shrines and most popular pilgrimage destinations in the Christian world. Every year, hundreds of thousands journey to Cologne to pray before it in the cathedral.

Twelve bells hang in Cologne Cathedral's bell tower. The largest of these is the Petersglocke, first struck in 1924. *D'r dicke Pitter* ("fat Peter"), as the citizens of Cologne lovingly refer to it, is at 24 tons the largest free swinging bell in the world.

The cathedral also has two organs, both of which can be played from a single keyboard. The so-called "choir" or "transept" organ was built in 1948, immediately after World War II, in the north-east corner of the crossing. It was needed because the nave would be closed off for repairs until 1956, making the nave organ inaccessible to those celebrating mass in the choir. In 1988, the organ in the so-called "Swallows Nest", located high up against the north wall of the nave, was finally in place. A famous concert series held in Cologne Cathedral every summer takes full advantage of its near perfect acoustics.

Cologne Cathedral has been on the UNESCO list of World Cultural Heritage Sites since 1996. Today, it is most threatened by the damage inflicted by its urban environment. Acid rain eats away at the masonry and exhaust fumes stain its light-coloured sandstone. The cathedral has been under continuous repair and renovation since its 1880 completion, and it will never really be finished. There is a saying in Cologne regarding what they refer to as The Eternal Building Site: "By the time the cathedral is finished, the end of the world will be upon us!"

Above: The transept of the cathedral is almost 70 m tall.

Left: A view of Cologne at its most beautiful shows the cathedral on the right and the Church of St Martin on the left.

ITALY

The Colosseum

THE COLOSSEUM WAS THE BIGGEST ROMAN AMPHITHEATRE AND LARGEST ENCLOSED STRUCTURE IN ANTIQUITY. UP TO 60,000 SPECTATORS COULD WATCH GLADIATOR FIGHTS, ANIMAL HUNTS, RE-ENACTED SEA BATTLES, ATHLETICS AND THEATRICAL ENTERTAINMENT.

The Colosseum is the most readily recognized ancient monument in Rome. Its name originated in the seventh century CE and referred not to the building, but to the many colossal statues nearby. Rome's architectural emblem bears witness to the majesty of the Roman Empire as well as the engineering abilities of its architects. But it also recalls the Romans' fondness for gruesome spectacles and bloody forms of entertainment.

Emperor Vespasian commissioned the amphitheatre in 72 CE. Like many other Roman monumental structures built at that time, it was financed by the spoils from the 70 CE sack of the Second Temple in Jerusalem. The Amphitheatrum Flavium, or Amphitheatrum Novum, as it was first called, was completed in 79, the year of Vespasian's death. It consisted of three superimposed arcades, each with 80 arches. The lowest storey was built in the Doric style; the middle, Ionian; and the uppermost, in Corinthian style. Vespasian's son and successor later added a fourth storey, a low masonry wall with small window niches. The Colosseum was built of tuffstone and brick with an exterior facing of fine travertine marble.

The amphitheatre was opened in the year 80. The inaugural games continued for 100 days and included gladiatorial contests, re-enactments of sea battles

This model of Ancient Rome revolves around the enormous, elliptical mass of the Flavian Amphitheatre, later known as the Colosseum.

FACTS

* **Size:** The Colosseum is 156 m wide and 188 m long. Its walls once stood 48.5 m high. The foundations of the building are 12 m deep.
* **Size of the arena:** The arena was 86 m long and 54 m wide.
* **Entrances and seating space:** The Colosseum had 80 entrances and 50 rows of seating. It had room for 50,000 seated spectators and a further 10,000 people could stand.

and animal hunts. Over 5,000 animals were supposedly killed in these staged hunts, many of them exotic creatures from Africa.

In plan, the Colosseum is an ellipse 156 metres wide and 188 metres long. Its walls were 48.5 metres high. Its circumference of 545 m enclosed stands to accommodate 60,000 spectators, who entered through one of 80 gates. The stair, tunnel and gallery circulation system remains the model for most large sports complexes today. Then as now, tickets had a number for the seat, but also numbers for the tunnel, stairway and entrance patrons should use to get there. The arena itself was an ellipse, a plan that denied gladiators and beasts any chance of saving themselves by hiding in a corner. The floor of the arena was made of wooden planks that could be removed so that it could be flooded for sea battles. Cells, cages and service areas were later installed below the arena floor, as well as complex, pulley-driven stage machinery for special effects or to move scenery.

Panem et circenses (bread and circuses) was the motto for many centuries at the huge amphitheatre in the city centre. The people expected to be fed, but also to be entertained. At the Colosseum and other Roman amphitheatres, they gorged on a steady diet of gruesome competitions and bloody executions. The varieties of contests and victims varied. Those condemned to death might be thrown to wild beasts, or forced to fight a professional gladiator, perhaps within a staged mythological context. Although many gladiators and animals died on the sand-strewn floor of the arena, the figures may not be as high as some sources and popular imagination suggest.

The first recorded protest against the arena spectacles came only in 404 CE, when the monk Telemachus leapt from his seat during a contest, declaiming against it. The spectators replied by stoning him to death. The last recorded gladiatorial contests and animal hunts took place in 523, after which the Colosseum began to decline. In the seventh century a monk wrote: "As long as the Colosseum stands, so stands Rome. When the Colosseum falls, Rome will fall with it." That the building would fall into ruin was a foregone conclusion, with earthquakes and stone robbing contributing to its demise. In the fifteenth century, Pope Nicholas, like so many others, made use of the Colosseum as a quarry, transporting 2,500 wagonloads of marble to build the Vatican.

Centre: The exterior walls of the Colosseum are made of travertine.

Bottom: Until at least 523 CE, gladiatorial combat was a favourite, if gruesome, Roman entertainment.

RUSSIA

Kremlin and Red Square

RUSSIANS HAVE ALWAYS HAD AN ESPECIALLY INTIMATE CONNECTION TO THE CITY ON THE MOSKVA RIVER. ALTHOUGH ST. PETERSBURG WAS THE NATION'S CAPITAL FOR CENTURIES, THE HEART OF RUSSIA HAS ALWAYS BEAT IN MOSCOW.

They all came to Moscow – the czars, Bolsheviks and democrats. The city has been the centre of the Russian Empire since the fourteenth century, when its czars resided in the Kremlin. After 1917, the "Red Czars" ruled from the Kremlin. Since 1991, the current democratic government chose to do the same.

An old Moscow proverb says: "Over the city, there is only the Kremlin, and over the Kremlin, there is only God." The cornerstone of the Kremlin Palace was laid in 1147, after Prince Juri of Suzdal built his hunting lodge here. It is hard to believe that one of the world's most monumental buildings and most important centres of power originated in this simple structure.

The fifteenth-century red-coloured wall enclosing the Kremlin complex is 7 metres thick and up to 19 metres high. Almost 2.5 km long, it encircles the earlier Czarist fortifications. Behind the wall lies a palace complex consisting of a number of impressive buildings. The oldest standing structures are the Cathedral of the Dormition (1479), the Church of the Virgin's Robe (1486) and the Cathedral of the Annunciation (1489), the latter sporting a 16-metre-tall iconostasis, an altar screen upon which icons can be displayed. The oldest surviving secular building is the Palace of Facets. It was built in 1491 for Ivan III in

FACTS

✻ **Function:** The Kremlin is currently the seat of the Russian Parliament.

✻ **Monuments:** Its most famous architectural features are its wall with 19 towers (15th century), the Dormition Cathedral (1479), the Church of the Virgin's Robe (1486), the Annunciation Cathedral (1489), the Palace of the Facets (1491), the bell tower known as "Ivan the Terrible" (1508), the Churches of the Twelve Apostles and Patriarchs (17th century), the Terem Palace (17th century), the Arsenal (1737), the Kremlin Senate Palace (1787) and the Great Kremlin Palace (1839–50).

✻ **The Kremlin,** Red Square, St. Basil's Cathedral and the Lenin Mausoleum were placed on the UNESCO World Cultural Heritage list in 1990.

An honour guard marches by the Lenin Mausoleum, where the preserved body of the "Father of the Soviet Union" is on permanent display.

Italian Renaissance style by specially imported architects. Also among the earliest structures are the tall bell tower, known as "Ivan the Terrible" (1508), and the St. Michael Archangel Cathedral of 1509.

The Great Kremlin Palace was built in 11 years, between 1839 and 1850. Inside, the Vladimirsky and Georgievsky Halls are truly exceptional. In these elaborately decorated salons, rulers and power brokers practised the art of government at any time of the day or night. After the Communists came to power in 1917, highly visible red stars were added to every tower and turret.

Red Square is a large (500 x 150 metres), open space directly in front of the Kremlin walls. It is not named for all the blood that has flowed here, nor is "red" a reference to Communism. In Russian, the words for "red" and "beautiful" are the same, and this has been the "Beautiful Square" since the seventeenth century, when the old wooden houses that used to stand here were cleared for its construction.

Many famous Russian heroes have been buried along the Kremlin walls, such as Josef Stalin and Yuri Gagarin, the first man in space. Most famous of all is probably Lenin, whose mausoleum is designed to resemble a stepped pyramid. It is built of dark red porphyry stone with details in black Labrador. The corpse of Vladimir Ilyich Ulyanov – Lenin, founder of the Soviet Union – lies here on permanent display.

St. Basil's Cathedral, with its nine vividly coloured domes, is the emblem of Red Square. Crowned by an Orthodox cross, the church is a symbol of victory and a declaration of faith. In 1552, the battle against the Mongols at Kazan had raged for eight days before Ivan the Terrible's army was finally able to force them back inside the city walls, where they were besieged and defeated. Ivan commissioned St. Basil's Cathedral in recognition of this hard-fought victory.

Above: The Kremlin Cathedrals are famous for their gilded domes.

Left: The Great Kremlin Palace, viewed from the Moskva River.

GREECE

Meteora Monasteries

THE METEORA MONASTERIES PERCH LIKE EAGLES ON TOP OF SANDSTONE PILLARS AS MUCH AS 400 METRES HIGH IN THESSALY'S PINDUS MOUNTAINS. HERMIT MONKS FLEEING THE TURKS BUILT THE FIRST OF 24 MONASTERIES HERE IN THE ELEVENTH CENTURY.

The name Meteora is derived from *meteorizo*, which means "place suspended in the air", a phrase that could not be more accurate in describing the precarious location of the monasteries. When the early morning fog swirls around the cliff face, the abbeys built on top of the soaring cliffs seem to float in the air. During Meteora's golden age in the late Middle Ages, 24 monasteries and hermitages were located here; today, only six survive. Monks occupy four of these: Megalo Meteoro, Varlaam, Agios Nikolaos Anapavsas and Agia Triada. Nuns operate the other two: Agiou Stephanou and the Rousanou Monastery. Though the other 18 monasteries lie in ruins, there are still men and women who, by living the life of a hermit, preserve the Byzantine spiritual and cultural legacy.

The earliest hermitage in the mountains was mentioned in reports from the eleventh century. The hermits fled the world and its diversions, sustaining a humble, ascetic existence in simple rock caves in order to better concentrate on God. As more and more hermits arrived over the years, they gradually organized themselves into monastic orders, following the example of the Monastic Republic of Athos.

A small group of hermits founded the first Meteora monastery, Doupani, which now lies in ruins. One

Right: The monasteries truly seem to be suspended in air.

Below: Agia Triada was founded in the middle of the 15th century.

small thirteenth-century chapel still stands witness to the first stirrings of monasticism at the site.

In 1334, the monk Athanasios fled to Meteora. With his arrival, monastic life began to truly thrive in the region. In 1370, Athanasios joined with fourteen others to found the Megalo Meteora monastery, which is also known as Metamorphosis. Encompassing an area of some 60,000 square metres, it is the largest Meteora complex. According to legend it was an eagle, or perhaps an angel, who carried Athanasios up to the mountaintop. Once there, he gave the local monks both spiritual and physical structure. His drive and personal charisma attracted both pious rulers and stern men of the church as patrons. Over time, he and his followers were able to found several additional monasteries.

Today, only six of the 24 monasteries are still inhabited. In the Church of John the Baptist in the Knolaos Anapavsas monastery complex, the skulls of all the monks who ever lived here are neatly stacked on shelves. The monastery is decorated with the frescos and paintings of Theophanes Steletzas (*circa* 1500–59), one of the most important members of the Cretan School, a group of artists that included Doménicos Theotocópoulos, later famous in Spain as El Greco. The Rousanou (or Arsanou) Monastery was founded in 1388. A convent since 1950, Rousanou was frequently attacked and plundered. Its sixteenth-century frescos are masterpieces. The Varlaam Monastery was built between 1518 and 1535, and is mentioned in a 1779 travel diary as being off limits to women.

Megalo Meteora, the largest complex, was named by its founder Athanasios after the cliff upon which it sits, the Meteora, "the floating one". Until 1923, the monastery could only be reached by climbing up a stick ladder or being hauled up in a net. Today, there are 143 steps and a tunnel cut through the rock. The monastery church is decorated with frescos dating to 1552. Agia Triada ("Holy Trinity") Monastery was probably built between 1458 and 1476, and its frescos date to 1741. The library houses an outstanding illuminated copy of the Gospels from 1539. In 1980, part of the James Bond movie *For Your Eyes Only* was filmed here, much against the will of the monks, who protested loudly but to no avail. Agiou Stephanou, a convent since 1961, was built sometime around 1400. The nuns who live here continue the Byzantine practice of icon painting as a form of meditation. Located at a lower elevation than the others, it is the most easily accessible of the monasteries.

DATES

* **11th century:** The first monks began living at Meteora in simple rock caves.
* ***circa* 1370:** The charismatic monk Athanasios founded Megalo Meteora.
* **1939–45:** Bombing heavily damaged the monasteries during World War II.
* **Since 1972:** Renovation of all of the functional monasteries has been ongoing.
* **1988:** UNESCO placed Meteora on the World Cultural Heritage list.

DENMARK AND SWEDEN

The Oresund Bridge

MORE THAN 8,000 YEARS AGO, NATURAL FORCES WRENCHED APART THE LANDMASSES THAT ARE NOW THE COUNTRIES OF DENMARK AND SWEDEN. THANKS TO AN INCREDIBLE ENGINEERING FEAT, THEIR COASTS ARE ONCE AGAIN JOINED TO ONE ANOTHER.

The Oresund Bridge is part of a larger project to create the "Oresund Region", linking the Danish capital of Copenhagen with Malmö, in Sweden. The central span of this combined road-and-rail bridge and tunnel system, called the High Bridge, is the longest cable-stayed bridge in the world. Completed in August 1999, it was opened to car and train traffic in the presence of the royal families of Denmark and Sweden on 1 July 2000.

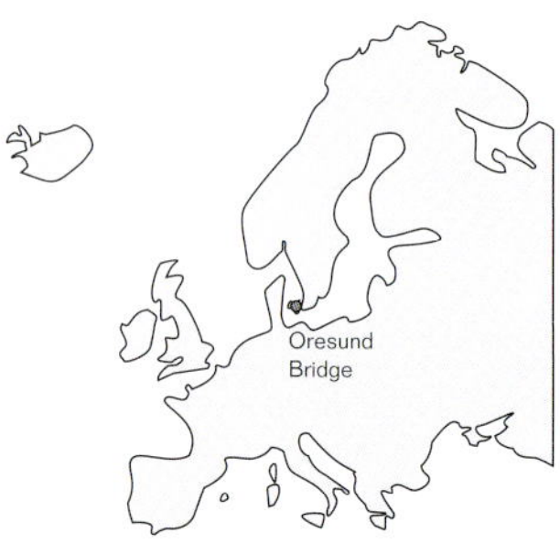

Planning and construction were the responsibility of the Oresund Consortium, a group formed to work out the details of this complex transport project. Half-Swedish and half-Danish, the consortium functioned as owner and contractor. It took out $12 billion in loans, which were projected to be paid back with income from bridge tolls within 27 years.

Architect Rotne's vision was realized in four years. It crosses the 18-km-wide Oresund Strait in several stages. On the Danish side, an artificial island, Peberholm ("Pepper Island" – Salt Island lies nearby), is the starting point of a 3,700-metre-long tunnel under the Drogden Strait to Copenhagen. From the eastern coast of the Peberholm, the Oresund High Bridge emerges and spans the water with a combined road-and-rail bed so high that even the largest container ships and tankers can pass beneath it.

FACTS

✻ **Location:** The Oresund Bridge, built between 1996 and 2000, joins Denmark and Sweden. It was designed by architect Georg Rotne.

✻ **Structure:** The structure is categorized as a two-storey cable-stayed bridge. The road and track beds are 23.5 m wide. Automobiles use the upper level and trains use the steel-framed lower section.

✻ **Length:** The Oresund High Bridge is suspended for 1,624 m. Its central cable-stayed span measures 490 m. It has a clearance of 61 m.

✻ **Size of the pylons:** The pylons are 203.5 m tall.

✻ **Weight:** The cable hung between the pylons weighs 2,300 tons. The steel suspended between them weighs approximately 145,000 tons.

✻ **Mass of concrete used:** 320,000 m^3 of concrete were poured for the complete construction.

The pylons of the Oresund Bridge are made of a specially mixed, super-strong concrete. Standing 203.5 m tall, they are the tallest structures in Sweden.

The Oresund High Bridge itself is one part of a multi-section span that extends more than 7.8 km. On the Danish side, the bridge is approached from Peberholm via a 3,014-metre ramp consisting of 22 weight-bearing modular segments. On the Swedish side, the ramp is 3,739 metres long and is composed of 28 segments. Both of the access ramp sections start out approximately 8 metres above the water's surface and gradually rise to the 65-metre height of the High Bridge.

The High Bridge section is the "real" Oresund Bridge that crosses the main body of water, the Flint Channel. It is 1,624 metres long, with a central cable-stayed span measuring 490 metres. Its superstructure is suspended from two cables, each 85 cm thick, strung between two gigantic pylons made of super-strong concrete. Standing 203.5 metres high, the pylons are the tallest structures in Sweden. In section, they measure 9.4 x 12.6 metres at their base and 2.6 x 5.8 metres at the top. The road and rail beds of the two-storeyed bridge are 23.5 metres wide. Four lanes of automobile traffic cross on the upper storey, with two train tracks on the lower deck.

During the Middle Ages, bridges were understood as the embodiment of the dangerous path we must travel to reach salvation, and thus chapels and holy images were erected along a bridge to ensure safe passage. In those days, donations and foundations paid for these works, but in the present, it is the traveller who pays the toll: a one-way trip across the Oresund Bridge costs around £22.00. The price is one of the reasons that this wonder of engineering has seen less traffic than the Oresund Consortium anticipated, leading to revised projections of when toll income will pay off the building costs. The current estimated date is 2035, more than three decades after the bridge's completion.

Above: The Oresund Bridge was officially opened to traffic on 1 July 2000 in the presence of the royal families of both Denmark and Sweden.

Left: The 7,845-metre-long Oresund Bridge connects the cities of Copenhagen and Malmö.

ITALY

St. Peter's Basilica

NOW THE SECOND-LARGEST CHRISTIAN CHURCH IN THE WORLD, ST. PETER'S BASILICA IS THE CENTRE OF THE ROMAN CATHOLIC RELIGION, ITS MOST IMPORTANT SANCTUARY AND THE MOST FREQUENTLY VISITED PILGRIMAGE DESTINATION IN ALL OF EUROPE.

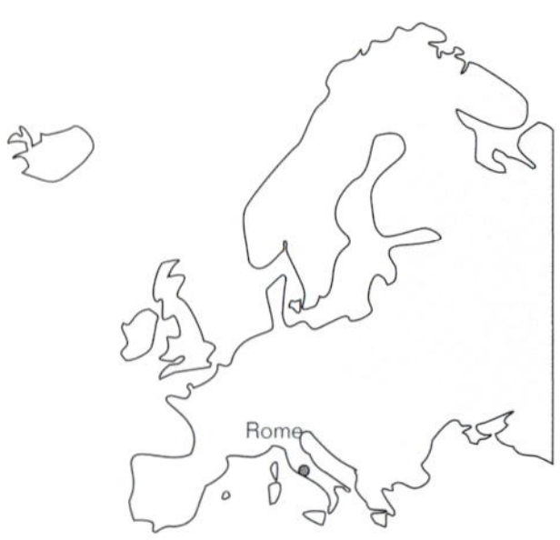

To reduce the meaning of St. Peter's to a mere description of its architectural brilliance does justice neither to its importance within the Eternal City or to its pivotal role in the development of Western art, architecture and culture. St. Peter's is much more than an art-historically significant building. Within the walls of Roman Catholicism's central sanctuary all manner of artistic, historical and spiritual influences are united. The first St. Peter's Cathedral began with an edict by Emperor Constantine the Great in the year 324, when he declared Vatican Hill to be the location of the grave of the apostle Simon Peter. In recognition of the hill's holiness, he commissioned a five-aisled basilica, a modest predecessor of the monumental church that stands there today.

During the fifteenth century, plans were made to expand the Constantinian basilica. It soon became clear that the structure of the original building was so unstable that it could not be salvaged. Instead, Pope Julius II commissioned a new, monumental building to replace it. The cornerstone for the new St Peter's Church was laid on 18 April 1506. The construction was financed by the rich and lucrative sale of indulgences and by tithes collected from lay members of the church, called "Peter's Pence".

Right: The interior of the enormous dome of St. Peter's

Below: Michelangelo's *Pietà*, a masterpiece of Renaissance sculpture, is in a side chapel just inside the entrance.

Bramante was the first "Renaissance man" to take on the task of designing this new, and newly monumental, house of God. After his death in 1514, the artist Raphael (d. 1520) took over management of the building project, followed by da Sangallo and Peruzzi. Until 1546, progress was slow, with a succession of highly ambitious project managers causing all manner of delays. Each tried to put their personal stamp on the design, causing frequent alterations to the plan, with each set of changes bringing work at the site to a halt.

In 1547, Pope Paul III entrusted the now 72-year old Michelangelo with the task and ordered the ill-tempered master to finish the building. Michelangelo bowed before the firm will of the pope and set to work. The artist worked on St. Peter's until his death in 1564. Michelangelo accepted no salary for the job, but instead received a promise from the pope that he would have a free hand in the new basilica's design and execution. Pope Paul III did not hold his end of the bargain. He was quite used to interfering in the work of his artists and would continue to do so with St. Peter's. This led to terrible arguments and disagreements between the two.

St. Peter's Basilica was finally completed on 18 November 1623, when Pope Urban VII formally consecrated the church. The great basilica had been under construction for nearly 120 years – through the reigns of no fewer than 20 popes, from Julius II through Urban VII – each one involved to a greater or lesser extent in the creation of this magnificent house of God. The list of building masters, architects and artists who contributed to the ultimate success of the project reads like a "Who's Who" of architectural history: Bramante, Raphael, Bernini and, of course, Michelangelo all worked on St. Peter's.

Together, they created a masterpiece. The architectural details, along with the artistic furnishings of the church's interior, are world famous. The fantastic dome, emblematic of the building as a whole and visible from a great distance, rises high above the rest of the structure. The dome is the largest freestanding brick dome in the world, with a diameter of 42.34 metres and a height of 43.2 metres. The dome's relationship to the rest of the building emphasizes the enormous scale of St. Peter's. Its lantern, including a cross that was added later, is more than 137 metres above the floor of the church! The dome sits on four massive, five-cornered pillars, each with a diameter of 24 metres.

In addition to the main dome, and eight smaller ones, the interior of St. Peter's contains 800 columns

DATES

✻ 324: The original St. Peter's, a five-aisled basilica, was built on Vatican Hill by order of Emperor Constantine the Great.

✻ 18 April 1506: The cornerstone was laid for the new St. Peter's.

✻ 1514: The church's first building master, the architect Bramante, died.

✻ 1515–46: Raphael, da Sangallo and Peruzzi served as building masters.

✻ 1547–64: Michelangelo was in charge of the design and construction of St. Peter's.

✻ 18 November 1623: Pope Urban VII consecrated the new St. Peter's, which had been under construction for almost 120 years.

The view from the lantern of St. Peter's dome over St. Peter's Square and the Eternal City of Rome.

and 390 colossal statues made of travertine, marble, plaster and bronze. It has 45 separate altars. Visitors enter the basilica through a massive bronze door. Nearby is the "holy door", which is opened only when the pope declares a Jubilee, or holy year.

An inscribed porphyry slab set into the floor of the nave marks the spot where the high altar of the old St. Peter's basilica once stood. Charlemagne knelt here to be crowned Holy Roman Emperor by Pope Leo III in the year 800.

The papal altar is located beneath the great dome, as is Bernini's famous bronze baldachin (or canopy), erected between 1624 and 1633. It stands over the site of the Confessio, the Chapel of the Confession, which houses a statue of Pope Pius VI. The Confessio marks the site that is traditionally identified with the actual site of St Peter's grave. Each of the four niches of the great dome's pillars contains a 3-metre-tall marble statue of a saint: Saints Veronica, Helen, Longinus and Andrew. The sculptural programme directly refers to the valuable relics now or previously held in the basilica. These include Veronica's cloth, a piece of the true cross discovered by Helen, Longinus Holy Lance and the apostle St Andrew's skull (returned to its original finding spot in Greece in 1964). The statues are the work of four different sculptors: Longinus is by Bernini; Andrew by François Duquesnoy; Veronica by the studio of Francesco Mochi; and Helen by Andrea Bolgi.

The dome of St. Peter's can be reached by climbing 537 steps to the lantern, or there is a lift. The frieze running around the base of the dome includes a Latin inscription citing the Gospel of Matthew. Translated, it reads: "You shall be Peter, the rock, and upon this rock I will build my church. To you I give the key to heaven."

Walking through St. Peter's, one encounters magnificent works of art everywhere. One of the most impressive is surely Michelangelo's sublime *Pietà*. It is located in a small chapel off the aisle to the right. The statue is 1.75 metres tall and rests on a base 1.68 metres wide. Michelangelo completed it in 1500, when he was just 25 years old. He signed the Virgin's sash in Latin: "Michael Angelus Buonarrotus Florentinus Faciebat", which means "Michelangelo Buonarroti, the Florentine, made this". It is the only sculpture he ever signed. Unfortunately, today one can only view the *Pietà* through a thick pane of

FACTS

* **Status:** In Rome, St. Peter's is known as San Pietro in Vaticano. It is the papal palace church and therefore not properly referred to as a cathedral.
* **Measurements:** The basilica is 211 m long, 132 m wide and, measured from floor to the top of the dome, 138 m tall.
* **Size of the dome:** The diameter of the dome is exactly 42.34 m. Its height from the base of the drum to the lantern is around 43 m.

A statue of the apostle Simon Peter from the basilica that bears his name

bullet-proof glass. In 1972, a mentally disturbed person smashed the statue with a hammer, doing great damage to it. When the carefully restored *Pietà* was returned to St. Peter's, it was decided that it needed to be protected against any future attacks.

The apse of St. Peter's houses the so-called Cathedra Petri, a bronze altarpiece created by Bernini in 1666. Its purpose is to cover a wooden chair concealed inside. This is purportedly the original Throne of Peter, the seat from which the apostle, as the first pope, directed the early church. Based on stylistic comparisons with Byzantine pieces, it is more likely that this is the chair in which Charlemagne sat to be crowned Holy Roman Emperor by the pope.

Another masterpiece of Bernini's in St. Peter's is the tomb of Pope Alexander VII. A life-size, gilded bronze skeleton emerges from underneath the folds of a red marble shroud, holding an empty hourglass aloft in the direction of the pope. High above, a marble statue of the pope prays, unmoved by the inexorable passage of time.

The baptismal font of St. Peter's is a porphyry sarcophagus lid originally from the mausoleum of Emperor Hadrian. Emperor Otto II was originally entombed on this spot, but his remains were later moved to a simple stone coffin in the Vatican crypt when this part of Old St. Peter's was levelled in 1600 as part of the construction of the new basilica.

The Gregorian Chapel in St. Peter's is named after Pope Gregory XIII (d. 1585), a great lover of mosaics. The interior of his burial chapel is covered with them. While pope, he had all the monumental paintings in the basilica replaced with mosaics. The original paintings can still be seen in the Vatican Museum, where many more art treasures can be viewed, though in less lofty surroundings than the Basilica of St. Peter's, the greatest masterpiece of all.

Above: The stupendous dome of St. Peter's.

Left: The main façade of St. Peter's on St. Peter's Square.

FRANCE

Pont du Gard

THE PONT DU GARD NEAR THE FRENCH CITY OF NIMES IS THE LARGEST AND BEST PRESERVED OF ALL THE ANCIENT AQUEDUCTS. NOW NEARLY 2,000 YEARS OLD, THE AQUEDUCT IS THE MOST IMPRESSIVE REMNANT OF ROMAN CIVILIZATION IN FRANCE.

The Pont du Gard strides across the Gardon tributary near the site of the Ancient Roman city of Nemausus, today the French city of Nîmes. The Romans built the Pont du Gard in the first century CE to supply the city with water, drawing it from the same natural spring that produces the world-famous Perrier brand sold today. The aqueduct bridge is but a small section of the 50-km-long water system that brought water from its source near the village of Uzes to Nîmes, all without a single pump. Roman engineers, using the simplest of measurement and surveying devices, correctly calculated the steady decrease in elevation necessary for the aqueduct to function with the force of gravity as its sole energy source. This was a masterful achievement, especially considering that the spring is located at an elevation just 17 metres higher than Nîmes, requiring that the water flow down with a gradient of 1:3000, around 25 cm per kilometre. The aqueduct supplied the city with water for over 300 years.

The Pont du Gard is an architectural masterpiece. The individual blocks, weighing up to 6 tons, were set in place seamlessly without the use of mortar, a technique that is known as "Opus quadratum". The Romans further improved the structure by altering

A tributary of the Gardon River is spanned by 52 arches organized into three levels of arcades supported by 35 pillars. The upper level encloses the stone-lined water channel.

DATES

✻ 1st century CE: The Pont du Gard was built as an aqueduct.

✻ 5th century: The water channel began to silt up due to lack of maintenance, leading to its decay.

✻ 19th century: Napoleon III restored the Pont du Gard.

✻ 1985: The Pont du Gard was placed on the UNESCO list of World Cultural Heritage Sites.

FACTS

✻ Function: The Pont du Gard is both an aqueduct and a footbridge. Its primary building material is local limestone.

✻ Size: It is 49 m high and 275 m long at its greatest extent.

✻ Width of the arches: Its widest arch has a diameter of 24.4 m.

✻ Slope: The 1.2-m-wide water channel slopes about 19 cm per km.

the standard pattern of ashlar masonry. Instead of alternating headers and footers within individual rows, they alternated rows consisting entirely of either headers or footers. This greatly increased the binding strength of the structure because it used friction to hold the blocks in place.

The pillars of the lower and middle storeys rest exactly on top of each other so as to ease the weight borne by the arcade arches. The width of the arches decreases from the middle of the bridge to the banks in either direction, a modification that decreases the total weight borne by each arch. The giant keystones of the arches weigh up to 6 tons each, each one carefully finished and precisely set. Probably some 1,000 workers laboured for three years to build the Pont du Gard, using only simple tools to shape the blocks and raise them into place. Block and tackle cranes powered by workers running on a treadmill did most of the heavy lifting.

The three levels of the Pont du Gard stand 49 metres high, with 52 arches. The lowest level of the aqueduct bridge is 142 metres long, 22 metres tall and 6 metres wide, with six arches. The middle level is 242 metres long, 20 metres tall and only 4 metres wide, with 11 arches. The top level contains the actual water channel. It is 275 metres long, 7 metres tall and 3 metres wide, with 35 small arches supporting the stone-lined passage through which water flowed. Accessible until recently, the channel is 1.8 metres high and 1.2 metres wide. The channel slopes about 19 cm per kilometre. In Roman times, 20,000 cubic metres of water flowed through it daily.

After the fourth century the aqueduct was only intermittently maintained, so that by the ninth century it was blocked by silt and went out of use as a water conveyance. It continued to be used as a footbridge into the eighteenth century. In order to widen the path across the Pont du Gard, several of the middle level pillars were shaved down, but this threatened the stability of the entire structure and they had to be completely restored in 1702. A new footbridge was built alongside it in 1747 as a replacement.

Today, the Pont du Gard is the most visited tourist destination in southern France. It can still be crossed on foot using the eighteenth-century addition. Recent development sponsored by UNESCO and the EU re-routed automobile traffic to create a large pedestrian area around this Roman wonder.

Centre: The limestone blocks weighed as much as 6 tons each.

Bottom: Visitors can get very close to the Pont du Gard by means of the footbridge, built in 1747.

SPAIN

La Sagrada Familia

THE CHURCH OF LA SAGRADA FAMILIA IS THE MOST FAMOUS BUILDING IN BARCELONA. AND YET IT IS STILL INCOMPLETE, DESPITE BEING UNDER CONSTRUCTION SINCE 1882. CURRENT PROJECTIONS ESTIMATE ITS COMPLETION SOMETIME IN THE YEAR 2026.

The towers of La Sagrada Familia are visible from far away, rising well above the sea of houses that constitute the Spanish city of Barcelona. Construction of the church, the full name of which is Temple Expiatori de la Sagrada Familia (Expiatory Temple of the Holy Family), began in 1882. It originally followed a plan in the historical neo-Catalonian style by the French architect Francesc del Villar. Envisioned as a "church for the poor", it was intended to be completed by 1910. However, after just one year, the architect quarrelled with the contractors and left the project.

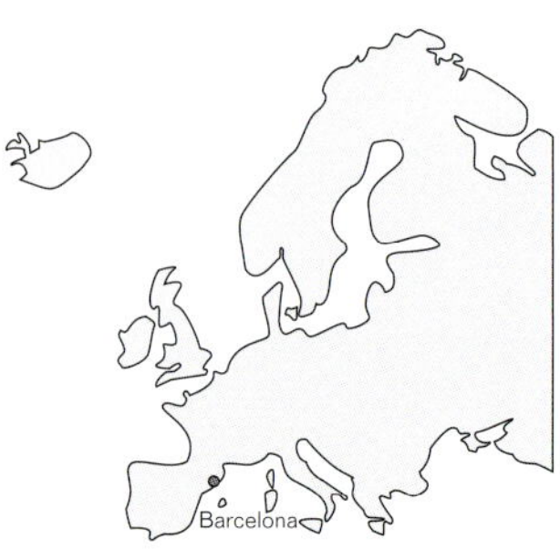

In 1883, the church's patrons decided to hand over the reigns of the project to the local Catalan architect, Antoni Gaudí. Gaudí discarded the plans of his predecessor, starting from scratch with an entirely new concept for the building. Instead of a church in a historical style, he would design a church using the elements of the then current Jugendstil (related to Art Nouveau), modernism and naturalistic forms,
all imbued with Gaudí's own unique personal spirituality and vision.

Construction still moved along slowly, in part because of financial constraints, but also in part due to the nature of Gaudí's creative process. His artistic

FACTS

✻ Location: La Sagrada Familia is in Barcelona, Spain. When construction began in 1882, the building site lay more than a mile from the city.

✻ Completion: Current estimates project the church's completion in 2026.

✻ Towers: There are 13 towers, 12 of them 115 m in height. One tower will eventually rise to 170 m.

✻ Visitors per year: La Sagrada Familia welcomes 2 million visitors a year.

✻ Financing: Construction is financed by donations and private sponsorship.

✻ Architect: The most important works of architect Antoni Placid Gaudí y Cornet (1852–1926) include La Sagrada Familia (1883–1926); Palau Güell (1886–90); the Bishop's Palace in Astorga (1887–94); Park Güell (1900–14); Casa Batilo (1904–06) and Casa Milà (1906–10).

The church has 12 towers stretching 115 m into the air. The tower over the main dome will eventually be 170 m tall.

exuberance led to a great many diversions, and work progressed in stops and starts as he continually re-imagined his masterpiece. Not infrequently, the gifted architect would disassemble entire sections of the building that had already been built in order to alter them to better harmonize with his changing conception. He would frequently work and rework parts of the building until they were perfect and fit his imaginative vision in every way.

As the construction process unfolded, the details and individual elements became more and more fantastic. The core structure sprouted spindle-topped towers and extensive sculptural ornamentation. The gables and ridges of its roof were crowned with elements related to the Cubist movement in art, while other details of the decoration were clearly derived from Art Nouveau. When asked when he thought his masterpiece might be finished, Gaudí replied, "my client isn't in a hurry".

On 10 June 1926, the 74-year old architect was run over by a tram, and he died two days later. He had devoted 40 years of his life to work on La Sagrada Familia, and for the last 15 years had worked on nothing else. Construction slowed to a crawl. Then, Gaudí's original plans were destroyed during the turmoil of the Spanish Civil War. After World War II, the architects Fransesco Quintana, Isidre Puig-Boada and Lluis Gari took over the project. Since that time, work on La Sagrada Familia has never ceased. The main tower over the central dome, when completed, will soar 170 metres into the sky. The 12 smaller towers, which symbolize the 12 apostles, reach as high as 115 metres and are for the most part complete. When the building is (finally) finished, La Sagrada Familia will be the largest and tallest, sacred building in the world. It is already one of the most unusual and beloved religious

Above: These fantastic tower tops illustrate Gaudí's love of detail. All the towers and, indeed, very nearly all the surfaces of the church, are covered with detailed ornamentation.

Left: The view from the towers over the city of Barcelona.

ITALY

Leaning Tower of Pisa

WHEN ITS PATRONS COMMISSIONED THE CAMPANILE FOR THE PISA CATHEDRAL, THEIR INTENT WAS TO CREATE AN ETERNAL SYMBOL OF THEIR POWER. INSTEAD, THE "LEANING" TOWER EMPHASIZES THE TRANSITORY NATURE OF POWER AND ARCHITECTURE.

In 1173, the artist Bonanno Pisano was given the task of building a bell tower for the cathedral in the city of Pisa in Tuscany. He designed a free-standing campanile resembling a column. It soon became clear that the foundations he had laid were too weak for the unstable sub-soil below. The tower was already starting to lean with the construction of the third storey, which visibly tilted 5 cm to the south-east. Worried about his reputation, Pisano halted work on the structure.

Construction of the tower would not begin again for almost a hundred years. In 1272, the well-known architect Giovanni di Simone took on the risky project. He tried to compensate for the lean by building the next four storeys perfectly straight. This looked a bit strange, leaving an odd angle in the profile. The end result was even more catastrophic. The tower began to lean even more than before as the added weight caused the foundations to sink even further into the soft earth. By 1298 the tower was 1.43 metres off the vertical, and in 1360 the tilt had increased to 1.63 metres. Nevertheless, in 1372 Tommaso Pisano decided to complete the building by adding the bell chamber, setting it vertically on top of the leaning tower. The (leaning) bell tower was finally complete after 200 years of intermittent construction.

Right: There are no landings along the spiralling path up the tower.

Below: The Leaning Tower is emblematic of Pisa as well as being its greatest tourist attraction.

Over the following centuries, the rate of increase of the tilt slowed. It has been suggested that the weight of the tower, estimated at 14,500 tons, has somehow compressed the subsoil, increasing its stability. In 1838, the architect Alessandro Gherardesca made an attempt at restoration. Digging a trench around the foundations, he removed the soft, muddy earth beneath the tower and replaced it with a marble basin to catch ground water. The results were disastrous. The foundation base flooded repeatedly and the tilt quickly became more extreme. By 1918 it measured 5.1 metres off the vertical! Until 1990, the campanile continued to gain 1–1.2 mm of lean per year. There was no question that the Leaning Tower of Pisa was in danger of collapsing. For safety reasons, this emblem of the city of Pisa was closed to the public in 1990.

The Italian government, however, led a concerted effort to save the tower. In 1994, as a counterbalance, 690 tons of lead bars were attached to the north side of the tower and then anchored 40 metres deep in the earth. It worked, at least insofar as it stopped the tower from tilting any further. Additional stabilization measures, however, such as injecting concrete into the foundation, have had no effect whatsoever. In 1998, to keep the tower from collapsing, the north side was tied down with two steel cables, each 100 metres long and weighing 4 tons.

Architects and art historians are not yet ready to give up on the world-famous Leaning Tower of Pisa. From February 1999 through June 2001, new technology has been brought to bear on the problem. Vacuum tubes eased under the north wall of the "Torre Pendente" gently removed some 30 tons of earth, enough to permit the tower to be straightened by about 50 cm. This new method does seem to be working: the Leaning Tower is straightening itself out. Its current angle is relatively moderate compared to its more recent extremes, and its tilt is close to where it was 250 years ago. Although the campanile will never stand completely straight, its once desperate situation has been remedied and the structure can finally be described, for the first time, as stable. The patient is no longer at death's door and is expected to survive without further damage for the next 200 or 300 years.

As a sign of these recent successes, since June 2001 the Leaning Tower of Pisa has once again been opened to visitors. The 55-metre-tall tower can now be safely climbed, and finally, for the first time in many years, the seven bells in the bell chamber of Italy's most famous campanile are allowed to chime.

FACTS

* **Name and function:** In Italian, the tower is known as the Torre Pendente di Pisa. It is a campanile (bell tower).
* **Building time:** The Leaning Tower of Pisa was intermittently under construction from 1173 to 1372, over a period of 199 years.
* **Size:** It is 56 m tall and has a diameter of 7.4 m at the base.
* **Storeys:** The tower has seven storeys, plus a bell chamber with seven bells.

GREAT BRITAIN

Stonehenge

LOCATED IN THE MIDDLE OF THE SALISBURY PLAIN IN SOUTHERN ENGLAND, STONEHENGE IS ONE OF THE MOST FAMOUS SACRED SITES IN THE WORLD. A GREAT MANY MYTHS AND LEGENDS SURROUND THE MEGALITHIC STONE CIRCLES AND BARROW GRAVES.

Few structures have guarded their secrets as long as this stone circle in Salisbury Plain. Stonehenge still poses many puzzles to archaeologists, historians and New Age enthusiasts. What is certain is that the site of what was later Stonehenge was already a cult site and burial place during the Mesolithic period (*circa* 8500 BCE) and that its name comes from the Old English *stanhen gist*, or "hanging stones".

Stonehenge was built during three distinct periods of construction in the course of some 2,000 years. This burial site and cult complex is built of megaliths, similar to other massive stone complexes found throughout Europe. At Stonehenge the megaliths are incorporated into post and lintel trilithons, giving this particular stone circle its unique character.

In the first phase, around 3100 BCE, a circular bank and ditch structure were created. The material used during the first phase is earth that was dug from the ground and heaped up to form a banked wall.

The second phase began sometime after 2500 BCE. In this phase, the first megaliths were put in place and the north-eastern entrance was moved slightly so as to be oriented towards the rising sun. The high level of precision involved is still astonishing.

The third phase took place around 2000 BCE. Additional megaliths were set up, weighing up to

FACTS

✽ **Place of worship:** The area around Stonehenge has been the site of religious activity since at least 8000 BCE.

✽ **Building phases:** The first building phase dates to around 3100 BCE, the second to 2500 BCE AND the third to *circa* 2000 BCE.

✽ **Building time:** The complex as a whole was built over the course of some 2,000 years.

The mighty megaliths still pose puzzles to researchers today. The joins of the trilithon show Bronze Age influences.

several tons, including what is called the "Sarsen Circle". This consists of 30 blocks of sandstone, each 4.25 metres high and weighing around 25 tons, laid out in a circle with a diameter of 30 metres. Lintel stones of 7 tons each were smoothed to fit perfectly into the arc of the circle. They were joined to the pillars by mortise and tenon, or tongue-and-groove, technique. That joints like these were used is a sign of Bronze Age influence and technology. In the centre of the circle, the five trilithons were arranged in a horseshoe formation.

Every stone, pillar and lintel was positioned with reference to the position of the sun both at equinox and during the solstice. Nevertheless, it is not certain that Stonehenge ever functioned as an astronomical observatory; it was more likely a religious centre. A greenstone altar lies at the centre of the circle. The other stones found inside are "bluestones", a type of basalt found in the Preseli Hills in Wales, 380 km away. To transport these gigantic stones over such a distance would have been an unbelievable achievement at the time. According to archaeologist Aubrey Burl, this never happened; rather the Stonehenge bluestones are local, isolated remnants left behind by glacial activity. Legend has it, though, that the magician Merlin ascribed the bluestones special powers.

The myth of Stonehenge lives on, and the site has lost none of its attraction. Every year, countless tourists visit Salisbury Plain. In 1986, UNESCO placed Stonehenge on the World Cultural Heritage list. No one is allowed to enter the stone circle, although twice a year, during the spring equinox and summer solstice, members of the Society of British Druids may continue to practise Celtic rituals. Precise radiocarbon dating shows that the latest use of Stonehenge predates any Celtic presence by far. The first verifiable Druid ceremonies occurred here in 1905 CE.

Above: Members of the Society of British Druids celebrate the summer solstice at Stonehenge.

Left: The cult site of Stonehenge remains mysterious and harbours untold secrets.

ICELAND

Þingvellir National Park

ÞINGVELLIR ("ASSEMBLY FIELD") IS THE NAME OF TWO PLACES IN SOUTHERN ICELAND. ONE OF THESE IS THE HISTORICAL SITE WHERE MEDIEVAL ICELANDERS ASSEMBLED TO GOVERN THEMSELVES AND RESOLVE DISPUTES, AND THE OTHER IS A NATIONAL PARK.

In the year 930, Viking settlers from Norway held their first legislative assembly, the Alþing, in Iceland. This makes the Alþing the oldest recorded parliamentary assembly in the world. It was also one of the most enduring. The Alþing continued to meet regularly until 1798, when the Danes, who had taken political control of Iceland, finally dissolved it. In 1928, the area around the historical site of the Alþing was turned into a national park. It was here, at this important place, that the Republic of Iceland was declared in 1944.

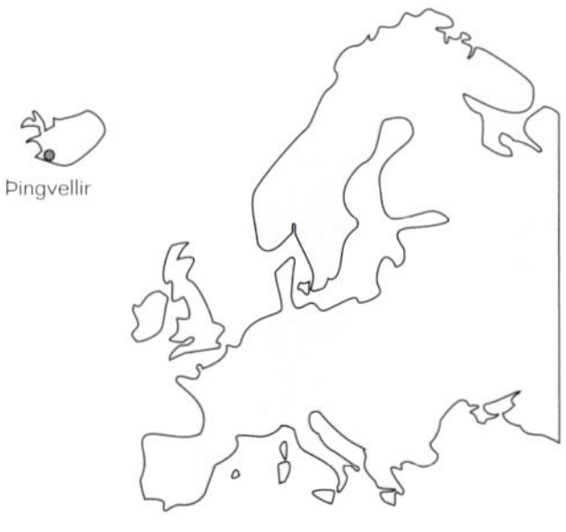

Established in 1928, Þingvellir National Park is located in south-west Iceland, some 40 km north-east of the capital, Reykjavik. It sits directly on top of a remarkable series of fault lines marking the place where the American and European continental plates meet. Every year, these two gigantic plates drift 2 cm further apart, causing a build-up of enormous tectonic pressure, which makes itself known in the form of earthquakes and volcanic eruptions when it is released. There are a total of four active volcanoes in the Þingvellir area, among these the famous Hengill, located on the northern coast of Þingvallavatn Lake. The lake is the largest in Iceland with an area of 83 km^2. It is also extraordinarily deep, plunging to around 114 metres at its deepest point.

Right: The "great crevasse" is the valley running through the Þingvellir where two continental plates meet.

Below: The Oxara River flows through the Þingvellir National Park.

Over the course of the last 9,000 years, a mere blip in the geological history of the Earth, the Þingvellir Valley has sunk between 60 and 90 metres. Visitors wandering through this unique landscape can witness the powerful effects of the forces of nature at work.

The drifting apart of the American and European tectonic plates has produced a landscape marked by deep fissures, gorges and cracks in the rocky surface. The prime example of a fissure of this kind is called the Alamnnagja ("Everyman Gorge"), which plunges deep into the volcanic subsurface. The Oxara River flows through the Alamannagja, terminating in an impressive waterfall called the Oxarafoss. The river is permanently shrouded in a haze of steam, a result of cold water coming into contact with rock warmed by subterranean volcanic activity.

The most beautiful waterfall in Iceland is only a stone's throw away from Þingvellir and the Oxarafoss. The Gullfoss ("Golden Waterfall") is a two-level waterfall that tumbles into the depths at the terminus of the Hvita River. It falls 32 metres over a relatively short distance, causing 30 cubic metres of water per second to cascade through the torrent in the winter, and up to 30 cubic metres per second in summer. This is by far the largest volume of any waterfall in Europe. At its base, the masses of water are literally sucked into a gorge. From certain angles, the river seems to simply vanish into the earth. This unique topography has made the Gullfoss the most famous of Iceland's many spectacular water features.

There are a number of reasons for Iceland's preponderance of magnificent waterfalls and geyser landscapes. Where the Gullfoss is concerned, a south-west/north-east crevice in the basalt bedrock runs in the same direction as the upper part of the cascading waterfall. The lower part of the Gullfoss is more affected by a fault line running in a north-west/south-east direction. When the water hits the first crevice, it is full of debris and gravel, giving the flow terrific erosive power, enough to cut a deep gorge in the Hvita river bed. Fossils found further down the river include a number of marine species, proving that the sea once penetrated far inland.

The Þingvellir National Park, the Gullfoss Waterfall and the nearby geyser landscape of Haukadalur, the most famous hot water springs in Iceland, form what is called the Golden Circle. The Golden Circle is one of the most visited natural sites in northern Europe. The national park and related features were added to the UNESCO World Natural Heritage list in 2004.

FACTS

* **Iceland,** with a total area of over 40,000 inhabited square miles, supports a human population of just over 300,000.

* **Unique:** The Icelandic alphabet has 32 characters, the majority of which correspond to those in the Latin alphabet. One of the extra letters is the Þ/þ, which comes from the Runic alphabet. It is pronounced like a hard "th", as in the word "thing", but with the tip of the tongue rolled under behind the teeth.

ITALY

Venice

AT DAWN, VENICE, THE FAMOUS CANAL CITY, RISES OUT OF THE MIST LIKE A MAGICAL CASTLE ON WATER. THE CITY ITSELF IS A WORK OF ART, A NEARLY INDECIPHERABLE MAZE OF NARROW STREETS, CANALS, BRIDGES, LANDINGS AND ISLANDS.

What we know as Venice developed out of a scatter of small settlements across the islands of a shallow lagoon. Venice sits in the middle of this lagoon, built on a series of islands and islets connected to each other and to the north Adriatic coast by causeways, canals and shallow bays. The lagoon and its islands developed during prehistoric times when alluvium began to accumulate near the mouth of the Po and Piave Rivers. To preserve the lagoon as a defensive feature, security-conscious Venetians diverted the rivers in the early fifteenth century. This stopped the flow of silt that would eventually have made Venice part of the mainland.

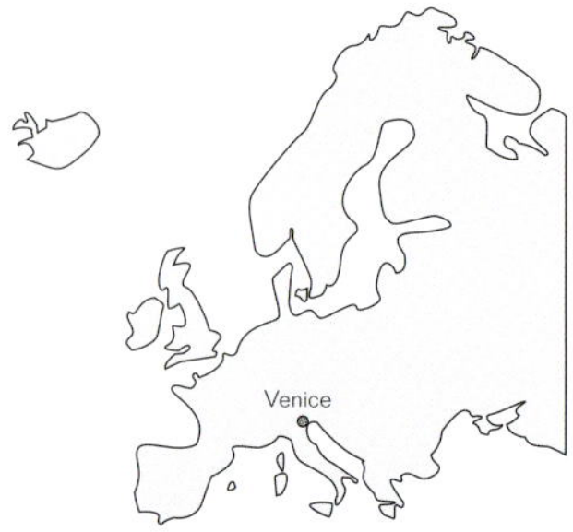

The Venetian Lagoon encompasses an area of some 550 km², of which only 8 per cent is solid land and 11 per cent is permanently submerged. The greatest part of the lagoon, around 80 per cent, consists of bog and marshland. In Venice, the landscape is defined by the transition between land and sea.

The northern part of the 50-km-long and up to 15-km-wide lagoon consists of stagnant fresh water known as *laguna morte* (dead lagoon). The southern half is predominantly salt water, subject to the tidal rhythm of the ebb and flow of the sea. The saltwater half is called *laguna viva* (living lagoon).

Life on water isn't all romance. The historic heart of the city is threatened by serious flooding several times a year, as shown here by the all too common site of a flooded St. Mark's Square.

DATES

* **421:** Likely date of the founding of the city by Roman refugees fleeing the Goths.
* **828/829:** The relics of St Mark the Evangelist were brought from Alexandria to Venice. To house them, the Basilica San Marco was built between 830 and 1094.
* **1309–1442:** The Doges Palace, Venice's most important secular building, was built.
* **1453:** Venice was the largest and most powerful Italian city-state, controlling most of the trade with the eastern Mediterranean and Near East.
* **12 May 1797:** Napoleon conquered Venice and the last doge, Lodovico Manin, stepped down.
* **1902:** St Mark's campanile collapsed. It was rebuilt in 1903–12.
* **1987:** Venice was placed on the UNESCO World Cultural Heritage list.

The historic centre of the famous canal city lies in the very heart of the lagoon. Today, Venice has a population of around 300,000, of which only 65,000 or so live within the lagoon area. This historic core is, in its own unique way, a work of art.

Over 3,000 narrow streets and alleys snake through the rows of houses, palaces, churches and secular buildings, all built up tightly against one another, interrupted here and there by large or small piazzas and squares. The most famous of these is Piazza San Marco (St Mark's Square), in front of the famous St Mark's Basilica. Around 180 canals and navigable waterways criss-cross through the city, which boasts over 400 bridges and landings. Venice's "Main Street" is the 3.8-km-long Grand Canal, the busiest waterway in the city. With all the other canals leading either away from it or to it, the Grand Canal pulses with the very life of the city. Vaporetti, Venice's water buses, carry commuters, locals and tourists to very nearly every corner of the city. Police boats make their rounds, on the lookout for boats breaking the strict traffic controls in place to ensure the safety of the narrow, heavily travelled waterways. Accidents are an everyday occurrence. The concert of horns and shouts between the drivers differs little from what one hears on the busy mainland roads. Medic boats take on the role of terrestrial ambulances, barrelling through the narrow canals with their sirens blaring. Even the fire brigade uses boats, equipped with extinguishers, hoses and ladders, just like fire engines on land. Darting in between it all are countless fishing boats, garbage scows, water taxis and traghetti, which are small personal vessels carrying passengers from one canal bank to another. There are also private motorboats, rowboats and pedal boats, as well as the famous gondola, of course, not to be forgotten, without which it is difficult to picture Venice at all.

The canals are the very arteries of the lagoon city and the city could not survive without its system of well-maintained waterways. It goes without saying that Venice is a singular city in a many ways. The Venetian comic poet Carlo Goldoni (1707–1793) recognized this when he said: "Venice is such an unusual city that it is impossible to form an image of it correctly without having seen it. Maps, plans, models and travel narratives are not enough. One simply has to see it."

Centre: Over 400 bridges span the canals of the lagoon city.

Below: The Grand Canal is the Main Street of Venice.

FRANCE

Versailles Palace

THE FIRST PALACE IN VERSAILLES WAS A SMALL HUNTING LODGE BUILT BY KING LOUIS XIII; LOUIS XIV DESIGNED THE PALACE FAMOUS FOR ITS POMPOSITY. MAGNIFICENTLY LANDSCAPED PARKS SURROUND THE BAROQUE ROYAL RESIDENCE AND SEAT OF GOVERNMENT.

Versailles! What a stage it was for courtly ceremonies, the theatre-like productions directed by the royal family, with king, queen and nobles as star players. Versailles was the cradle of absolutism, symbolic of the decadence of court life and indicative of everything the French Revolution set out to destroy. Every room, hall and gallery of the palace has stories to tell about life among the high nobility in prerevolutionary France. **King Louis XIV (1638–1715)** was, like no other ruler, a master of stage-managing his own image. Favouring grand entrances and dramatic gestures, life for the Sun King was a theatrical production with himself playing the lead role. When the narrow spaces of the walled, densely packed city of Paris proved too small for his performances, he built Versailles Palace, his own stage, one large and elaborate enough to accommodate his ambitions. In 1688, he had his father's hunting lodge transformed and expanded into an imposing royal residence surrounded by fantastical parks. **The sheer size of the palace** is impressive. The park façade alone is 570 metres long. Visually, horizontal lines dominate, with only thin pilasters breaking up the dominant visual rhythm. The enormous Hall of Mirrors takes up the entire width of the first floor of the main building. It is an ornate gallery separating

FACTS

✻ Construction: Versailles Palace was built primarily during the reign of King Louis XIV, the Sun King, in the years 1668–1710.

✻ Construction costs: Construction costs are estimated to have been 5.7 million livres (1 livre = 409 grams of silver), the equivalent of about $2 billion.

DATES

✻ 5 October 1789: King Louis XVI was forced to vacate Versailles Palace by revolutionaries.

✻ Since the 19th century: Renovation and conservation of the building began in earnest and continues to this day.

✻ 18 January 1871: Prussian King Wilhelm I was crowned German emperor (Kaiser) in the Hall of Mirrors.

✻ 26 February 1871: The peace treaty ending the Franco-Prussian War was signed at Versailles.

✻ 28 June 1919: The Treaty of Versailles, setting terms for the end of World War I, was signed.

Versailles Palace's building master was the Sun King, Louis XIV himself, a point reinforced in this painting, in which he gestures towards the architectural plans.

two salons, one named for war (*de la guerre*) and the other for peace (*de la paix*). The elaborately decorated surfaces of the Hall of Mirrors include not only the eponymous and expensive mirrors, but also magnificent paintings, columns, arches and pilasters. **Every room of the palace** had a symbolic meaning, and no room – not even those within the residential quarters of the nobles or of the royal family – was private. The entire palatial city always had to be ready to stand at attention to bask in the light cast by the absolute power of the Sun King. The centre of the palace was not the throne or administrative offices; the king's bedroom received much more attention. Court ceremonies were performed there every day, bizarrely cultlike in nature. Up to 100 members of the court might be present to perform a series of precisely choreographed rituals every day when the royal couple awoke and went to sleep, the daily "lever", celebrating the rising of the king and queen in the morning, and the "coucher", when they went to bed. Each ceremony was conducted according to the strictest rules and protocols.

Versailles Park served as a complement to the palace it surrounds. It, too, was used as a stage for the frequent refined parties and festivals where the Sun King danced in the company of thousands of guests.

The park was laid out in three phases from 1662 to 1689, following the master plan of landscape architect André le Nôtre. Sublime gardens extend for miles, making it one of the largest formal parks ever created in Europe. Designed to ascend towards the palace in a series of terraces, it replicates the spirit of the palace architecture with its lawns, fountains, orangery and artificial lakes, accompanied by monumental sculpture and a wealth of decorative details. Louis XIV was so pleased with his park that he decreed that he would publish the first guidebook describing its wonders.

Above: The palace's park is a masterpiece of Baroque landscape architecture.

Left: The famous Hall of Mirrors (*Galerie des Glaces*) is one of the most remarkable and ornate spaces in the palace.

Many civilizations left their traces throughout the land between Mexico and Patagonia. The Incan, Mayan and Aztec cultures generated magnificent cultural monuments, temple complexes and unique pyramids we can still see today. These, as well as a variety of grandiose natural wonders, are the very essence of the richness of Central America and the South American continent.

CENTRAL AND SOUTH

AMERICA

AMAZONIA

The Amazon Basin

THE AMAZON BASIN IS A LOWLAND PLAIN COVERED BY RAINFOREST THAT OCCUPIES MOST OF THE NORTHERN HALF OF SOUTH AMERICA. IT EXTENDS OVER 6.5 MILLION SQUARE KILOMETRES, AN AREA EQUIVALENT TO 5 PER CENT OF THE EARTH'S SURFACE.

The Amazon Basin, the location of the world's largest forest, extends over the borders of nine countries: Brazil, French Guinea, Suriname, Venezuela, Colombia, Ecuador, Peru and Bolivia. The Basin drains the Amazon River, which meanders in all directions through the rainforest on its way from its source in the Andes to the Atlantic Ocean. It is so large that only satellite images from outer space can capture it in its entirety.

Despite the deep wounds left by illegal logging and construction, the Amazon Basin is still almost entirely covered by thick rainforest. The green carpet of lush vegetation conceals the Amazon River and its tributaries. The Amazon River is better described as a river system, of which the Rio Amazonas is but one part. The low-lying Amazon Basin, just 200 metres above sea level, is frequently flooded and rich in watercourses formed by the run-off.

Over 1,100 Amazonian tributaries, large and small, make their way beneath the forest canopy, branching out from the mountains and highlands in every direction throughout the enormous area of the Amazon Basin. Of the rivers that flow into the Amazon, 17 of them are over 1,500 km long, and about 20 per cent of the Earth's fresh water flows through the Amazon Basin as a whole. Since the

FACTS

✲ Location: Amazonia extends over the boundaries of nine countries: Brazil, French Guinea, Suriname, Guyana, Venezuela, Colombia, Ecuador, Peru and Bolivia.

✲ Area: It covers approximately 6.5 million km^2, or 5 per cent of the total surface area of the Earth.

✲ Length: Amazonia is named after its largest river, the Amazon, which is 6,275 km long, 5–12 km wide and 30–100 m deep.

The Rio Negro winds through the rainforest like a giant anaconda. Over 50,000 km of the Amazon and its tributaries are classified as navigable river.

basin is relatively flat, the currents generated by the river are not very strong. The Amazon River falls only about 5 mm per kilometre, giving it less of a slope than the water in the average bath! Most of the year, water flows into the Atlantic at a fairly placid rate of between 100,000 and 200,000 cubic metres per second, depending on the season.

Many of the largest tributaries of the Amazon are distinguished by the colour of their water. The Rio Negro is black and the Madeira is golden red like the wine that gives it its name. Others are named after indigenous tribes, such as the Rios Tapajos and Xingu, which have crystal clear water. Near Manaus in Brazil, the Rio Negro meets the yellow, sediment-rich water of the Rio Solimoes rushing down from the Andes. The two rivers, one black, the other yellow, merge in a single river bed like two chemical elements that refuse to combine. Eighty km further down the river – the yellow – water of the Solimoes triumphs.

The source of the Rio Solimoes, only discovered in 1971, is the likely source of the entire Amazon system. In its upper reaches, which extend to Peru and Ecuador and continue on into north-western Brazil, the river changes names six times, with only the middle stretch called Solimoes. The final stretch, about one-third of the total length, is called Amazon.

The Amazon is 6,275 km long, the longest river, one made up of many rivers. During the high water season, 280,000 cubic metres of water per second rush through its river bed, which is so deep that enormous transoceanic container ships and tankers can travel up to 3,700 km inland on it. This takes them through much of the northern part of the continent, as far as the Peruvian rainforest city of Iquitos, far further inland than any terrestrial highway reaches. The navigability of the river is what makes the riches of Amazonia accessible, for better or for worse.

Above: The theatre in Manuas, the Brazilian city where the Rio Negro and Rio Solimoes meet.

Left: The muddy, yellow water of the Solimoes only mingles with the black water of the Rio Negro 80 km downriver from where they first converge.

MEXICO

Chichén Itzá

MYSTERIOUS AND EVER PUZZLING, THE HISTORY OF THE MAYA AND THEIR MAGNIFICENT CIVILIZATION CONTINUES TO POSE QUESTIONS THAT REMAIN UNANSWERED. WHAT BROUGHT ABOUT THE SUDDEN COLLAPSE OF THE ANCIENT MAYAN CULTURE?

During their golden age, the Maya built temples, cities and architectural monuments of imposing size and beauty. The jewel of the Mayan civilization and centre of its highly advanced culture was the city of Chichén Itzá, on the Yucatán Peninsula in southern Mexico. It is still not clear when the Maya first came into the region, nor from where. Chichén Itzá came into being in the second half of the first millennium when a Mayan ruler ordered that a large city be built around three natural sinkholes, or *cenotes*. Springs in the sinkholes provided plentiful fresh water year-round.

Several thousand Maya took part in the construction of a city that would be inhabited solely by the rulers, priests and their families. Everyone else lived in the fields in simple straw and mud huts as farmers, supplying the city with maize, animal products and labour. The Maya were not, however, a peaceful agricultural civilization. Their rulers were locked in a constant, violent struggle with each other. With a band of warriors serving as their instrument of power, the Mayan kings were constantly planning or leading military expeditions that had everything to do with perpetuating their own wealth and fame. Using Chichén Itzá as a base, they conducted an endless series of raids on other Mayan settlements and cities.

The throne of the Maya ruler of Chichén Itzá was modelled in the form of a jaguar with inlaid jade eyes. A symbol of power, this one dates to around 1050.

DATES

✻ circa 435 – 455: According to the much later manuscript of Chumayel, Chichén Itzá was founded around 435–455. It is assumed that the city was mostly abandoned by the late 9th century. Invading Toltecs took it over in 987.

✻ 999: The Mayan ruler of Tula, named Quetzalcoatl after the god, died.

✻ 1533: The Spanish conquistadores invaded the region.

✻ 1841 – 42: The first scholarly investigation of Chichén Itzá began with the work of John Stephens.

✻ 1904 – 1907: Cave divers investigated the sinkhole, known as "holy" or "sacrificial".

✻ 1923: Systematic excavation and preservation of the ruins began.

✻ 1988: Chichén Itzá was named a World Cultural Heritage Site by UNESCO.

The Mayan rulers grew more powerful every year, which makes the sudden collapse of Mayan civilization at the end of the ninth century puzzling. Chichén Itzá seems to have been abandoned around that time. There is evidence of a catastrophe – drought, failed harvests, famines, or a combination of all three – but why the civilization declined so rapidly is unknown. A much-reduced population survived, only to be overcome by the Spanish in the sixteenth century. Spanish accounts describe the Maya as a small tribal group eeking out a living from the forest. The Spanish soon decimated the Mayan.

The power of Chichén Itzá's ruler was symbolized by his throne atop the Kukulan Pyramid. Over 30 metres tall, the pyramid towered above all other buildings. The complex iconographic references in its decorative programme and number system of its proportions demonstrate the Mayas' knowledge and advanced technical skill. As an example of Mayan "number magic", the pyramid consists of a socle step, on which stand four flights of stairs, each with 91 steps. 4 x 91 plus 1 (the socle) = 365, the number of days in a year. The Temple of the Warriors (*Templos de los Guerreros*) stands opposite the Kukulan Pyramid. Its distinguishing feature is the Hall of 1,000 Columns, where the warriors presumably lived. It backs onto a 91 x 36-metre ball court.

The Mayan ball game "pok ta pok" (team against team) held an important place in Mayan culture. Two teams competed to manoeuvre a ball a little larger than a basketball through a vertically oriented stone hoop high on a wall and decorated with images of snakes. Wearing heavy padding, the teams had to score without using their hands or feet. Games went on until one team was thoroughly beaten. Pok ta pok was a bloody game with religious significance: the captain of the losing team was beheaded on the field as a sacrifice. In Mayan culture losing one's life this way was an honour. Some accounts claim it was the captain of the winning side who would be sacrificed.

Images of snakes are everywhere in Chichén Itzá. Kukulcan, the "snake-that-climbs-out-of-the-temple," and Quetzalcoatl, the feathered serpent, were the most important Mayan gods. For the gods, there would be no collapse. The feathered serpent was still worshipped in Yucatán and by the central Mexican Aztecs when the Spanish arrived in the sixteenth century.

Centre: The ball court at Chichén Itzá is the largest surviving example in Mexico.

Bottom: The Hall of 1,000 Columns is part of the Temple of the Warriors.

ECUADOR

The Galápagos Islands

THE GALÁPAGOS ISLANDS, ALSO KNOWN AS THE ARCHIPIÉLAGO DE COLON, LIE IN THE PACIFIC OCEAN 1,600 KM WEST OF THE COAST OF ECUADOR, THE COUNTRY THE 61 LARGE AND SMALL ISLANDS BELONG TO.

Charles Darwin wrote in his journals about the Galápagos Islands: "in that little world within itself, we seem to be brought somewhat near to that great fact – that mystery of mysteries – the first appearance of new beings on this earth." In 1835, the great British naturalist had travelled to the Galápagos Islands in search of evidence to support biblical creation. What he found instead was a much better theory: the "Evolution of Species by Natural Selection". His work in the Galápagos would radically and permanently alter humankind's view of itself and its role in nature.

The Spaniard Tomas de Berlanga, bishop of Panama, discovered the Galápagos Islands by chance in 1535 after his ship was blown off course while on the way to Peru, leaving him and his companions temporarily stranded on one of the Archipiélago's volcanic islands. After they returned home safely, he told of the place he had named the Islas Encantadas.

No one had ever suspected that there might be undiscovered islands so far out in the ocean. The strong currents that plagued the area led some sailors to suspect that the islands moved around, always changing their location.

In the seventeenth century, the islands functioned primarily as pirate hideaways. Buccaneers could

Right: The namesake of the islands is the Galápagos tortoise.

Below: A view of the Galápagos Islands from outer space clearly shows their volcanic origins.

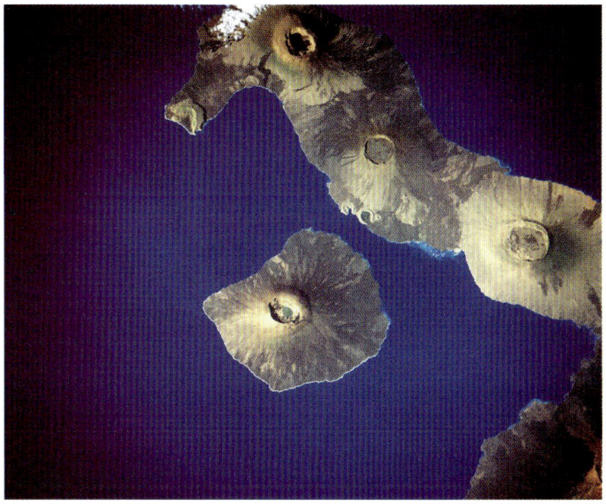

launch their attacks on the gold-laden ships of the Spanish who sailed from Mexico, then quickly retreat to the safety of the isolated islands.

In the nineteenth century, the islands were finally given a name, Galápagos, after the giant land tortoises that lived there. In 1832, General José Maria Villamil claimed the islands for Ecuador, renaming them the Archipielago del Ecuador and founding the first permanent settlement. The islands were officially renamed the Archipielago de Colon in 1892, in honour of the 400th anniversary of Christopher Columbus' discovery of the New World.

The Galápagos Islands are all of volcanic origin. The Nazca tectonic plate lies directly below them, right on top of an enormous magma chamber that to this day is the source of frequent volcanic activity. The volcano Mt Cumbre on Fernandina last erupted in 2005. The islands sit almost exactly on the equator, although the climate is closer to temperate because the sea water surrounding them is relatively cool (around 18–20 °C) due to the Humboldt Current. The nutrient-rich deep seas around the islands sustain the remarkable diversity of animal and plant species that live there. The rainy season lasts from January until June, with almost no precipitation at all at any other time during the year. In the so-called El Niño years, when the warmer, swirling El Niño current is active, its effect on the sensitive climatic regime can dramatically alter both the rainfall and the viability of the flora and fauna.

In 1835, Charles Darwin arrived in the archipelago, hoping to find evidence for the biblical paradise. What he found instead revolutionized science, challenging its norms and preconceptions. New forms of life were coming into being on the islands due to environmental pressures that were unique to each habitat. In some species, very early, primitive adaptations had been retained that had long disappeared in similar life forms outside the Galápagos. Darwin's theory rests on the presence of the giant land tortoise and the adaptations of Galápagos finches. The island plants had also adapted to the unique conditions here, many exhibiting features found nowhere else. As the place where the evolutionary process can be followed as in a laboratory, the Galápagos Islands are highly worthy of preservation. In 1978, the islands were placed on the UNESCO list of World Natural Heritage Sites. However, this has not completely shielded these wonders from pollution, development and the effect of global warming on its sensitive ecosystem. The islands and their unique plants and animals remain under threat to this day.

FACTS

* **Name and location:** The official name of the Galápagos Islands is the Archipiélago de Colon. The islands belong to Ecuador and lie 1,600 km off its west coast.
* **Population:** The 61 islands have a total population of 25,000.
* **World Natural Heritage of the UNESCO:** The Galápagos Islands were declared a UNESCO World Natural Heritage Site in 1978.
* **Charles Robert Darwin,** (1809–82) was a British naturalist, one of the most important scientists in all of history. His theory of evolution by means of natural selection and gradual variation (collectively called 'Darwinism') revolutionized 19th-century science. It explained the diversification of organisms into different types as a slow process responsive to specific environmental pressures.

ARGENTINA AND BRAZIL

The Iguazú Falls

"POOR NIAGARA!" WAS ELEANOR ROOSEVELT'S COMMENT AS SHE GAZED UPON THE IGUAZÚ FALLS, A BREATHTAKING DISPLAY OF THE POWER OF NATURE LOCATED ON THE BORDER BETWEEN ARGENTINA AND BRAZIL.

What impressed the First Lady back then continues to fascinate the countless visitors from all over the world who make the journey to see the great Iguazú Falls. In the language of the local Guarani native peoples who live on the Iguazú River, the name means "big water" (*y guaso*). The river, 2.7 km across, cascades in the form of more than 270 individual waterfalls over the edge of a gorge that is up to 75 metres deep, called Garganta del Diablo (the "Devil's Throat"). A great many indigenous tribal folk tales, legends and myths have to do with the creation of the "big water". The most dramatic, and poetic, legend is the myth of Naipi, the beautiful daughter of the chief. It goes like this:

On the banks of the Iguazú lived a beautiful chief's daughter named Naipi. She was in love with the bravest warrior in her tribe. Alas, she was already promised as a bride to the snake god, M'boi. Desperate, Naipi and the warrior fled in a canoe on the Iguazú, which at that time was a gently flowing river. Then, suddenly, M'boi awoke and noticed that his bride was gone. Enraged, he churned up the water so much that the river could never again be calmed. With a powerful blow he cracked the bedrock so that the water fell into the depths. No boat would ever cross

FACTS

✻ **Location:** The Iguazú Falls straddle the border between Argentina and Brazil.

✻ **Size:** The falls are 2,700 m wide, of which 800 m are in Brazil and the remaining 1,900 m in Argentina.

✻ **Water masses:** The falls cascade up to 75 m into the gorge below. As much as 7000 m³ of water per second fell before the recent construction of a dam reduced the output by two-thirds. Currently, the Salto de Caixas Dam regulates the flow by means of an adjacent reservoir.

✻ **Discovery:** In 1542, Spanish sailor Alvar Nuñez Cabeza de Vaca (1490–1557) was the first European to see the falls.

✻ **World Natural Heritage Site:** The Iguazú Falls and two adjacent national parks were added to the UNESCO list of World Natural Heritage Sites in 1986.

The best view of the Iguazú Falls is from the Brazilian side. The falls are surrounded by lush rainforest.

this threshold again. M'boi changed the warrior into a large rock to be whipped and pummelled for all eternity by the rushing water. The beautiful chief's daughter Naipi was turned into a palm tree on the bank of the "big water", from where, when the evening wind blows, she can mournfully stretch her branches out to the rock in the waterfall, incessantly, and in vain.

This is how myth explains the origins of Iguazú Falls, but science takes a more sober approach. Geologists explain their origin as the product of tectonic movements taking place over the course of 100,000 years. The Garganta del Diablo came into being when the Iguazú delta sank, leaving behind the sharp edge over which the falls cascade today.

The Iguazú River, some 1,320 km long, is formed where the Irai and Atuba rivers meet near the Brazilian city of Curitiba. Its last few miles flow through the Brazilian province of Parana, where it defines the border between Argentina and Brazil. This means that the waterfall straddles the border between the two countries, with about 800 metres of the Iguazú Falls in Brazil, and the greater part, about 1,900 metres, in Argentina. While it is only possible to come close to the "Devil's Throat" from Argentina, the best overall view is from the Brazilian side. Until recently, as much as 7,000 cubic metres of water cascaded over or edge and down into the Devil's Throat every second. Now, however, following the highly controversial building of a dam in Salto de Caixas, the flow has been reduced by two-thirds. Scientists and environmentalists fear for the survival of native flora and fauna in an already sensitive rainforest environment. Despite being named a World Natural Heritage Site by UNESCO in 1986, along with two national parks on its banks, the Iguazú falls and the region around them remain under threat.

Above: The "big water" cascades into the gorge in more than 270 individual waterfalls.

Left: The Garganta del Diablo, or "Devil's Throat", is the gorge at the foot of the falls.

BRAZIL AND PARAGUAY

The Itaipú Dam

THE ITAIPÚ DAM ON THE BORDER OF BRAZIL AND PARAGUAY IS THE LARGEST HYDRO-ELECTRIC DAM AND POWER PLANT ON EARTH. GROUND WAS BROKEN IN 1971, AND 12 YEARS LATER TWO OF ITS GIGANTIC TURBINES WERE PRODUCING ELECTRICITY.

In the language of the local Guarani tribes, Itaipú means "singing stones". Planning for the world's largest hydroelectric dam was already under way in the mid-1960s, when it was decided that the Paraná River forming the border between Brazil and Paraguay should be dammed over more than 170 km between two waterfalls-the Sete Quedas and Foz do Iguaçu. On 26 April 1973, Brazilian president Medici and Paraguayan head of state Stroessner signed the contract for the gigantic complex, with Brazil responsible for most of the immediate financing for the the costly mega-project. In return, Paraguay promised to provide Brazil with electricity free of charge until it had paid off its part of the construction costs. In total, the price for the Itaipú Dam would run to over $20 billion.

It took 12 years to build the wall of the dam together with its hydroelectric power plants. Environmental groups and human rights organizations protested against the project. The ecological and social effects of the dam were severe indeed. Some 40,000 people, most of them from the Guarani tribes, had to be resettled. In addition, the Itaipú Dam and reservoir swallowed up some 800 km² of farmland and 600 km² of forest. The dam would flood 600 km of roads as well as 50 km of railway line. Most

The power plant integrated into the main retaining wall of the dam attracts thousands of visitors every year from all over the world. The foaming mass of the water as it exits the turbines makes for an impressive show.

FACTS

✽ Name: The official name of the dam is the Itaipú Binancional ("bi-national").

✽ Size: The dam wall is 7,700 m long and 196 m high. It is capable of retaining water to a height of 190 m. Under normal conditions, the level of the Itaipú reservoir lake is 100 m at its deepest point. The dam can retain up to 29 million m³ of water.

✽ Size of the lake: The surface area of Lake Itaipú is around 1460 km². The lake is 170 km long, with a width of 7–12 km.

✽ Mass of water: Around 62,200 m³ of water per second pass through a turbine, giving the dam's 18 turbines an output of 14,000 MW. The Itaipú Dam holds the world record for gigawatt hours of electricity generated within a calendar year with over 93,000 GWh in 2000.

✽ Building material: Over 15.57 million m³ of concrete were poured for the Itaipú Dam complex.

damaging environmentally were the areas of rainforest that would have to be cut down to facilitate construction and to provide space for the complex. Many more hectares would end up underwater when its reservoir was filled. The region's ecological balance would be essentially destroyed.

Up to 30,000 people were employed on the Itaipú Dam's construction, pouring so much concrete that the sheer amount would have been enough to rebuild Rio de Janeiro. The tons of iron and steel built into the dam could have built the Eiffel Tower 380 times over. The main dam wall, at 196 metres, is as tall as a 65-storey skyscraper.

The Itaipú Dam was completed on 13 October 1983. Just two weeks later, its reservoir was flooded to a depth of over 100 metres. Once Lake Itaipú was full, the power plant could be activated and energy production began. Since 1991, the hydroelectric plant has been running at full power, with its 18 turbines capable of producing 14,000 MW of electricity per year. This is eight times the output of the Aswan Dam in Egypt, and just over twice the production of the Grand Coulee Dam in Washington state, the largest in America. A conventional power plant has to burn 434,000 barrels of oil to produce the same amount of electricity. Every second, 62,200 m³ of water flow through the turbines, 40 times the flow of the Iguazú Falls. A single turbine provides electricity for a city with 1.5 million inhabitants.

The main retaining wall of the Itaipú complex is 7.7 km long and 196 metres high. The power plant, with 18 turbines producing electricity, is fully integrated into the central part of the dam wall. It is 968 metres long, almost 100 metres wide and 112 metres high! The static diameter of an Itaipú turbine is 16 metres. In 2000, it broke the world record for the amount of energy generated within a calendar year by producing 93,428 GWh, more than twice the previous record. The Itaipú Dam's only competition is the Three Gorges Dam on the Yangtze River in China. which became operational in 2010.

Today, the hydroelectric complex provides much of the energy used in Brazil and Paraguay. Itaipú has become a popular destination, with the beaches on the west shore of Lago Itaipú, the dam's reservoir, becoming a tourist attraction and recreation area. With an area of around 1,400 km², the lake offers many opportunities for leisure activities.

Centre: Water cascades into the spillway of the Itaipú Dam, heading for the power plant.

Bottom: The Itaipú Dam is the world's largest hydroelectric power plant.

PERU

Machu Picchu

THE LEGENDARY CITY OF MACHU PICCHU LIES HIDDEN IN THE ANDES AT AN ALTITUDE OF OVER 2,400 METRES. NESTLED BETWEEN TWO STEEP MOUNTAIN PEAKS, THE ANCIENT CITY OF THE INCAS REMAINS AS MYSTERIOUS AND FASCINATING AS EVER.

It was the year 1532. Invading Spanish conquistadores stormed the highlands of Peru, easily defeating and dominating the indigenous peoples. They carried off their legendary treasures as plunder and replaced the Incan rulers with puppet kings. But Manco Capac II, also known as Manco Incan Yupanqui (1516–44), a proud Incan noble, was not content to be a henchman in service to the Spanish crown. He gathered his devoted warriors around him and revolted against the Spanish occupation. The power imbalance proved to be too great and, after several years of bloody battles, Manco Capac II retreated with his remaining followers to the inaccessible mountain peaks of the Andes.

High in the mountains, they searched for a site for a new Incan city, eventually coming across a plateau lying between two mountain peaks, the "Young Peak" (Huayna Picchu) and "Old Peak" (Machu Picchu), high above the wild torrent of the Urubamba Valley. Manco Capac II named his new city in the clouds Vilcabamba, where his Incan Empire would survive for another 30 years. After the Spanish burned that city in 1872, its location was forgotten. When Hiram Bingham rediscovered Machu Picchu in 1911, he believed that he had found the legendary lost city. Recent archaeological evidence disputes this,

Right: Machu Picchu is built entirely of local stone.

Below: Astronomers, scholars and priests used the sundial for a number of different calculations.

however, identifying Vilcabamba with another site 100 km further west.

Whoever built the city at Machu Picchu planned it down to the very last detail. On one side stand the houses of the nobles, along with the palace and temples. The houses of the scholars, scribes and artisans are organized around the main plaza. The peasants lived further down the slope, amid animal stalls and storage buildings. Every part of the city is built from stone quarried right on the site, from the plateau itself. Incan masonry, with each block fitted precisely to another with no gap in between, has to this day never been bettered.

The Incas planned Machu Picchu so that it could function independently of the outside world; people could live there without ever having to leave. The southern slope was adapted for agriculture, with terraces cut into the mountainside that could be filled with earth brought up from the fertile Urubamba Valley. These terraces, called "andenes" (from which we get the name "Andes") were retained by low walls. This let them be irrigated artificially without the soil washing away. The water was brought down to the terrace fields from the higher mountains by means of an ingenious network of canals and channels. This system of irrigation still functions today much as it did 500 years ago.

Machu Picchu's impressive Sun Temple serves as evidence of the sheer magnificence of Incan architecture. This architectural masterpiece, with its trapezoidal doors and windows – which are typical of the Inca – was where they worshipped the sun, their central deity, the very basis of their religious life. The word "Inca" means both "the one" and "son of the sun". The religious centre of Machu Picchu is the hill where one bowed to the sun's majesty, the "Intihuatena", which in the Incan language means "the place where one captures the sun". On top of it lies a sacred stone resembling a sundial. It is thought that astronomers, scholars and priests used the sundial to calculate the year, months, day and time of day. Whether they used other instruments as well remains unknown.

The demise of Machu Picchu is also shrouded in mystery. It seems to have fallen out of use around the time of the Spanish conquest of 1532, and once the city was abandoned, the surrounding forest quickly took over. Machu Picchu could no longer be seen from the valley, the road leading up to it was quite hidden, and the site became nearly inaccessible. It would be almost 400 years before it would be rediscovered.

DATES

* **15th century:** Founding of Machu Picchu, according to archaeological evidence.

* **1776 and 1782:** Bills of sale related to the purchase of the terraced fields around Machu Picchu.

* **1895:** The road to Cuzco leading into the lower part of the "Holy Valley of the Incas" was built, greatly increasing accessibility to the region.

* **1911:** An expedition sponsored by Yale University and led by Hiram Bingham rediscovers the site of the city. Bingham visited the site again in 1912 and 1915.

* **1934:** Archaeological research began under the leadership of the Peruvian archaeologist Luis E. Valcarcel. In 1940–41 Paul Fejos took over the excavation. Work at the site continued into the 1960s.

* **1983:** Machu Picchu was placed on the UNESCO list of World Cultural Heritage Sites.

PERU

The Nazca Lines

THE NAZCA LINES HAVE NO PRECEDENT OR SUCCESSOR ANYWHERE ON EARTH. THE QUESTION REMAINS: WHY WOULD ANYONE TAKE ON THE ARDUOUS TASK OF DRAWING LINES AND FIGURES ACROSS THE WASTES OF THE ATACAMA DESERT?

The Nazca Lines, some of which are thousands of feet long, are the remains of an advanced civilization about which archaeologists still know very little. Until recently, even their age was uncertain. What is known is that the Nazca Lines are among the most puzzling legacies left behind by humankind.

The Nazca Lines were discovered in the 1920s when the first aeroplanes flew over the Atacama Desert. In those days of open cockpit planes, passengers and pilots took photographs of the ground below. In the meantime, archaeologists have concluded that the lines stem from the Nazca culture, named for a nearby city, which flourished between 500 BCE and 600 CE. Its apogee was around 200 BCE, when Nazca came under the influence of the Paracas culture. There was also a late phase of Nazca culture in the seventh and eighth centuries, when the region was influenced by the Wari peoples.

Why did these people choose to cover the ground of the Atacama Desert with monumental etchings? This central question has yet to be adequately answered, though theories abound. That they represent an enormous astronomical calendar is no longer considered valid, with few scientists supporting this view. One of the problems is that our knowledge about Nazca culture is extremely fragmentary. It

FACTS

✻ **Drawings made on the ground** are known as geoglyphs and the Nazca Lines are the most famous in the world. The Nazca etchings were created by scratching away or excavating a thin surface layer of dark gravel or earth, exposing the light-coloured layer that lies directly below.

✻ **In 1994**, the Nazca geoglyphs were described on the UNESCO World Cultural Heritage list as "Lines and drawings on the ground from Nazca and the Pampa de Jumana".

This is a mummy of a native of the Nazca culture. The Nazca people buried their dead in the hot, dry sand of the Atacama Desert, where well-preserved mummies are still found today.

seems likely the lines have some astronomical and religious significance. There are observable correlations between certain lines and the position of the sun at solstice, for example. The animal figures may have marked pathways that were walked in procession during religious ceremonies, perhaps ceremonies that ended with the sacrifice of those animals. **Author Hoimar von Ditfurth** put forth the theory that the high plateau of Nazca was some kind of giant sports arena. Other investigators have interpreted the lines as marking the location of a groundwater system that could have been tapped to irrigate the desert, making the land arable. Erich von Däniken proposed the most widely discussed theory: namely, that the Nazca Lines, represent landing strips for ancient visitors from outer space. To this day, no solid proof has been found to support any of these theories. The most recent interpretation is based on the proposition that the Atacama Desert was once a fertile plain, based on finds of very small silicate plant fragments called 'phytoliths'. If these plants could grow here, there must once have been rainfall and sufficient water. Accordingly, the Nazca people could have fallen victim to an extreme climatic shift that left the region with virtually no rainfall and allowed the desert to advance to its current extent. The people fell back on the water in the rivers of the Andes, but something had to be done to stop those sources from drying up as well. In response, the Nazca people scratched lines in the desert as a message to the gods, using motifs that conveyed their request for water. **For a long time,** it must have seemed as though the prayers had worked. Over a period of 400 years, people continued to scratch figures and symbols in the desert. Eventually, as desertification continued, even the reliable water sources dried up and the Nazca disappeared into the shadows of history.

Above: This pair of gigantic hands is etched into the rough ground of the Atacama Desert.

Left: This famous geoglyph shows a giant monkey.

CHILE

Easter Island

ON EASTER SUNDAY 1722, CAPTAIN JAKOB ROGGEVEEN CAME ACROSS AN ISLAND IN THE MIDDLE OF THE PACIFIC OCEAN, THE FIRST EUROPEAN TO VISIT THIS ISOLATED PART OF THE WORLD. ON HIS NAUTICAL MAP HE GAVE THE PLACE A NAME: EASTER ISLAND.

One can only imagine the astonishment of Roggeveen and his crew, not to mention how surprised the islanders must have been. The sailors did not expect to find an inhabited island in the empty vastness of the south-central Pacific Ocean, and the islanders had certainly not anticipated the arrival of a boatload of "white gods". The sailors were fascinated by the colossal stone sculptures that ringed the coastline of the island. **Who were these people** who could carve and set up these giants in stone? How did they come to settle such an isolated place? Where did they get the stone they used for their sculptures? According to legend, around the year 1400, a small group of men and women commanded by Polynesian chief Hotu Matua set off in canoes searching for an uninhabited island in the Pacific. With them they brought everything they needed to make the island livable: seeds, plants, domestic animals and tools. They found their island and named it Te Pito o te Henua – the "Navel of the World". Its new inhabitants brought their customs and rituals with them as well. Hotu Matua had cult sites set up along the coast. On the islands where he was born, probably the Marquesas, it was customary to erect *moai* – memorials to dead tribal leaders in the form of monumental stone statues.

This Easter Island moai has long ears and a large nose. Up to 10 m tall, moai can weigh as much as 150 tons.

FACTS

* **Name and size:** Easter Island is also known as Rapa Nui. It has a total area of 162.5 km².
* **Location:** The island lies at latitude 27° south and longitude109° west. Politically, it is part of Chile. The nearest inhabited land is Pitcairn Island, more than 2,000 km to the west. Chile lies 3,700 km away, and Tahiti is 4,000 km distant.
* **Unique:** Easter Island is famous for its colossal stone figures carved from the local volcanic tuff stone. They are as tall as 10 m and some weigh over 150 tons.
* **World Heritage site:** Easter Island was added to the UNESCO World Cultural Heritage list in 1995.

The figures – over 900 finished pieces have been catalogued – are as much as 10 metres tall, with the majority around 4.5 metres, and there is an unfinished piece in the quarry that would have stood 22 metres high. They were probably transported using tree trunks from the thick forests of giant palms that once covered the island. The enormous figures were first set on trunks used as rollers or sleds, and then slowly pushed and pulled over many miles to their positions. This difficult task would have required the strength of several hundred men.

Captain James Cook visited Easter Island in 1774. What he found was very different from the Dutch reports of a flourishing, advanced civilization comparable to the Old World. Instead, Cook found many of the magnificent stone colossi had been knocked over or otherwise destroyed. The island was depopulated, with the few remaining inhabitants living in fear in inaccessible caves. What had happened? The islanders' reports were contradictory. Archaeology would provide the best information. Some time after the departure of the Dutch, the islanders suffered catastrophically from overpopulation and starvation. The cult of the stone images had led to deforestation, which led to a sharp decline in food resources. A series of failed harvests added to the misery. A series of violent conflicts broke out and cannibalism was widespread. When Cook arrived on the island, he counted 4,000 inhabitants instead of the 20,000 Roggeveen had reported in 1722. Worse was yet to come. In 1862, Peruvian soldiers arrived and carried off 900 people as slaves to work the guano fields; only 15 of them survived. When they returned, they brought smallpox and other diseases with them. By 1877, there were only 111 people living on Easter Island. In 1888, it was annexed by Chile. The islanders were denied local jurisdiction until 1966, when they elected their own governor for the first time.

Since 1964, Easter Island has had an airport, bringing it closer to the outside world. Some 20,000 tourists visit the still mysterious island each year. For the present population of around 3,800, sheep herding, introduced in the late nineteenth century, is an important part of the economy. The deforestation and subsequent ecological disaster has left Easter Island covered with little more than thin grassland, and even that meagre remnant of the once lush biosphere is threatened by overgrazing and erosion.

Centre: The stone heads of Easter Island are as mysterious and puzzling as they are impressive.

Bottom: Round huts made of stone are found all over the island.

PANAMA

The Panama Canal

THE PANAMA CANAL IS ONE OF THE MOST IMPORTANT MAN-MADE WATERWAYS IN THE WORLD. JOINING THE GREAT OCEANS OF THE ATLANTIC AND PACIFIC, THE CANAL CUTS THROUGH THE ISTHMUS OF PANAMA AND TRIUMPHS OVER THE CONTINENTAL BARRIER.

Back in the sixteenth century, the Spanish conquistadores were already thinking of digging a navigable waterway that would connect the two great oceans. But the Spanish king, Philip II, was strongly opposed to the project, setting the death penalty as punishment for anyone who continued to waste time on bold plans for a canal. It would be 300 years before anyone would try again. Flushed with triumph following his success with the Suez Canal, Ferdinand de Lesseps also made plans to join the Atlantic with the Pacific. He started work in 1881, but this time the result was a fiasco. The ambitious project completely shut down only seven years after it was begun. The consortium in charge of the finances was ruined by mismanagement, corruption and bribery scandals. It went bankrupt soon afterwards.

In 1902, the consortium's liquidators sold what was left of the canal to the United States of America for $40 million. At this time, Panama still belonged to the political jurisdiction of Colombia, making it impossible for the Americans to simply pick up and start construction again. President Theodore Roosevelt supported a coup instigated by a Panamanian independence movement, helping it to victory. By

Right: The container ship *Cape Charles* is one of the largest allowed on the canal.

Below: A freighter passes through the Gatun locks.

1903, Panama was an independent, sovereign nation and work on the canal could begin. The first ship passed through the new Panama Canal on 15 August 1914. The contract between the United States and Panama stated that the canal would remain an American possession "forever".

Roughly 80 km long, the Panama Canal runs between the city of Colon on the Atlantic through to the dammed Lake Gatun on the Pacific side. Its construction shortened the sea journey from New York to San Francisco from around 26,000 km to just 10,000 km. The level of the Atlantic Ocean is only 24 cm lower than the Pacific. Nevertheless, the landscape is hilly and ships on their way through the isthmus must pass through three sets of locks that raise the water 26 metres to the level of Lake Gatun, a process necessitated by the rolling topography. The canal is wide enough to permit travel in both directions for almost the entire passage. The locks determine the size of the ships that can pass through, and those dimensions are known as the Panamax. Panamax ships can be no larger than 294 metres long and 32 metres wide. They also cannot have a draught, or depth, greater than 12 metres.

Since the Panama Canal was opened in 1914, more than one million passages have been recorded, with 14,000 in the year 2005 alone. The Panama Canal Authority collects tolls for every transit. When the United States relinquished control of the canal to Panama in the year 2000, the nation of Panama became solely responsible for its operation and administration. The tolls, based on the size and tonnage of the ship, average around $70,000 per passage. However, it has long been clear that the canal's capacity is no longer sufficient. Freight shipping between the USA and Asia has increased dramatically while using more and larger ships. The measurements of ships in the so-called post-Panama class, of which there are currently around 300 sailing the world's seas, do not permit them to pass through the canal's locks. Soon there will be many more of these giant tankers and freighters. The largest container ships now in existence can carry up to 10,000 containers, twice as many as the largest Panamax-class freighter.

For the nation of Panama, the canal is a veritable gold mine. In order to ensure continued demand and secure the long-term income of the state, the Panamanian government intends to renovate the canal to accommodate larger ships, with much higher tolls planned as a means of financing the project. This highly controversial renovation which begun in 2007, will be complete within seven years.

DATES

* **1881:** A French consortium broke ground for the construction of the canal.
* **1902:** Remainders of the French attempt were sold to the US for $40 million.
* **1903:** Panama gained its independence and work on the canal resumed.
* **15 August 1914:** The first ship passed through the Panama Canal.
* **1920–1999:** The canal was owned by the US.
* **1 January 2000:** The US transferred ownership of the canal to Panama.

FACTS

* **Length:** The canal is 80 km long, with three locks along the way.
* **Passage:** There have been over 1 million passages since 1914. The average toll per ship is $70,000. Up to 45 ships traverse the canal daily.
* **Panamax class:** Panamax-class ships can be no more than 294 m long and 32 m wide. They cannot have a draught greater than 12 m.

ARGENTINA

Perito Moreno Glacier

THE PERITO MORENO GLACIER IN PATAGONIA IS THE ONLY GLACIER IN THE WORLD THAT GROWS CONTINUALLY, UP TO 450 METRES A YEAR. THE GLACIER AND THE LOS GLACIARES NATIONAL PARK WERE PLACED ON THE LIST OF WORLD NATURAL HERITAGE SITES IN 1981.

The landscape of Patagonia, the southernmost part of the South American continent, has a wild, bizarre look to it. Nature plays out here in a unique fashion, with an irregular, but always impressive, performance. As often as once every four years, or as seldom as once a decade, the waters of the Lago Argentino, a lake periodically dammed by the Perito Moreno, burst forth, dramatically rupturing the icy carapace of the glacial giant. **The Patagonian icefield** covers the greater part of the Los Glaciares National Park. Second only to the Antarctic ice cap, the Patagonian icefield is one of the largest in the world, with a total area of 4,459 km^2, a length of 350 km and a width of 50 km at its widest point. It originates in the north of the national park on the slopes of the Fitzroy Massif at an elevation of only 1,500 metres. The three main tributaries of the primary glaciers – the Perito-Moreno, Uppsala and Viedma – all end at around 1,300 metres above sea level. Their melt-water has formed enormous lakes characterized by an intense turquoise colour, from which the edges of the glacier rise like giant icebergs. The pointed, steep, fissured protrusions project up to 60 metres. As is true of icebergs, the great majority of the glacier, some 130 metres, lies below the water's surface.

FACTS

Name: Los Glaciares National Park was founded in 1945.

Area: Consisting of 13 glaciers, it has a total area of 4,500 km^2.

Unique: The glaciers make up the second largest continuous ice mass: only the Antarctic ice cap is larger.

Etymology: The Perito Moreno Glacier is named after its discoverer, the Argentinian geographer and anthropologist Pascasio "Perito" Moreno (1852–1919).

World Heritage Site: The glaciers and national park were added to the UNESCO list of World Natural Heritage Sites in 1981.

Wide prairies called 'pampas' cover large parts of Los Glaciares National Park. In the background loom the snow-covered peaks of the southern Andes.

The Perito Moreno Glacier is the largest one in Los Glaciares National Park. The icy giant is approximately 60 km long and up to 5 km wide. Everywhere in the world, the great glaciers are retreating as they slowly (or in some cases, quickly) melt away. The Perito Moreno, in contrast, is the only glacier in the world that is still advancing. Every day, the heavy snows in its originating icefield create 1 metre of new ice, pushing the glacial stream forwards by about 450 metres per year.

Metre for metre, it advances. When it reaches Lago Argentino it is nearly 2 km broad and rises as much as 60 metres above the water's surface. In many years, the glacier actually divides the lake into two parts. The northern half of the lake can empty itself as always, while the waters of the southern half are blocked, dammed behind the glacial barrier. Water levels on the northern and southern sides of the ice dam can vary by as much as 30 metres. Eventually, the immense pressure and weight become too much and, with almost primeval power, the water breaks through the glacial. This unique natural phenomenon is known in Argentina as *la ruptura*, or 'rupture'.

When this happens, blocks of ice as big as houses give way all at once. The ice mass is blown into the air, to fall again with a deafening crack into the floodwaters of the Lago Argentino. The water eats away at the ice until it has bored a tunnel or canal through the glacial barrier large enough to allow the water to run off into the northern part of the lake. This creates an enormous flood wave that races onward towards the Atlantic Ocean. The "performances" of *la ruptura* take place somewhat unpredictably every four to ten years. The most recent one took place before thousands of fascinated spectators in March 2006, captivating each and every one of them with its icy magic.

Above: Large pieces of fractured ice frequently break off the edge of the glacier.

Left: The Perito Moreno Glacier is the only glacier in the world that continues to advance rather than retreat.

MEXICO

Teotihuacán

TEOTIHUACÁN WAS THE CENTRE OF THE EARLIEST ADVANCED CIVILIZATION IN CENTRAL MEXICO. NOTHING HAD MORE INFLUENCE ON THE DEVELOPMENT OF MESOAMERICA THAN THIS MYSTERIOUS PLACE LOCATED 40 KM NORTH OF MEXICO CITY.

The founding of Teotihuacán marks the beginning of the classical period of Mesoamerican history. Undisputedly, it served as the capital of a kingdom that surpassed even that of the much later Aztecs in size, power and influence. Still, the identity of the people who built the monumental city with its soaring pyramids remains unknown. When the Aztecs settled in the ruins of Teotihuacán in the fourteenth century, they were impressed by the size of the buildings, but knew little about who had created them. **There are several legends,** most of which probably date back no further than the Aztec Empire. In them, Teotihuacán appears as the site where the gods assembled to organize the creation of humankind. More likely is that the first settlers were indigenous farmers emigrating from the north, who began to build the city around 300 BCE. They must have been experienced and highly skilled farmers, because Teotihuacán quickly became an important place. Its inhabitants involved themselves in trade with other Mesoamerican regions, enhancing Teotihuacán's wealth and prosperity. The city became an important economic centre with a population of around 200,000 at its height between 300 and 600 CE. The powerful city nevertheless fell around 650, with all but a few

The Avenue of the Dead is 1.6 km long, running from the Pyramid of the Moon past the Pyramid of the Sun to the Temple of Quetzalcoatl.

DATES

* **500 BCE:** Earliest pottery in the region.
* **200 BCE:** Construction of the Pyramid of the Sun began.
* **50 CE:** The Quetzalcoatl Temple was built.
* **100 CE:** The golden age of the city, when it had around 200,000 inhabitants and covered an area of 30 km^2.
* **200:** The city was first attacked by nomadic tribes.
* **400–420:** The city was laid waste by enemy nomads, leading to the first phase of emigration from the site.
* **650:** Teotihuacán was abandoned by nearly all its inhabitants.

inhabitants abandoning the site. When and why this happened is still one of Teotihuacán's greatest mysteries. Scorch marks on many of the buildings suggest that a catastrophe took place, causing most of the people to flee. Nearly 100 years later, around 750, the Toltecs plundered what remained of Teotihuacán and left it as a ghost town.

In the fourteenth century, the Aztecs took possession of Teotihuacán and resettled its ruins. They gave the city its name, which means "the place where one becomes a god" or "city of the gods". The Aztecs were impressed by its immense size. They were convinced that only giants could have built Teotihuacán, and that both the moon and sun were born here.

The smaller of the two pyramids that dominate Teotihuacán is called the Pyramid of the Moon. It is located at the beginning of the main street, the Avenue of the Dead. The Aztecs used both sides of this street as a burial place. It runs from the Pyramid of the Moon to the Temple of Quetzalcoatl, crowned by a pyramid covered with relief sculptures of snakes. Quetzalcoatl was the god of rain, depicted as a feathered serpent. This was the most important religious building in Teotihuacán.

Between the temple and the Pyramid of the Moon lies the Pyramid of the Sun, the most elaborate monument in Teotihuacán. It is the third largest pyramid in the world, 63 metres high, and covers an area 222 by 225 metres. Almost 1 million cubic metres of material were used in its construction. Engineers estimate that this pyramid, which was painted bright red, weighs around 3 million tons. In contrast to other Mesoamerican pyramids that grew over time, as smaller pyramids were enclosed by larger ones, the Pyramid of the Sun at Teotihuacán, like the Pyramid of the Moon and many other buildings, seems to have been built all at once. Unlike the Egyptian pyramids, the Mesoamerican ones are not grave monuments, but temple platforms. In 1971, archaeologists discovered a 100-metre-long tunnel leading into the structure. Its walls were covered with religious scenes, though they are of little help in identifying what deity was worshipped in the temple on top of this artificial mountain. The Aztecs thought the sun was worshipped here, and thus called it the Sun Pyramid, much like they named the other monuments at the site. Like so much about Teotihuacán, their original names remain a mystery.

Centre: The Pyramid of the Sun towers over the ruins of Teotihuacán. The third largest pyramid in the world, it is 63 m tall.

Bottom: The rain god, Quetzalcoatl.

GUATEMALA

Tikal

STONE MONUMENTS RISE HIGH TOWARDS THE HEAVENS FROM THE MIDDLE OF THE DENSE RAINFOREST, MAGNIFICENT REMAINS OF A LONG-VANISHED CULTURE. THESE ARE THE PYRAMIDS, TEMPLES AND PALACES OF THE LEGENDARY CITY OF TIKAL.

The people who lived in Tikal, the Ancient Mayan, are shrouded in myth. They appeared as if from nowhere 3,000 years ago, and over time developed a phenomenally advanced civilization that remained strong longer than the Roman Empire. Then they disappeared in a mysterious manner, much like their first appearance upon history's stage.

Mayan culture reached its apogee in the fifth century. Ornate cities, magnificent palaces and monumental temples were built, with Tikal its most important religious centre. The competing Mayan dynasties spread their culture by invading and dominating smaller bordering states, pulling them into their vast sphere of influence. Then, in the eighth century, only 300 years later, Tikal lay abandoned in the middle of the dense forest. Its inhabitants seem to have fled the once flourishing city in a very short period of time. All over Central America, the highly advanced culture of the Mayan vanished along with its people. What happened?

The mystery gave rise to a myth. For a long time, the Mayan were seen as peaceful people living in harmony with nature. In this respect at least, new studies have shown the Mayan of Tikal were quite different.

In Tikal, everything revolved around the power, influence and eventual apotheosis of the members of

Right: During the height of the classic Mayan period, more than 100,000 people lived in Tikal.

Below: Tikal was the most important Mayan ceremonial centre.

the ruling elite. They ruthlessly exploited their subjects and environment to the point of self-extinction. Years of poorly managed economies and egoistic political manoeuvres designed solely to increase the power and wealth of a small elite led to ecological disaster. This contributed to the end of one the most important advanced civilizations in antiquity.

The Mayan rulers exploited their subjects' belief in divine kings. Perhaps at one time they had to wrest power from influential shamans. In declaring themselves god-kings, only they were in the position to intercede with the gods. According to popular belief, a healing energy flowed through the divine rulers. The god-kings established a strict, hierarchal system to ensure their nearly absolute power. The most important instrument was the invention of a written script with which the rulers could catalogue their deeds. These served as proof of their all-powerful nature, securing their immortality.

Access to advanced knowledge, from writing to advanced mathematics, was limited to a chosen few. Apart from the ruling caste, there were also carefully chosen scholars and scribes who were trained to record the rulers' triumphs and keep track of time using a ritual calendar. The Mayan were the first to use the number zero and their calendar, based on a long series of astronomical observations, was more accurate than the one used in Ancient Rome. Those in power were always a small group, and the ruling caste reacted with great brutality to any threat to their power, influence and knowledge. Thousands went to their deaths in sacrificial rituals and blood-splattered competitions. The more monumental a palace or temple in Tikal was, the more elaborate its decoration. Plaster ornamentation completely covered columns, steles, staircases and roof ledges. Making plaster for this purpose meant burning a great deal of limestone, requiring tons of wood. The rulers ordered the forest around Tikal completely cleared, as well as that maize be planted where the trees had grown. Planned as a means of securing food for the population, instead it was a disaster. Tropical rains washed away the thin topsoil, which deforestation left exposed and unprotected. Soon, nothing grew any more, resulting in food shortages and famines. This led to a sharp decline in the rulers' power and to the collapse of Tikal. Once abandoned, the forest returned, completely taking over the empty city. What remained of Tikal to be rediscovered in the modern period remains an impressive monument to a flourishing civilization, but also to the impermanence of the power and riches that built it.

DATES

* ***circa* 400 BCE:** Tikal was first settled.
* **250 CE:** Tikal was the most important religious centre of the Mayan.
* **292:** King Balam Ajaw ("Decorated Jaguar") began his reign. He left behind two of the earliest extensive historical texts carved on steles.
* **360–378:** Rule of King Yax Moc Xac ("Great Jaguar Paw"), who built the first great palace at Tikal.
* **682–734:** King Double Moon, also known as Prince Chocolate ("Ah Cacao") reigned. He was entombed in the great Temple Pyramid I; his queen occupies the tomb in Pyramid II. Archaeologists from the University of Pennsylvania have excavated both tombs.
* **900:** Tikal had been completely abandoned.

In the USA and Canada, nature and high tech exist side by side in a unique symbiosis. Magnificent modern buildings and monuments designed and built by human hand testify to an unstoppable drive for progress and a high level of technical know-how. At the same time, the beauty of its natural resources make North America a plant and animal paradise of unimaginable wealth.

NORTH AMERICA

CANADA

The CN Tower

APPROACHING THE CANADIAN CITY OF TORONTO FROM THE SOUTH, TRAVELLING BY BOAT ACROSS LAKE ONTARIO, THE CN TOWER IS VISIBLE LONG BEFORE THE REST OF THE SKYLINE COMES INTO VIEW.

The CN Tower, gigantic yet elegant, is the tallest freestanding structure in the world. Designed to function as a television signal tower, it stands exactly 553.33 metres tall and is therefore often described as "Canada's World Wonder". It is named after the Canadian National Railway (CNR) which, in consortium with the Canadian Broadcasting Company (CBC), built the tower during the 1970s.

The cornerstone for the CN Tower was laid on 6 February 1973. Around 62,000 tons of earth and shale rock had to be dug up and removed for the foundation, which is a concrete slab 6 metres thick and 70 metres in diameter. Over 57,000 tons of concrete were poured to support the 130,000-ton weight of the CN Tower.

The concrete shaft of the tower was constructed by using hydraulic jacks to raise a metal slip, a kind of mould for the concrete, approximately 6 metres each day. This allowed each layer of concrete to set as the form was moved higher up the structure. This was by far the most difficult part of the entire construction process. The construction method meant that the tower could not be allowed to tilt away from the vertical; even a few inches would be too much. The engineers ensured that this would not happen by

Right: The CN Tower rises high above downtown Toronto.

Below: At night, Toronto is a sea of lights on the northern shore of Lake Ontario.

suspending a 100-kg steel cylinder on a rope down the centre of the tower's six-sided core. This acts as a giant plumb bob.

Throughout the construction period, highly sensitive instruments regularly checked the tower's measurements. The result is remarkable. The tower, which stands over 550 metres tall, is just 2.7 cm off the vertical over its entire height.

A radio transmitter crowns the top of the tower. The steel needle was put together from 39 individual parts, each flown up and set in place with the help of a very large Sikorsky helicopter. This shortened the construction period for the antenna to three and a half weeks. With conventional methods, involving a fixed crane, the antenna alone could have taken half a year to build. The last piece was put in place on 2 April 1975.

In 1976, after just three years of construction, the innovative, daring, yet stable CN Tower was officially opened. The structure itself is quite unusual. In section, the shaft of the tower is not round, as would be typical, but hexagonal. In retrospect, this has proved problematic for a number of reasons. It is much more sensitive to wind than round towers, for example, and as a result it had to be built to withstand winds three or four times as strong. It is therefore not surprising that the top of the tower sways back and forth as much as a metre or more in high winds.

Four glass-walled lifts travelling at a speed of over 6 metres per second take visitors up and down the outer wall of the CN Tower, from ground level to the Sky Pod at a height of 447 metres. The 7-storey tower pod in which it is located has a maximum diameter of 36.5 metres. Restaurants, a nightclub and two observation decks are also found in this pod. The lower vantage point, at the base of the pod, offers an unbeatable view straight down through a floor made of 6.35-cm thermal reinforced glass, strong enough to support a weight of 38 tons. Nevertheless, visitors have great difficulty trusting the invisible floor. A carpet has been laid over most of it.

The lower part of the pod is coated in a Teflon-like substance reinforced with glass filaments concealing the tower's antennae. The upper part is clad in stainless steel that reflects the sun, making it visible from very far away. The highest accessible point on the tower, the Sky Pod observation deck, 447 metres above the ground, is the highest one in the world. The view from here is simply unbelievable, provided the extraordinary height doesn't make you dizzy!

FACTS

* **Location:** The cornerstone for the CN Tower was laid in Toronto on 6 February 1973. It was completed in April 1976.

* **Size:** The CN Tower is 553.33 m tall. It stands on a foundation consisting of a 6-m-thick concrete slab with a diameter of 70 m. The foundation weighs 57,000 tons, supporting the 130,000-ton weight of the tower itself.

* **Lifts:** There are six glass-walled lifts travelling up and down the outer wall at a speed of 365 m per minute.

* **Main observation deck:** The round observation deck, about 340 m above the ground, is 36.5 m in diameter. This lower deck offers an unbeatable view, straight down, through a floor made of 6.35-cm thermal reinforced glass that is strong enough to support 38 tons.

* **Number of steps:** 2,570 steps lead up to the Sky Pod ad the top of the tower.

USA

Death Valley

IF YOU EVER PASS THROUGH THE HEAT OF DEATH VALLEY IN AN AIR-CONDITIONED CAR, YOU WILL FIND IT HARD TO BELIEVE THAT THE DESERT WAS ONCE COVERED IN A METRE OF ICE. TWICE IN ITS HISTORY, THE VALLEY OF DEATH HAS BEEN A GLACIAL LANDSCAPE.

Hot, hotter and hottest: Death Valley is unbearably hot and dry. The air shimmers with dust particles. It is not uncommon for summer temperatures to reach over 49 °C. The highest temperature ever documented in the United States, 57 °C, was recorded in the valley at Furnace Creek Ranch. Although Death Valley lies only a few hundred kilometres from the Pacific Ocean, it is one of the driest regions on Earth. Rain captured by moist winds blowing in from the sea has already fallen well before reaching this far inland. By the time the wind gets to Death Valley, all that's left is hot air.

Despite the difficult and dangerous conditions, there is life in Death Valley. Archaeologists have found rock drawings, hearths and other remains of human settlement all over the desert. Today, only a few Native Americans from the Timbisha-Shoshone tribe live year-round in the valley, near Furnace Creek. **The national park also supports** a thriving population of bighorn sheep. These exceptionally adaptable beasts have overcome the inhospitable environment of Death Valley in magnificent fashion. Plants are few, although spring storms can awaken Death Valley, bringing forth a carpet of wildflowers from seeds lying long buried in the dry soils. For a short time, the landscape will be covered with tender blooms.

FACTS

✻ History and location: Death Valley National Park was named a national monument in 1933 and a national park in 1994. It lies in the states of California and Nevada, covering an area of 13,628 km^2.

✻ Elevation: Death Valley Park is notable for its extreme variations in elevation. Badwater Basin lies 85.5 m below sea level, while Telescope Peak soars 3,368 m above it.

✻ Number of visitors: Over 1 million people visit Death Valley National Park every year.

✻ Etymology: The name "Death Valley" comes from a tragic accident. In 1849, a group of 49-ers on their way to the California Gold Rush tried to take a shortcut through the desert. Many of them met their death in the valley due to dehydration and heat.

A really "hot" putting green! Even the nighttime temperature at the Devil's Golf Course seldom falls below 38 °F.

Geologically, Death Valley is a relatively young formation, just a few million years old. The region can nevertheless look back at an active geological past. At least four active volcanic periods formed the valley, along with three or four periods of sedimentation. There has also been considerable tectonic activity and two periods when glaciers dominated.

There are many fascinating natural features within Death Valley National Park, most of which are known by colourfully descriptive names. Artists' Palette is a site known for its multicoloured rock formations, and Badwater Basin is famous for being the lowest point in the continental United States at 85.5 metres below sea level. Nearby is the weather station where the hottest temperature ever documented in the USA was recorded on 10 July 1913, when it reached 56.7 °C. Dante's View is a flat-topped mountain that rises 1,669 metres above Death Valley. Its summit offers visitors a panoramic view that stretches from Badwater Basin to the Great Salt Sea (also known as the Devil's Golf Course) and on to Telescope Peak, which at 3,368 metres is the highest point in Death Valley National Park.

The northern half of Death Valley is home to the Mesquite Flat Dunes, enormous sand dunes that can be up to 50 metres tall. Film director George Lucas filmed part of his famous *Star Wars* series here. Another remarkable feature are the so-called Wandering Rocks of Racetrack Playa. Large boulders seem to move along the hot sand and gravel as if guided by a ghostly hand. A more likely explanation is that the occasional strong nighttime rains transform the sand into a slippery surface for a short period of time. When the strong winds blow, they push the stones over the temporarily wet sand. The movement leaves telltale tracks behind as the moisture quickly evaporates in the hot Death Valley sun.

Above. After the storms and flash floods of spring, Death Valley briefly shows its friendly side.

Left. The Mesquite Flat Dunes are located in the northern half of Death Valley National Park.

USA

The Empire State Building

ON 1 MAY 1931, THE EMPIRE STATE BUILDING WAS OFFICIALLY OPENED WITH GREAT FANFARE. FOR NEW YORKERS, IT WAS LOVE AT FIRST SIGHT. THE NEW EMBLEM OF THE CITY ADDED AN EXCLAMATION MARK TO THE END OF THE ROARING TWENTIES.

Only a year after Black Tuesday, that day in 1929 when the Wall Street Stock Market collapsed, construction of the Empire State Building began, a new skyscraper located far uptown between 33rd and 34th streets. The crash put a stop to nearly every major building project in New York City, because their financing had been secured by investments in a booming stock market that had ceased to exist overnight. Developers and investors alike were suddenly broke, and the construction industry came to a standstill. **The Empire State Building** was an ambitious project developed by John Jakob Raskob, a stock-market speculator and founder of General Motors. He was also one of the few who came out ahead after the crash. Raskob commissioned architect William F. Lamb to build the tallest building in New York. New Yorkers said that the building would either be a great triumph, or a total disaster, but no one really believed the undertaking would succeed. Construction began in late March 1930, with its cornerstone officially laid in September of that year by the former governor of New York, and current presidential candidate, Alfred E. Smith. **William F. Lamb developed** a magnificent system of logistics for the Empire State Building's construction. Inspired by automobile manufacturer Henry

Completed during the worldwide financial crisis brought on by the stock-market crash, the Empire State Building stood as an irrefutable symbol of American courage and perseverance.

FACTS

✻ Location: The Empire State Building is located in the borough of Manhattan in New York City.

✻ Material: It is built from 55,000 tons of steel, 10 billion bricks and 5,660 m³ of sandstone. The Empire State Building contains 30,000 m² of marble flooring and weighs around 331,000 tons.

✻ Wires and pipes: The Empire State Building has 760 km of electrical wiring, over 110 km of water pipes and 1,700 km of telephone cable running through it.

✻ Windows: The skyscraper has 6,500 windows, filled by 2 km² of glass.

Ford's success with the assembly line, Lamb installed a vertical rail system inside the building for quickly delivering tools, building materials and manpower via crane or transport vehicle to wherever it was needed. Minutely calibrated according to a set timetable, this clever, exceptionally efficient adaptation drastically reduced the hours of work lost to waiting around for a load of steel, a piece of equipment or a crew of men to arrive on the job.

Over 50,000 steel beams were incorporated into the Empire State Building, and Lamb's vertical transport system ensured that every one of them was in place in record time. The building shot out of the earth in a little more than a year, with an average of 4.5 floors completed per week. The record for the Empire State Building was 14 floors in only ten days. The clear heroes among the construction workers were the ironworkers, many of whom were Native Americans from the Mohawk tribe. They were responsible for walking the steel frame of the towering building and riveting the beams together. Working in teams at dizzying heights, they hammered up to 800 rivets per day.

The Empire State Building's opening celebration took place on 1 May 1931 in the presence of President Herbert Hoover. Although New Yorkers loved the building from the very first, it would be many years before its vast quantity of office spaces were filled. For the first few years, income from the fees charged for admission to the observation deck was greater than income from office rental. New Yorkers had a nickname for the building in those years: they called it the 'Empty State Building'.

As early as the 1930s, Hollywood realized the skyscraper's potential as a magnificent backdrop. Who can forget King Kong, the giant gorilla that clung for dear life to the Empire State Building with Fay Wray clasped in his hand? Many an unforgettable Hollywood kiss has taken place on the observation deck of the Empire State Building.

Although the Empire State Building never succeeded in moving the centre of Manhattan's financial world uptown from Wall Street, no one can call it a failure. Its soaring, freestanding form is still New York's emblem. At a height of 381 metres (or 443 metres including its antenna), it was, as John J. Raskob had intended, the tallest building in the world, a position it held for a record 41 years.

Centre: Many Native Americans of the Mohawk tribe worked on the construction of the building.

Bottom: With a height of 381 m, the Empire State Building was the tallest building in the world until 1972, when the Sears Tower was built in Chicago.

USA

The Everglades

AUTHOR AND NATURE PRESERVATION ACTIVIST MARJORY STONEMAN DOUGLAS TITLED HER BESTSELLING 1947 BOOK *RIVER OF GRASS*. HER WORK WAS A LOVE LETTER TO THE WORLD-FAMOUS PRIMEVAL LANDSCAPE WE CALL THE EVERGLADES.

Despite a hundred years of intense efforts on the part of Marjory Stoneman Douglas and many others before and after her, the once natural landscape of the Everglades remains seriously threatened. These subtropical marshlands in southern Florida are on the brink of complete ecological collapse. The Everglades had already been badly damaged during the early twentieth century by drainage and deforestation directed by agricultural interests. More recently, increasing population in the cities of Miami and Orlando has led to unfettered residential development and further demands on freshwater supplies, accelerating the destruction of the wetlands. The Everglades National Park, which has been in existence since 1947, includes only 20 per cent of the original extent of the Everglades system. Its creation was considered a last-chance attempt to save what humankind cannot simply let slip away.

For many thousands of years, the same natural drama had unfolded, day after day. With the sunrise, the Kissimee Lakes come to life. The fresh water of the lakes is what feeds this unique ecosystem. In south Florida, freshwater lakes, the "source" of the Everglades, lie only 5 metres above the level of the Gulf of Mexico some 500 km away. The water makes

FACTS

✻ **Location:** Everglades National Park is located in southern Florida. It was established in 1947.

✻ **Size:** The total area of the Everglades is some 6,100 km². It is categorized as a subtropical marshland.

✻ **UNESCO World Heritage:** The Everglades have been on the UNESCO list of World Natural Heritage Sites since 1979. The region has been on the Red List of Endangered Environments since 1993.

✻ **Unique:** A wide variety of flora and fauna, including orchids, mangroves, alligators and manatees, make their home in the Everglades.

Agricultural land encroaches on the primeval Everglades landscape.

its way slowly to the sea, fanning out broadly into a fantastic marshland over an area up to 80 km wide. The water can only travel 30 metres per day, which means that it may take as many as 40 years to reach the sea. The longer it takes, the saltier the water becomes, partly due to evaporation and in part due to the gradual mixing of the fresh water of the Everglades with the salt water of Florida Bay. The lush vegetation in the marshes, which provides a habitat for a phenomenal number of bird and animal species, is held in check in the coastal area by a tangle of mangrove trees.

By the time the water from the Kissimee Lakes reaches the Gulf of Mexico, it has covered an area of over 6,000 km², making the Everglades the largest marshland region on the Earth. But how much longer will they last?

When the Spanish conquistadores landed on the coast of Florida in the sixteenth century, they travelled only a few miles inland before coming upon an enormous, mosquito-ridden swamp fit to be inhabited only by the alligators, poisonous snakes and biting insects that lived there. The Spanish did not realize they had come upon an ecological jewel, the largest continuous marshland on Earth. For them, it was a dangerous place with worthless land. For all intents and purposes, they were happy to leave the Everglades alone.

Human exploitation of the Everglades first began in the late nineteenth century. American agricultural and estate-agent speculators began to drain the marshes, ignoring the warnings of scientists. Within a very short period of time, 1.2 million km² of land had been dried out. Moisture-sucking melaleuca trees were imported from Australia to help the proess along. The melaleuca, a kind of myrtle, absorb four times as much water as the native flora.

Above: The unique landscape of the Everglades at sundown.

Left: Lush mangrove forests cover many small islands in the Everglades.

Suburbs of Miami and Orlando penetrate further and further into what was recently marshlands.

An ecological catastrophe of unanticipated proportions loomed. The goal of the developers had been to create land where houses could be built, as well as fertile, productive agricultural land for sugar cane and fruit plantations. Once begun, the destruction of this essentially untouched natural ecosystem could not easily be stopped. Marshlands were rigorously converted into farmland. The thousand-year water cycle was interrupted.

With plantation owners firmly in control, economic interests took precedence over ecological concerns. But all was not well in this apparent paradise. During the hot summer months, wild fires raged through fields and swamp meadows as the ground dried out completely due to lack of moisture. Many plantations were only profitable for a couple of years, after which the soils were exhausted of nutrients. Reacting quickly to the threatening fires, farmers created enormous reservoirs that drew still more water out of the Everglades. The water cycle was not only destroyed, but also poisoned by unfiltered pesticides and fertilizers that had infiltrated the groundwater. The Everglades stood on the brink of extinction.

It is thanks to active nature preservationists, such as Marjory Stoneman Douglas, that attitudes began to change around the middle of the twentieth century. It was a long time before people in Florida began to realize that the destruction of the Everglades water system directly threatened their own existence. A billion dollar marshland rescue and restoration project was initiated, and giant pumping stations were put in place to regulate the water flowing through the region. For a large portion of the Everglades, however, it is already too late. What was once paradise is already almost gone for good.

Today, around 50 per cent of the area originally occupied by the Everglades is used for agricultural purposes, and the other 50 per cent is protected wetland. The southern half of the Everglades has been a national park since 1947, and has been on the UNESCO list of World Natural Heritage Sites since 1979. The extent to which the Everglades nonetheless remain endangered is illustrated by the continued presence of its flora and fauna on the Red List of Threatened Species. As an ecosystem, the Everglades first made the list in 1993, despite all the protective measures in place.

FACTS

✻ **Flora:** Over 950 different kinds of plants are found in the Everglades, of which 65 are unique to southern Florida – 25 orchid species, 120 types of trees and 3 varieties of mangrove are represented.

✻ **Fauna:** 36 different animals that live in the Everglades are listed as threatened and endangered. These include the Mississippi alligator, caiman, Florida panther and the manatee.

The alligator is the king of the Everglades. Encroaching residential development has led to more and more alligators wandering into gardens and swimming pools.

The Everglades are a subtropical mosaic of life forms. An unbelievable number of species call the marshlands home, including 950 different kinds of plants, of which 65 are unique to southern Florida. There are 25 species of orchid, 120 kinds of trees and three distinct varieties of mangrove. Thirty-six different animals that live in the Everglades are listed as threatened and endangered, and many pieces of the mosaic have already been lost forever. The environments supporting the Mississippi alligator, fierce caiman, Florida panther and placid manatee are all under severe threat. Despite the protected areas, the decimation of the biosphere continues today almost unhindered.

Stoneman Douglas' famous, bestselling book, *The Everglades: River of Grass,* reads like a love letter to the one-of-a-kind landscape she held so dear. Excerpts from her descriptions can be read in nearly every Florida travel book. The author praises, in particular, the almost surreal silence that could still be experienced deep in the marshlands in 1947.

Today, the Everglades attract visitors from all over the world, with over 1.5 million tourists coming to the national park every year. Needless to say, uncontrolled leisure activities take a toll on the marshlands, too. Development associated with the growth of Miami and Orlando, however, whose suburbs penetrate ever deeper into what was originally the Everglades, is an even bigger threat. Every day, 850 additional people move to the Everglades to live, pushing back the boundaries of the protected areas before them. Their new houses have gardens and swimming pools, leading to an average water usage of 470 litres per person per day. More and more frequently, confused alligators emerge from the marshes in search of a pond or stream, only to find a swimming pool instead.

Above: The Everglades are a hunter's paradise. The population of the Florida panther is under acute threat.

Left: Tourism is another factor that disrupts the natural balance of the Everglades.

USA

The Statue of Liberty

FOR MORE THAN A CENTURY SHE HAS HELD HER TORCH HIGH. IMMIGRANTS, REFUGEES, NEWCOMERS, TOURISTS AND THOSE RETURNING HOME: STANDING TALL AT THE ENTRANCE TO NEW YORK HARBOUR, THE STATUE OF LIBERTY WELCOMES THEM ALL.

The Statue of Liberty was a gift from the French government to the United States on the occasion of the centennial of the American Declaration of Independence. The giant figure the French call "Liberty Enlightening the World" is the product of ten years of work by the studio of sculptor Frédéric Auguste Bartholdi. Gustave Eiffel, the builder of the Eiffel Tower, designed the statue's steel internal structure. The dedication date was meant to be 4 July 1876, but a lack of funds, which were supposed to be raised almost entirely by donations, led to delays. Finally, on 28 October 1886, US president Grover Cleveland accepted the Statue of Liberty with great fanfare on Bedloe's Island, where donations from the American side had paid for her pedestal to be built. In 1956, the island was renamed Liberty Island in her honour.

Early on, the two governments had agreed that the French would oversee the construction and transport of the statue, while the Americans secured a location and built a monumental pedestal. Both the Americans and the French agreed that the small islet in New York harbour would serve their purposes well. The star-shaped foundations of Fort Wood, already in place, would provide a stable foundation for the

Right: A look at Lady Liberty's interior framework.

Below: One of the most famous faces in the world.

pedestal, the cornerstone for which was laid in 1884. **By the time the financing** of the pedestal and site preparation costs were being discussed in America, Bartholdi and Eiffel had long been at work on the statue and her inner workings. For the exterior of a statue that would be 47 metres tall, Bartholdi chose a lightweight, copper-sheet skin no more than 2.4 mm thick. The copper would then be hammered over a specially prepared wooden form. Altogether, Bartholdi and his helpers finished 350 different pieces to be transported to Bedloe's Island by ship in July 1884. Once there, the pieces were fitted together like some kind of three-dimensional puzzle and mounted on Eiffel's steel frame.

The frame consists of four enormous iron pylons that run through the statue from bottom to top. These support elements are attached to the pedestal with strong bolts. Attached to the pylons is a filigree steel frame, to which Bartholdi's hundreds of puzzle pieces could be attached. Every piece of copper on the outer skin was stabilized by its own individual beam in order to give the statue both strength and flexibility. For the construction of his fixed framework, Eiffel made use of the fact that copper bends, folds and stretches easily. This left a lot of room for the thermal expansion and contraction of the entire structure. All in all, the Statue of Liberty is a masterpiece of the art of engineering.

Together with the classical-style socle designed by the American architect Richard M. Hunt, the total height of the statue from the base of the ground-level foundations to the tip of the gold-plated flame of the torch is around 95 metres. The seven beams radiating from her crown symbolize the seven seas. For many people who have crossed the Atlantic to come to America, the Statue of Liberty is a one-of-a-kind symbol of freedom, liberty, independence and prosperity. Hundreds of thousands of immigrants from all over the world have passed under her gaze at the entrance to New York Harbour. Arriving with high hopes and great expectations, many of them would succeed and make themselves a new home in America, but many also failed. The museum in the main hall on Ellis Island relates many such tales, both the success stories and the stories of shattered American dreams.

On the occasion of her 100th birthday in 1986, Lady Liberty received a "face lift". The salty air had so eroded her construction that extensive restoration work was necessary. Donations from citizens all over the United States covered nearly $2 million of the renovation costs. She is worth that much to them, and more.

FACTS

* **Name:** The official name of the statue, translated from the French, is "Liberty Enlightening the World". She is also known as the Statue of Liberty, Lady Liberty and Miss Liberty.
* **Design:** French sculptor Frédéric Bartholdi designed the statue. Gustave Eiffel was the engineer responsible for its steel structure. The total weight of the statue is 254 tons.
* **Size:** The statue is 46.5 m tall and stands on a 47-m-tall pedestal. 192 steps lead up to the top of the pedestal, with a further 354 steps leading up to the crown.
* **UNESCO World Heritage:** The Statue of Liberty was added to the UNESCO list of World Cultural Heritage Sites in 1984.

USA

The Golden Gate Bridge

PLANS TO BUILD A BRIDGE ACROSS THE ENTRANCE TO SAN FRANCISCO BAY WERE IN THE WORKS IN 1872, BUT CONSTRUCTION OF THE GOLDEN GATE BRIDGE ONLY BEGAN IN 1933. FOR OVER 30 YEARS, IT WAS THE LONGEST SUSPENSION BRIDGE IN THE WORLD.

The first plans came to nothing because late-nineteenth-century technology was not up to the task; architects considered the distance between the banks too great. In the early twentieth century, engineer Joseph B. Strauss took up the idea again. Stubborn and ready to meet any opposition, he insisted on his plan for the bridge. Nevertheless, a suspension bridge joining the northern and southern sides of the bay was still considered an impossible undertaking.

The preconditions for construction of a bridge of this size were formidable. The Golden Gate Straits were recognized early on as an exceedingly difficult place to build. The currents are exceptionally strong and solid, and stable bedrock in which to anchor the bridge pillars lay very deep. A further unsettling factor was that the bay was an area prone to earthquakes. Finally, shipping was heavy in the strait, which was the gateway to San Francisco Harbor. Building a bridge here would not be easy, and Strauss had his work cut out. Still, he persevered and construction of the Golden Gate Bridge began on 5 January 1933.

There were construction problems from the very beginning, particularly regarding the foundations for the southern bridge pillar. The instability of the bedrock in shallow water made it necessary to build

Two massive steel cables, each with a diameter of 92.5 cm, carry the roadbed. The cables were spun from over 27,000 individual steel wires.

FACTS

*** Building time:** Construction of the Golden Gate Bridge began on 5 January 1933. The bridge was opened on 27 May 1937.

*** Construction:** The Golden Gate Bridge is a suspension bridge with a total length of 2,727 m. The 25-m-wide roadbed is suspended from cables attached between two 227-m-tall support pillars.

*** Traffic:** There are six lanes for vehicular traffic as well as bicycle and pedestrian paths across the bridge.

*** Suicide bridge:** Since its opening, the Golden Gate Bridge has been highly attractive to would-be suicides. Over 1,100 suicides have been attempted from the bridge so far. Only a few have survived the leap from the pedestrian path some 70 m above the water's surface.

the foundations far out in the straits, 335 metres from shore, in water 30 metres deep. The current in this location was so strong that it was only possible to work underwater when the tide was turning, which allowed for no more than 20 minutes of workable time per day. Each bridge pillar is 227 metres high and constructed of modular steel units stacked on top of one another and joined together by approximately 1.2 million stainless steel rivets. In honour of the bridge's completion, the final rivet pounded into place was made of pure gold.

The roadbed is suspended from two mighty steel cables joining one side of the bay to the other. Each cable was formed by spinning 27,000 individual 5-mm wires into dense ropes of steel, each with a diameter of 92.5 cm. The cables were tied to heavy concrete anchors set on each shore.

Despite all obstacles, the Golden Gate Bridge was built and opened with great fanfare on 27 May 1937. It was a "pedestrian day", and over 200,000 people crossed the bridge on foot. Ultimately, six lanes were opened to traffic, plus a bicycle and footpath. On its first fully operational day, 32,000 vehicles drove over the Golden Gate Bridge. Today, that figure is closer to 100,000.

Joseph B. Strauss was a very careful and thorough builder. The safety and security of his workforce was a top priority. Nevertheless, eleven men died during the bridge's construction. This was an amazingly low figure for bridge projects at the time. Many more would have died working on the Golden Gate Bridge had it not been for the safety nets Strauss had strung underneath. Nineteen workers survived with minor injuries after plummeting from the bridge at breakneck speed, their lives saved by the nets. After construction was completed, those 19 workers formed the "Halfway to Hell Club".

In addition to being a major engineering achievement, the Golden Gate Bridge is frequently praised for its outstanding aesthetic appeal. With its engraved pillars, it has been referred to as the largest piece of Art Deco ever made. Strauss and his team succeeded in integrating an enormous bridge structure into the stunning panorama of San Francisco Bay and its shining city. The harmony between the technological wonder of the Golden Gate Bridge and the natural landscape is perhaps Strauss's greatest achievement. Few would be able to match it.

Centre: The bridge pillars are 227 m tall.

Bottom: A pillar emerges from the fog in the light of the morning sun over 'Frisco Bay.

USA

The Grand Canyon

VISITORS TO THE GRAND CANYON IN NORTH-WESTERN ARIZONA ARE OVERWHELMED BY THE MAJESTIC SCENERY. THE GORGE WAS FORMED AS THE COLORADO RIVER CARVED A CHANNEL THROUGH THE ROCK OF THE KAIBAB PLATEAU, IN PLACES ALMOST 2 KM DEEP.

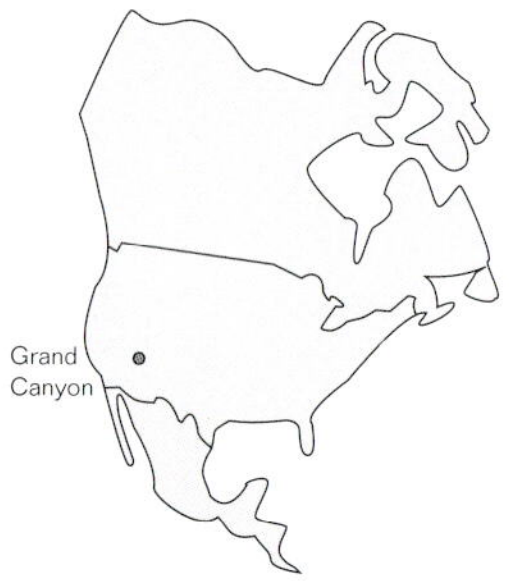

Ancient Navajo legends tell of the mythical hero Packithaawi. He brought an end to the Great Flood by taking a heavy club and pounding the Grand Canyon out of the inundated earth. Geologists estimate that the gorge formed around 40–50 million years ago as the Colorado River continually wore away the rock to make its bed.

In 1540, a troop of Spanish soldiers searching for the legendary Seven Golden Cities of Cibola came upon the rim of the ravine. Overwhelmed by what they saw before them, the men dropped onto their knees in terror and prayed. For three days they tried to find a way into the gorge, without success. When their water and supplies became low, they disappointedly returned to Mexico. With their search for the golden cities a failure, the region around the Grand Canyon was considered worthless. The magnificent ravine was soon forgotten.

In 1858, Joseph Ives sailed his steamship *Explorer* from the Gulf of California up the Colorado River. He was trying to determine the river's navigable distance, but did not get very far before running aground. Ives had to break off his expedition and turn around before reaching the Grand Canyon. It was 1869 before Major John Wesley Powell became the first man to travel the length of the Colorado

FACTS

* **Name:** Grand Canyon
* **Location:** Arizona, USA
* **Age:** 40 – 50 million years.
* **Size:** The Grand Canyon is close to 450 km long, 30 km across at its widest point and 1.8 km deep in places.
* **National Park and UNESCO World Heritage:** Grand Canyon National Park was established in 1919, one of the first in the USA, and it was added to the UNESCO list of World Heritage Sites in 1979.

River. His expedition marks the beginning of scientific investigation of the Grand Canyon.

Since Powell's trip, many scientists have followed. The Grand Canyon is a true El Dorado for geologists, with the layers of ancient bedrock exposed by the river a veritable library of the history of the Earth. Rock formations that are 1.7 billion years old have been identified here, the oldest exposed bedrock found anywhere. And the Colorado River continues to work for geologists; every day it cuts deeper into the rock, bringing new formations to light.

Two billion years ago, what is now the Grand Canyon was completely covered by an expansive sea. As the water retreated, it left large deposits of sediments behind. Volcanic eruptions covered them with glowing lava, sealing them off. Then, over millions of years, the heat and pressure generated by tectonic forces deformed the bedrock strata, pushing the layers up into tower-like formations that were pressed into mountains. Later a great sea once again flooded the region and the entire process began anew, with new layers of sediment and volcanic stone laid down over the strata already in existence.

Forty or fifty million years ago, the Rocky Mountains were created as tectonic forces raised the land south of the canyon by some 3,000 metres. It is this uplift that provided the necessary gradient for the Colorado River to begin cutting through the rock, a process accelerated during the melting at the end of the ice ages. The majority of the depth of the Grand Canyon was cut as recently as 1.2 million years ago.

Today, the elevation of the land around the Grand Canyon is around 1,000 metres lower than it was at the time of the tectonic uplift. The ongoing process of differential erosion is responsible for most of the loss. Some day, far, far in the future, the Grand Canyon itself will cease to exist.

The Grand Canyon offers breathtaking views and vistas in every direction.

Above: The Havasu Waterfalls fall into the Colorado River at the base of the Grand Canyon.

Left: Over the course of millions of years the Colorado River has cut its channel deep in the Kaibab Plateau.

USA

The Guggenheim Museum

FRANK LLOYD WRIGHTS' MOST MAGNIFICENT WORK IS LOCATED RIGHT ON 5TH AVENUE IN THE HEART OF MANHATTAN. WITH ITS RADICAL DESIGN AND UNIQUE BEAUTY, THE GUGGENHEIM MUSEUM BEARS WITNESS TO THE ARCHITECT'S CREATIVE GENIUS.

In 1943, artist Hilla von Rebay was the personal curator of industrialist and art collector Solomon R. Guggenheim. It was she who chose star architect Frank Lloyd Wright to design a museum to house part of Guggenheim's extensive private collection of modern art. Originally named the Museum of Non-Objective Painting, it was bursting at the seams on opening day in 1959. The invited politicians, art lovers and general public were amazed by what they saw, and not entirely complimentary. But there was one thing that everyone could agree on: Wright's museum definitely broke the mould.

In a 1943 letter to Wright, von Rebay described her idea for a new museum for the Guggenheim collection. She wrote: "I need a fighter, a lover of space, a tester and a wise man, ... I want a temple of spirit, a monument!" At first, Wright showed little interest. He made no secret of his dislike of the original site chosen for the museum in New York.

Finally, after a long period of discussion and negotiation, Hilla von Rebay, Solomon R. Guggenheim and Frank Lloyd Wright agreed on a different site in Manhattan. The chosen plot was on 5th Avenue, near Central Park. Proximity to the park had been one of Wright's conditions. The new museum would celebrate the symbiosis between architecture and

DATES

✲ **1937:** The Solomon R. Guggenheim foundation was founded.

✲ **1939:** The first Museum of Non-Objective Painting housing the Guggenheim collection was opened in a New York townhouse.

✲ **1943:** Frank Lloyd Wright began designing the current building.

✲ **1956–59:** The Guggenheim Museum was constructed on Fifth Avenue.

✲ **1991–92:** The building was completely restored and expanded.

With the Guggenheim Museum Frank Lloyd Wright created a masterpiece, one that continues to attract art lovers and architects from all over the world.

nature. The building was designed to bring art, architecture and nature into harmonic unison with the hectic life of a densely populated city.

Wright spent many years designing the new building, and construction only began in 1956. By that time Solomon R. Guggenheim, the museum's patron, was no longer alive. He had died in 1949.

Today, the Guggenheim Museum in New York is one of the most famous contemporary art showcases in the world. It is not just the art that is outstanding; the building itself continues to attract art lovers and architects from all over the world. Visitors stand before the Guggenheim Museum in amazement. In his effort to join architecture and nature, Wright designed a building that is organic right down to its basic structure, which resembles a snail shell.

Inside, a ramp spirals upwards along the walls, creating a space that gives the impression of being open on all sides. Exhibitions begin on the top floor and follow the ramp down. Visitors' visual perspective is constantly changed and refined as they move around the space, providing them with what is literally a new "point of view" with every step. The details of the interior space are a symphony of triangles, ovals, circles and squares. The forms repeat and rearrange themselves, creating a fantastic spatial environment.

Critics accused Frank Lloyd Wright of subordinating the art to the architecture, which they claimed overwhelmed the many superb works of art on exhibit rather than enhancing them. Wright disagreed, and defended his building as a complete symbiosis of architecture and art in which both were equally represented, working together in perfect harmony. History has shown him to be correct. The works of art from the Guggenheim collection in New York are today as famous as the museum Frank Lloyd Wright designed to house them.

Above: Patron and art collector Solomon R. Guggenheim (1861–1949) died before construction of the museum that bears his name began.

Left: Inside the building a spiral ramp winds its way to the top.

USA

The Hoover Dam

WHEN THE HOOVER DAM WAS COMPLETED ON THE COLORADO RIVER AT THE BORDER BETWEEN NEVADA AND ARIZONA, IT WAS THE WORLD'S LARGEST DAM BY ANY MEASURE. IT WAS ALSO IMMEDIATELY RECOGNIZED AS A MODERN WONDER OF THE WORLD.

In reality, the Hoover Dam isn't really a dam, but a retaining wall blocking the Colorado River at Black Canyon some 50 km south-east of Las Vegas, Nevada. The concrete colossus rises over 220 metres from base to crown. It holds back Lake Mead, the largest artificial reservoir in the United States.

Technically, the Hoover Dam is a concrete arch-gravity wall, bowed in the direction of Lake Mead. It is the arc of the wall that supports the immense mass of what can be as much as 35 billion cubic metres of water. Building the dam wall was the greatest engineering challenge of its time. The high temperatures of the summer months, as high as 50 °C, plagued the construction with problems from the very beginning. The temperature made it impossible to simply pour the concrete on-site all at once. Had this been attempted, the desert heat would have kept the concrete from setting completely for 125 years. Instead, it was decided to try a different technique. The engineers assembled the Hoover Dam from individual concrete blocks that would be cast on-site.

Piping was run through the block moulds and the pipes filled with ice water to help the concrete cool down quickly. Once it had cooled sufficiently, the pipes themselves were also filled with concrete.

FACTS

✻ Building time: The Hoover Dam was built between 1931 and 1935. Construction costs totalled $165 billion.

✻ Generating electricity: The power plant went into commission on 12 September 1936. It now has 17 modern turbines generating around 2,000 MW electricity per year. This equals more than 4 billion KWh of electricity, enough to cover the energy needs of 1.3 million Americans living in the south-western states.

✻ Building material: The Hoover Dam is built of 2.6 million m^3 of concrete and weighs around 6.6 million tons.

✻ Size of the lake: Lake Mead is 177 km long, with an area of 640 km^2 and 885 km of coastline. Its maximum depth is 180 m, and its capacity is up to 35 billion m^3 of water.

The dam wall is 221 m high, 379 m long and 14 m wide at its crown. The foundations of the dam extend 200 m underwater.

This also helped increase the stability of the structure. The pipes functioned like the metal bars used in modern reinforced concrete (rebars), and also bound the blocks tightly to one another. Each block was a uniform 1.5 metres tall, with the other dimensions varying, based on where the block fit into the wall. The smallest was 7.6 x 7.6 metres and the largest was 7.6 x 18 metres. Around 2.6 million cubic metres of concrete were built into the dam, a quantity that is difficult to imagine. It is enough concrete to build a 5-metre-wide, 20-cm-thick road stretching across the United States, from San Francisco to New York.

The Colorado River had to be diverted so that the building site would be dry during construction. Enormous tunnels were driven through both cliff faces of the valley to draw off the water. Four tunnels were bored altogether, the largest with a diameter of 17 metres and a length of 5 km. Approximately 3,500 workmen worked on the dam full time, 96 of whom died in construction accidents.

The original estimate for the cost of building this ambitious dam came to $49 billion. In the end, however, the actual total was more than three times that much; a staggering $165 billion. The construction costs were so high that income generated by the sale of electricity and through tourism only paid them off in 1985. Since then, finally, the Hoover Dam has been out of the red and earning a profit.

During the design phase the name attached to the project was "Boulder Dam", a name that better described the original location for the dam. Geological investigation, however, showed that the Black Canyon site would be much more favourable. Its current name is in memory of the 31st president of the United States, Herbert Hoover, the instigator and greatest champion of this most daring and wondrous dam project of his time.

Above: The turbines in the Hoover Dam power plant generate electricity for the south-western states and California.

Left: The Hoover Dam is a masterpiece of engineering.

USA

Mount Rushmore

NESTLED IN THE BLACK HILLS OF SOUTH DAKOTA, MOUNT RUSHMORE NATIONAL MEMORIAL CONSISTS OF FOUR COLOSSAL PORTRAITS OF US PRESIDENTS CARVED OUT OF A CLIFF FACE, A WORK OF ART THAT IS THE MOST AMERICAN OF ALL AMERICAN WONDERS.

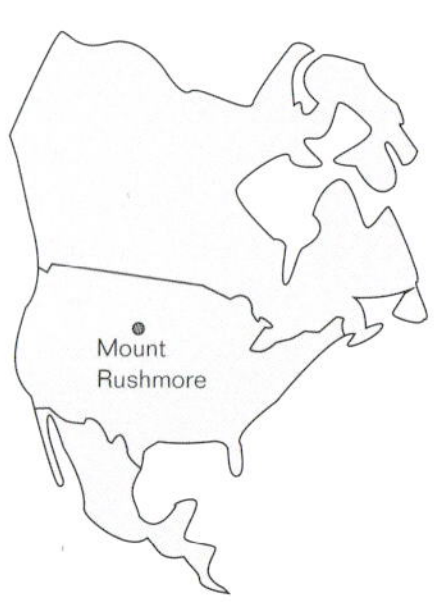

It was the sculptor and painter Gutzon Borglum (1867–1941) who came up with the concept of a powerful, everlasting national monument. He wanted his sculpture to embody the principles and ideals of the American nation. Colossal portrait heads of four great US presidents fit his vision perfectly.

The impetus for the monument was a serendipitous meeting of minds. Doane Robinson, the state historian of South Dakota, wanted a tourist attraction to draw visitors to the Black Hills region. In 1923, he invited Borglum, who was at the time well-known for his monumental historical works, to design a gigantic sculpture depicting four important American Presidents: George Washington, Father of the Country; Thomas Jefferson, author of the Declaration of Independence; Abraham Lincoln, who kept the country from being divided during the Civil War; and Theodore Roosevelt, builder of the Panama Canal and protector of thousands of acres of wilderness. Borglum chose the site of Mount Rushmore and began chiselling out the portraits on 10 August 1927.

Borglum and nearly 400 workers toiled on the enormous project under less than ideal conditions. Unfavourable weather kept them from working on the mountain except during late spring and summer.

Right: Abraham Lincoln is honoured because he kept the country from being divided by fighting the Civil War. With the Emancipation Proclamation, he ended slavery.

Below: The giant portrait head of George Washington gazes out over the Black Hills of South Dakota.

It took them 14 consecutive years to finish the sculptures, chiselling, hammering, boring and dynamiting Borglum's dream into the rock. The artist would not live to see its completion. Borglum died on 6 March 1941, seven months before his son, Lincoln, directed the work to its completion. Mount Rushmore National Memorial was officially dedicated on 31 October 1941.

Gutzon Borglum planned his project down to the very last detail. Each portrait would be between 18 and 20 metres tall. Over 450,000 tons of stone had to be blasted away before the finer work could begin. The coarse fashioning of the figures was done using jackhammers and dynamite. The positioning of the explosive charges was so precisely worked out by Borglum and his demolition specialists that more than 90 per cent of all the stone cut away for the sculptures could be removed using these labour-efficient methods. He also developed a specialized variety of jackhammer that left a smooth surface behind. The final, extraordinarily difficult fine work was supervised by Borglum himself. Working on the steep rock wall was labourious, exhausting and dangerous. The stone of Mount Rushmore is an extremely hard variety, called Harney Peak granite. It is notoriously difficult to work. While its resistance to weathering was one of the reasons Borglum chose the site in the first place, the granite's density forced him to change his original plans. The portraits of Thomas Jefferson and Abraham Lincoln, in particular, had to be extensively altered.

The project was first financed entirely by private donations and the corporate support of the powerful railways that hoped to profit by shuttling tourists to and from the remote site. The monuments' financing only became secure after the US government took over the project in 1938. The total cost of the Mount Rushmore National Memorial was exactly $989,992.32.

A team of experts watches over Mount Rushmore National Memorial continually for signs of instability, including fissures that could lead to rock falls. Once a year, geologists and demolition experts set off small, controlled explosions as a preventative measure. Tiny cracks are filled in with a special silicon-based cement. The presidential portraits themselves are most affected by the extreme variations in temperature, because even the hardest rock can fracture as it expands and contracts. Erosion is much less of a problem: Harnery Peak Granite weathers less than 1 cm over the course of 200,000 years. Conservation of the memorial currently costs the US government around $250,000 each year.

FACTS

* **Location:** Mount Rushmore is located in the Black Hills of South Dakota. It is named after the New York lawyer Charles Rushmore, the original owner of the mineral rights for the land.

* **Controversy:** The monument has long been a subject of controversy. The local Lakota Native American tribes consider the mountain, which they call Six Grandfathers, part of their traditional territory. They see the sculptures as a desecration of a sacred mountain. The Black Hills Crazy Horse monument, a colossal sculpture of the "spirit" of the Lakota chief, is located nearby.

* **Movie scene:** Film director Alfred Hitchcock used Mount Rushmore as the setting for the breathtaking conclusion to the film *North by Northwest* (1959), in which his star, Cary Grant, dangles from Abraham Lincoln's nose.

CANADA AND THE USA

Niagara Falls

NIAGARA FALLS IS PROBABLY THE MOST IMPRESSIVE AND SPECTACULAR NATIONAL BORDER ON EARTH. LOCATED 100 KM SOUTH OF TORONTO, THE MASSIVE CASCADE DEFINES THE BOUNDARY BETWEEN NEW YORK STATE AND THE PROVINCE OF ONTARIO.

The Niagara River, the waterway that connects Lake Erie with Lake Ontario, plummets more than 50 metres over a brink more than 1,000 metres wide, an awesome display of nature that takes one's breath away. The Niagara Falls are one of the most beautiful natural wonders of the North American continent.

The Niagara Falls have changed a great deal since they were first sighted in 1678 by Jesuit priest Louis Hennepin. While erosion, the natural result of centuries of cascading water, has played a role in changing the falls' looks, the changes are also to a large extent the result of human interference. It is the extent of the latter that is currently being re-evaluated by environmentalists and conservationists.

At the end of the last Ice Age, 12,000 years ago, the retreat of an enormous glacier carved out the five Great Lakes: Superior, Michigan, Huron, Ontario and Erie. The melt-water from the glacier filled Lake Erie to the point where it overflowed. This led to the formation of the Niagara River, which cascades over a cliff known as the Niagara Escarpment into Lake Ontario. The Niagara Falls are made up of three separate waterfalls. The Horseshoe Falls, by far the largest, are located on the Canadian side of the border, with the American and Bridal Veil Falls on

FACTS

✻ Location and size: Niagara Falls straddles both Canada and the United States. They are 1,155 m wide, with 792 m on the Canadian side and 363 m on the American.

✻ Height: The tallest part of the falls is 58 m above the water level in the plunge basin.

✻ Water mass: Up to 6,000 m^3 of water per second flow over Niagara Falls, 90 per cent of it over Horseshoe Falls on the Canadian side.

✻ Erosion: In 1931, 70,000 tons of rock fell from the cliff face on the American side. A few years later 27,000 tons fell from the cliff under Horseshoe Falls in Canada. Another major rock fall on the American side took place in 1954, when 170,000 tons thundered down.

✻ Rare freezing: If it gets cold enough, Niagara Falls can freeze completely. The last time this happened was in the winter of 1936.

The Niagara River and Niagara Falls lie on the border between Canada and the United States.

the American side. The waterfalls are separated by a chain of small islands, of which Goat Island on the Canadian side is the most famous. Some 90 per cent of the Niagara River water mass cascades over the Horseshoe Falls, and the remaining 10 per cent falls in American territory.

The bedrock underneath the Niagara Escarpment is quite unusual. The surface is hard dolomite that resists weathering. The lower part, however, is slate, which is prone to erosion and greatly affected by the cascading water of the falls. The slate breaks up, undermining the hard dolomite layer above, eventually causing large parts of the escarpment to break off and fall into the river bed below. Up to 2 metres of bedrock collapse this way every year, which is why the Niagara Falls have receded some 11 km back upriver since the first scientific survey of their position over 200 years ago. Human intervention has interfered with this natural process. The energy industry has long been diverting the Niagara River to supply electricity to industrial areas in the Great Lakes area. This has dampened the force of the water flowing over the falls, effectively halting erosion.

Nevertheless, extensive industrial use of the Niagara River as an energy source is not without controversy. So many hydroelectric plants feed off the river near Niagara Falls that when they are all operational, they reduce the maximum 6,000 cubic metres of water per second that naturally falls over the escarpment by half. The Niagara River and its falls are today a completely regulated system, controlled by the press of a button. During the tourist season visitors are treated to a foaming torrent of water sending spray kilometres into the air. But once the last tour bus has departed, the water is diverted through hydroelectric plants to generate electricity upstream, diminishing the power of the mighty falls.

Above: The 160-m Skylon Tower in the city of Niagara Falls, Ontario, offers panoramic views.

Left: The Niagara Falls are without a doubt one of the most beautiful natural wonders in the world.

USA

Old Faithful

YELLOWSTONE NATIONAL PARK, IN THE NORTH-WEST OF WYOMING, WAS FOUNDED IN MARCH 1872. THE OLDEST NATIONAL PARK IN THE WORLD IS FAMED FOR ITS GEOTHERMAL LANDSCAPE AND ITS GEYSERS, INCLUDING THE REMARKABLY REGULAR OLD FAITHFUL.

They bubble, burble and smoke: unbelievably, over 60 per cent of all the natural hot springs in the world are found within Yellowstone National Park in Wyoming. Of the over 300 geysers in the park, the one called Old Faithful is probably the most famous. It is not the largest – that title belongs to the nearby Steamboat geyser – but is certainly the most diligent and dependable. Old Faithful currently erupts at regular intervals of between 60 and 120 minutes, spouting anywhere from 14,00 to 32,000 litres of water vertically into the air. It is a magnificent performance.

Geysers are hot springs from which water shoots forth, regularly or irregularly, as if from a fountain. They are formed by a specific combination of geological and climatic conditions. Old Faithful bubbles and steams in the middle of Yellowstone Park's upper Geyser Basin. It was officially discovered in 1870 and was the first geyser in the region to be named. Since then, tens of thousands of visitors, as well as a good many scientists, keep Old Faithful under near constant observation. This is how we know that the geyser has erupted more than a million times since records began to be kept in the late nineteenth century. At that time, the geyser followed a schedule as if set by a Swiss watch. On average, Old Faithful

Lights, camera and...action! Old Faithful shoots forth a fountain of water as high as 55 m against the backdrop of a blue sky in Yellowstone National Park.

FACTS

✻ Location: Yellowstone National Park is mostly in Wyoming, with smaller parts in Idaho and Montana. It is the oldest National Park in the world, founded on 1 March 1872. It was added to the UNESCO list of World Natural Heritage Sites in 1978.

✻ Etymology: The name "Yellowstone" comes from the gold-coloured stones found in the canyons and gorges of the Yellowstone River.

✻ Area: Yellowstone National Park has a total area of 8,983 km², an area larger than 6 of the 50 US states. It is 39 km long and 86 km wide at its greatest point.

✻ Highest and lowest points: The highest point in the park is Eagle Peak, at 3,462 m. The lowest point is near the north entrance gate, at 1,620 m.

now erupts every 91 minutes, spewing a column of boiling water and steam from the interior of the Earth high up into the air. Each eruption lasts between 2½ and 5 minutes, in which tens of thousands of gallons of hot water and water vapor shoot forth from the ground under immense pressure. The column of water shoots between 30 and 55 metres high, generating a cloud of steam and water vapour visible from afar.

Old Faithful is categorized as a cone geyser, which means that it erupts with a narrow, steady jet of water emerging from a small channel that extends 7 metres below the ground, yet has a diameter of just over 11 cm. The water, at a temperature of 118 °C to 129 °C, shoots forth through this channel at high pressure, literally exploding through the surface of the Earth.

Yellowstone National Park has such a large number of geysers, hot springs and mud pots due to an enormous magma chamber lying directly underneath it. All of central Yellowstone is really an enormous volcanic crater, a caldera that formed over 600,000 years ago during a series of major eruptions. The specific eruption that formed the caldera was so powerful that it shook the entire planet, causing the magma chamber to collapse near the surface. Originally filled with lava, later eruptions, some comparably strong, emptied the caldera once again.

Ever since then, the Earth's crust at this location has been remarkably thin, only a few kilometres thick. Rain and melt-water easily seep through the fissures and cracks down to the volcanic bedrock. On the way down, the water is heated to very high temperatures by the molten rock. The boiling water leads to the build-up of intense pressure below the ground, forcing the water back to the surface where it shoots out like a fountain.

Old Faithful is not the only geothermal feature attracting scientific attention. The behaviour of all 300 Yellowstone geysers is closely monitored. Any change in their eruption rhythm – for example, as the result of earthquakes – is meticulously recorded and analysed. Research shows that the magma chamber underneath Yellowstone Park has erupted just three times, at intervals of 600,000 years. Everyone agrees that there is little doubt that it will erupt again. When it will erupt, however, is something no one can say with certainty.

Centre: The Grand Prismatic Pool is famous for its magnificent colours.

Below: Geothermal features bubble and boil all over the place in Yellowstone National Park.

USA

Redwood National Park

THREE STATE PARKS WERE JOINED IN 1968 AND 1994 TO FORM REDWOOD NATIONAL PARK IN NORTHERN CALIFORNIA. THE PARK WAS FOUNDED TO ENSURE THE PROTECTION OF THE LAST CONIFEROUS RAINFOREST WITH ITS SOARING, ANCIENT GIANT REDWOOD TREES.

Today, the region where the giant trees grow is limited to a narrow coastal strip extending from the Oregon border to central California. The redwood and giant sequoia trees can still be seen here on the Pacific coast, but destruction of their environment through years of irresponsible logging has greatly reduced their number. At the time the national park was formed, 90 per cent of all the redwood trees in the American Pacific North-west were already gone.

The native inhabitants of America had lived in the redwood forests for thousands of years in harmony with nature. White men knew nothing of the region before the nineteenth century. Jedediah Strong Smith came across what is today national parkland in 1828 searching for new hunting grounds with a group of fur trappers.

The first wave of emigration to northern California came in 1848 with the Gold Rush. The big logging companies arrived along with the gold seekers and other adventurers. They immediately began systematically cutting down the giant trees as quickly as they could. The demand was great. The wood was dense, but easily split into planks because of its linear grain. It was also resistant to both insect infestation and decay. The Native Americans were pushed out, with the last survivors forced to resettle on reserva-

Right: Redwood National Park has been recognized as a biosphere preservation zone since 1983.

Below: The trunk of a coastal sequoia can have a diameter of up to 11 m.

tions. The Gold Rush was over almost as quickly as it began, but the logging industry stayed, and unrestricted exploitation of the forest continued. There were also those who sought to preserve the forest. Jedediah Strong Smith was one of the first to warn of the consequences of clear-cutting the redwoods.

Unfortunately, logging companies paid no heed to the warnings. By 1965, the redwood forest had been reduced to 15 per cent of its original stand. In 1968, the US government was able to set aside a relatively small area of 430 km² for a national park. This was only around one-third of the 1,200 km² area where redwood trees could still be found. In the areas outside the protected zone, the destruction continued undiminished. The national park reached its current extent in 1994, when three small groves under state protection were added to the federal preserve. Still, this left almost half the known redwood trees without protection.

The coastal redwoods (*Sequoia sempervirens*) and the related giant sequoia (*Sequoiadendron giganteum*) belong to the same family – the cypresses. They owe their name to the distinctive red-brown core of their wood. Trees in the cypress family dominated the planet some 250 million years ago, when they were widespread. Changes in climate reduced the size of once extensive redwood forests.

In the wet climate of the Pacific North-west, monoculture redwood forests were once common. These giant trees can live for 2,000 years, growing to a height of over 100 metres. This is due to the presence of a chemical substance in their bark that protects it from wood beetles, fungi and other infestations. Sadly, this innate biological protection against decay is one of the characteristics that made the redwoods so attractive to loggers. The largest sequoia known, based on volume, is 'General Sherman'. Its trunk would produce an astonishing 1,500 cubic metres of wood. The logging companies are said to have cut down trees that were still larger.

The tallest sequoia in Redwood National Park is called the 'Stratosphere Giant'. The name is certainly fitting for a tree that is 113 metres tall with a diameter of 6 metres. It is currently the tallest tree on Earth, and is estimated to be at least 600 years old. Keeping in mind that redwoods can live for 2,000 years, one can only wonder how tall this Giant will grow as it enters the prime of its life.

The coastal redwoods and giant sequoia remain in demand. Only extensive measures for their protection and preservation, as in Redwood National Park, can save these wondrous trees.

FACTS

* **Redwood National Park** was founded in 1968 when 430 km² were placed under protection of the US government. The national park later absorbed three smaller state preserves: Prairie Creek State Park, Del Norte Coast State Park and Jedediah Smith Redwoods State Park.
* **Redwoods:** The redwoods have been on the UNESCO list of World Natural Heritage Sites since 1983. In that same year the national park was recognized as a biosphere preservation zone.
* **Unique:** Along with other natural wonders and beauties of the land, the giant redwoods are among America's most unique treasures. The trees are referred to again and again in poems, novels and songs. Folksinger Woody Guthrie immortalized redwood forests in his song, "This Land is Your Land", written in 1943.

USA

Volcanoes National Park

HAWAII IS OFTEN ASSOCIATED WITH ITS SANDY BEACHES, SURFERS, GIGANTIC WAVES, FLOWER LEIS AND HULA DANCERS. YET THE FIFTIETH STATE TO JOIN THE UNION HAS MORE TO OFFER IN ONE OF THE WORLD'S MOST UNIQUE NATIONAL PARKS.

The earth and rock beneath this dreamy South Sea island is seething. The entire island chain of Hawaii is of relatively recent volcanic origin: its 137 islands and islets are the peaks of an undersea volcanic ridge. The archipelago lies directly above the edge of the great Pacific tectonic plate, which is moving 10 cm to the north-west every year. The volcanoes of Hawaii's Volcanoes National Park are on the main island of Hawaii, locally called "Big Island". They are the most active volcanoes in the world. Measured from the floor of the sea, they are also among the world's tallest mountains.

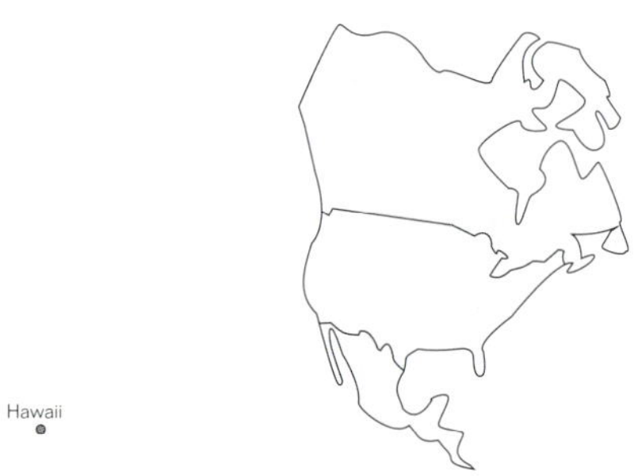

The national park was founded on 1 August 1916, and was originally called Hawaii National Park. The over 1,300 km² park was rededicated under its current name in 1961. Hawaii Volcanoes National Park encompasses a unique and complex ecosystem ranging from black sand beaches to fire-spewing mountains.

With an elevation of 4,169 metres above sea level, Mauna Loa is the tallest volcano on Earth. Its base actually lies far below in one of the deepest parts of the Pacific Ocean, adding 5,000 metres to that figure. This gives Mauna Loa a total height of over 9,100 metres, making it taller than Mount Everest (8,848 metres). Mauna Loa's "little brother" is

Right: Kilauea spews liquid lava hundreds of metres into the air.

Below: The 4,169-m summit of Mauna Loa is frequently covered in snow.

Kilauea. Not nearly as large as Mauna Loa, Kilauea has long held the title of the most active volcano in the world. Both mountains are shield volcanoes, as are Hawaii's other major volcanoes. On the Big Island scientists can directly investigate the volcanic activity that created the Hawaiian Islands.

The locals have a legend explaining why Kilauea is always erupting, sometimes violently. Native Hawaiians say that Kilauea's crater, the Halemaumau, is the home of the fire goddess Pele, who is moody and irritable. Whenever she's in a particularly bad mood her fiery temperament leads her to behave badly. Enraged and out of control, she spits fire and hot lava everywhere. When Pele manages to calm down, she falls into a restful sleep. No one can tell how long she will remain at peace. To placate the fiery goddess, and above all to keep her from becoming enraged, locals would leave gifts at the edge of the crater for Pele. This custom continues today.

Geologists explain Kilauea's frequent eruptions more scientifically. The most common explanation is the so-called hot spot theory. A 'hot spot' is any area that experiences volcanic activity over a long period of time rather than intermittent violent eruptions. The theory presupposes the existence of chambers beneath the Earth from which magma rises slowly to the surface, rather than explosively. The Pacific tectonic plate floats on a giant magma lake. The pressure exerted by the process of continental drift forces it to the surface. When this happens under the sea, a new island is created, one that will remain volcanically active. It is therefore no surprise that Kilauea is in a constant state of eruption, spewing out thin strands of glowing lava day and night. The lava collects in pools, or flows like a river down to the sea, which is permanently covered by a cloud of fine steam in the area around this mountain of fire.

The landscape and vegetation on the volcanic slopes is particularly impressive. Despite the high level of local volcanic activity, Mauna Loa is frequently covered in snow. Lichens and ferns grow on its lower slopes, right alongside freshly cooled lava. Older lava fields are covered in thick tropical rainforest. The south-western flank of the volcanic massif, which receives very little precipitation is, in contrast, a desolate landscape known as the Kau Desert. There the sharp edges and cliffs formed by lava flow stand out starkly against the horizon. The landscape remains stark because it is not subject to the weathering effect of heavy rain. On that side of the volcano, the lava flows almost daily over the cliffs and down to the sea, which boils from its heat.

FACTS

* **Foundation:** Hawaii Volcanoes National Park was founded on the island of Hawaii on 1 August 1916. Its total area today is 1,309 km^2.

* **Elevation:** The national park ranges in elevation from sea level to 4,169 m above sea level at the summit of Mauna Loa, the highest mountain on the island. Measured from the sea floor, it is the highest mountain on Earth at over 9,100 m.

* **Eruptions:** Since 1983, Kilauea has been erupting without pause. It has long been the most active volcano in the world.

* **UNESCO World Heritage:** Hawaii Volcanoes National Park was named a UNESCO World Natural Heritage Site in 1987.

USA

Yosemite National Park

CONSERVATIONIST JOHN MUIR DESCRIBED THE YOSEMITE VALLEY IN CALIFORNIA'S SIERRA NEVADA RANGE AS "NATURE'S MOST GLORIOUS WONDER". NATIVE AMERICANS TRIBES CALLED IT AHWAHNEE, "THE VALLEY THAT LOOKS LIKE A GAPING MOUTH".

Yosemite National Park is world famous. It is nature, pure and simple, and very likely the most magnificent national park on the continent. On the UNESCO list of World Natural Heritage Sites since 1984, its vast forests, prominent granite dome formations, giant trees and wide variety of plant and animal life make it a unique ecological treasure. Even its waterfalls are spectacular. One of them is the tallest in the United States.

The aboriginal inhabitants of the valley seem to have been overpowered by the beauty of the valley before them, or at least this is the impression one gets from their myths and legends. The Miwok people, for example, say they lived here for many generations until sometime in the eighteenth century, when their numbers were greatly reduced by "the black sickness", probably plague. Years later they returned to the valley of their fathers to find it had been occupied by another tribe. There was a confrontation, which led to the Miwok's changing the valley's name to Yosemite. In the Miwok language, Yosemite means "those who kill", a likely reference to the fierceness of the Paiute tribes who hunted there.

Yosemite's incredible natural beauty draws visitors from all over the world. The national park is like a treasure chest full of nature's most precious jewels.

FACTS

✻ **John Muir:** John Muir (1838–1914) was a pioneering conservationist known as the "Father of the national park". The author, adventurer, inventor, geologist and engineer is depicted on the back of the California State quarter.

✻ **Pohono:** Local tribes called Bridal Veil Falls "Pohono", which means 'Spirit of the Puffing Wind'. According to legend, one spring day a maiden was pulled inside the waterfall's curtain of mist. Her friends searched for her in vain. Her spirit became one with the cascading waterfall.

✻ **Sierra Nevada:** The Sierra Nevada Mountains are a high mountain range running 600 km through California and Nevada. Their highest peak is Mount Whitney, at 4,418 m.

There are several stunning waterfalls in Yosemite National Park.

Its four major waterfalls include Yosemite Falls, which at almost 800 metres is the tallest in the United States. Vernal Falls, a churning wall of white water, cascades down a nearly vertical cliff face. Nevada Falls is as wild and primal as the Sierra Nevada itself. Last but not least is Bridal Veil Falls, a torrent of ice-cold water cascading into a valley.

Prominent rock features known as granite domes are found at Yosemite. These soaring monoliths include the famous El Capitan (2,307 metres) and Half Dome (2,695 metres). Rock climbers are drawn to their 1,000-metre walls, but they are nearly vertical and rubbed smooth by glacial moraine, presenting a serious challenge. Half Dome was formed some 85 million years ago. It is hard to imagine the incredible temperatures and force that must have been at work to force a giant rock like this out of the Earth.

Yosemite's plant and animal life is also impressive. In the Mariposa Grove, a giant tree lies fallen on its side. Its name is The Fallen Monarch. Because sequoias, indeed, all redwoods, don't decay like other trees, no one knows how long ago it fell. Yosemite is home to at least 37 different kinds of trees, including giant sequoias that are over 2,000 years old. Rare pines and fir trees predominate. Yosemite is also home to some 1,400 different plants, 74 kinds of mammals and 230 species of birds. Coyotes, bighorn sheep, marmots and black bears roam the forests and mountainsides.

In 1864, landscape architect Frederick Law Olmstead was one of the first to call for Yosemite's protection. He described it as home to "the deepest beauty of nature, not in one feature or another, not in one part of one scene or another, not any landscape that can be framed by itself, but all around and wherever the visitor goes". It would be a generation before Yosemite's future was secured.

Above: Half Dome (2,695m) is covered in snow during winter.

Left: Local tribes called Bridal Veil Falls "Pohono", which means 'Spirit of the Puffing Wind'.

"Down Under" in Australia and New Zealand, breathtaking natural wonders have been fascinating indigenous peoples and visitors alike for thousands of years. On land and underwater, nature's paradise never fails to amaze. Ancient cult sites and masterpieces of modern architecture are the icing on the cake.

OCEANIA

AUSTRALIA

The Great Barrier Reef

THE GREAT BARRIER REEF RUNS PARALLEL TO AUSTRALIA'S EASTERN COAST. COMPOSED OF LIVING ORGANISMS, IT HAS BEEN CALLED NATURE'S GREATEST CONSTRUCTION SITE. THE ABORIGINES OF NORTHERN AUSTRALIA CALL IT 'WAGA GABOO'– THE GREAT REEF.

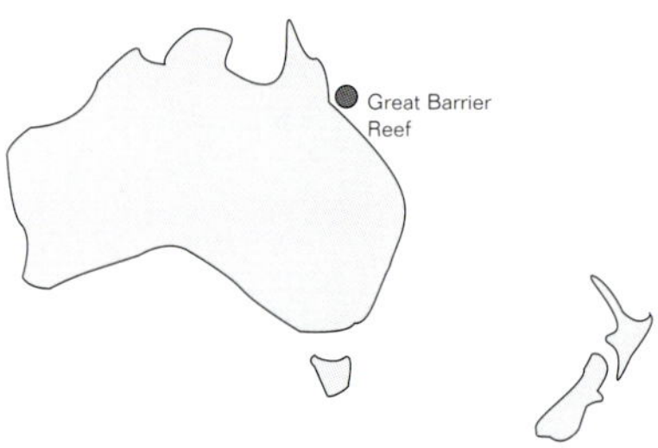

Great, indeed: over 2,300 km long, Australia's famous coral reef covers an area greater than all of Italy. Millions of coral polyps, among the world's tiniest creatures, are the architects of nature's greatest construction, building a unique ecosystem and imposing natural monument. The "foundations" of this fascinating paradise were laid millions of years ago. The Great Barrier Reef, the largest coral reef on Earth, was voted one of Seven Natural Wonders of the World in a poll of the international news organization CNN and became a UNESCO World Natural Heritage Site in 1981.

Although European's discovery of the gigantic coral reef off Australia's eastern coast was almost entirely by chance, it is unlikely that any ship captain forgot his first encounter with the razor sharp banks of coral just below the water's surface. On the night of 11 June 1770, the *Endeavour*, captained by the explorer James Cook, ran aground on the Great Barrier Reef. Until that point, the reef had never appeared on a European nautical map. The damage was such that the ship was nearly lost. After extensive repairs Cook was able to continue his journey north along the reef, and in mid-August 1770 he discovered what is today called Cook's Passage, the best and safest way through the Great Barrier.

Right: Every year, humpback whales give birth to their young near the reef.

Below: The reef shark is one of the greatest predators in the sea.

Cook must have been amazed as he completed a survey and cartography of the reef. His measurements would show that the Great Barrier Reef ran between the 10th and 24th southern lines of latitude, making it more than 2,300 km long with an area of 347,800 km². It begins on the north-west coast of Australia off what is now Queensland and continues into the Torres Straits of Papua New Guinea, terminating near Lady Elliot Island. It lies directly on the edge of the Australian continental plate. The reef is only 30 km off the Australian coast near Cairns, and as far as 250 km off the shore of Gladstone. Given its extreme size, the Great Barrier Reef is more easily understood divided into four sections, called the Far Northern, the Cairns, the Central and the Mackay Capricorn Reefs.

The entire Great Barrier lies in the tropical zone in an area frequently threatened by typhoons. The oldest section of the reef is the Far Northern, which, based on deep cores into sediments far below, may have come into being some 20 to 25 million years ago. The first clear reef structure is 500,000 years old. The so-called "living reef" of organisms dates to the last glacial period some 20,000 years ago. The reef itself is really a continuous chain of over 2,900 individual reef structures, 1,000 small islands and thousands of shifting sandbanks. The reef can only be seen in its entirety from outer space.

Every year, with the first warm days of summer, a marvellous performance takes place around the Waga Gaboo. A few days after the full moon, when the water temperature climbs and the ocean currents are at their weakest, millions of tiny coral polyps release their genetic material into the ocean, where it combines before being washed out into the open sea. Theoretically, any fertilized coral egg has the ability to start a new coral reef.

Less than a square kilometre of living coral reef produces 4 tons of limestone exoskeleton. The Great Barrier Reef is therefore constantly growing, providing an ever-larger ecological niche for countless plant and animal species. There are 359 different types of reef coral at work on nature's largest construction. Eighty types of soft corals attach themselves to the rock. The reef is home to 1,500 different sponges and 5,000 other invertebrates, many living deep in cracks and crevasses; 800 spiny echinoderms, a class that includes starfish and sea urchins, live there too. Over 1,500 kinds of fish frequent these waters, feeding and seeking shelter. For large predators, like the reef shark, the Great Barrier Reef is the perfect hunting ground. Mother nature has set a rich table, and not

FACTS

*** Location:** The Great Barrier Reef is part of Australia. It is located between the 10th and 24th southern latitudes. It is 2,300 km long and covers an expanse of 347,800 km².

*** Age:** The oldest part of the reef, the Far Northern section, may be over 20 million years old.

*** Composition:** The Great Barrier Reef consists of over 2,900 individual reefs and over 1,000 islands, as well as numerous sandbanks.

*** UNESCO World Heritage:** The Great Barrier Reef was added to the UNESCO list of World Natural Heritage Sites in 1981.

The Great Barrier Reef consists of over 2,900 individual reefs, 1,000 islets and countless sandbanks.

only for creatures that spend their entire lives underwater. At least 215 kinds of birds live off the reef and several endangered species of turtle survive only in this environment. Of the seven species of sea turtle worldwide, six can be found regularly on the Great Barrier Reef. The dugong, or sea cow, also threatened with extinction, is commonly sighted here and almost nowhere else on Earth.

A highlight of each year is the humpback whales. These magnificent animals stop here to give birth to their young in the warm reef waters on their way northward from the Antarctic. The Great Barrier Reef is, so to speak, their delivery room.

Sadly, the Great Barrier Reef is in danger. Coral reefs are extraordinarily sensitive ecosystems. The smallest change can lead to unforeseeable damage. In order to survive and successfully reproduce, reef coral require a marine environment with a relatively constant temperature range, preferably between 18 °C and 29 °C. A rise in water temperature can lead to both infertility and, should the algae die out, starvation. The algae are symbiotic with the coral, which ingest the one-celled plants, using them as a source of energy. Coral also derives its bright colours from algae, which protects the reef from the hot tropical sun. If the protective mantle is absent, the coral bleaches out as the calcified exoskeleton is exposed. If the water temperature continues to rise, the algae will not grow, or the coral will eject algae that show signs of stress. Without the algae, the living coral will die and all that will be left is the exoskeleton. This phenomenon, called 'coral bleaching', is currently the greatest threat to the survival of the Great Barrier Reef. By the year 2002, the warming caused by the increased greenhouse effect had affected between 60 and 95 per cent of the reef as a whole.

In addition to the effects of global warming, the reef must also withstand an annual influx of some 1.8 million tourists, as well as the effects of overuse of pesticides and chemical fertilizers on sugar cane and banana plantations. Every year, the monsoon washes these poisons into the coastal waters, leading to the extinction of reef coral many miles away. Additional chemical substances enter the water through increased construction and island development for tourism throughout South-east Asia and the Pacific.

Right: An anemone fish looks for protection among the tentacles of the poisonous sea anemone.

Below: Coral is the architect of the Great Barrier Reef.

Protective measures are difficult to institute and even more difficult to enforce: there are simply too many diverse factors that are contributing to the reef's distress. The pollutants themselves cross several national borders before reaching the reef, making practical legislation limiting their use a diplomatic nightmare. Then there is the problem of how little we really understand the specific biological effects on the coral itself.

Nature herself is reacting, violently, to global warming, in the form of stronger storms and devastating typhoons in the Pacific region. These, too, adversely affect the Great Barrier Reef. Tidal waves caused by these enormous low-pressure systems physically tear the reef apart. Large parts of the Great Barrier Reef have been affected by the increasingly catastrophic storms over the past decade.

Finally, the Great Barrier Reef is under threat from coral's natural enemy, the poisonous crown of thorns starfish. In the normal course of events, these starfish increase in population to the point of infestation every few years, feeding off the living coral polyps. Once the starfish have moved on, nothing is left alive in whole sections of reef. Perhaps due to the weakening of the reef due to warming and other factors, the crown of thorns starfish now seems to have settled permanently throughout the Great Barrier Reef in large numbers.

The Great Barrier Reef was placed on the UNESCO list of World Natural Heritage Sites in 1981. Soon afterward, scientists presented a 25-year research plan aimed at the preservation of this unique natural wonder. The first results are already available, and they are encouraging. Nearly all the coral stocks, including those among the 95 per cent affected by the massive coral bleaching that took place between 1998 and 2002, were able to recover following the institution of protective measures. Just 5 per cent of the Great Barrier Reef remains so severely damaged that it will take years before its wounds are healed.

The coral ridge that is the Great Barrier Reef, in all its beauty and complexity, remains an extremely fragile ecosystem. The smallest disturbance can drastically affect the many complex biological and symbiotic systems that constitute this natural paradise. Environmental pollution and global warming are two of the factors that negatively affect the entire life cycle of the reef. The establishment and enforcement of measures to protect this underwater Garden of Eden must remain one of humankind's highest priorities.

FACTS

* **Flora and fauna:** The Great Barrier Reef is home to 359 varieties of reef coral and 80 kinds of soft coral. Among the 1,500 types of invertebrates are 5,000 sponges and 800 spiny echinoderms, such as starfish and sea urchins. Also, 1,500 species of fish, 215 kinds of birds, 6 sea-turtle species, the dugong and humpback whales frequent the reef's waters.

NEW ZEALAND

Milford Sound

MILFORD SOUND IS A FJORD IN THE SOUTH-WESTERN CORNER OF NEW ZEALAND'S SOUTH ISLAND. LIKE THE FJORDS OF THE NORTHERN HEMISPHERE, MILFORD SOUND IS THE PRODUCT OF MANY THOUSANDS OF YEARS OF GLACIAL ACTIVITY.

The famous British author and world traveller Rudyard Kipling once visited the Milford Sound. Overpowered by its unique natural beauty, he declared it the eighth wonder of the world. In this far corner of the earth, Milford Sound, surrounded by Fiordland National Park, remains a magnificent and wild landscape of first growth forests and other fascinating natural wonders.

From a geological perspective, Milford Sound is a classic fjord that came into being millions of years ago. Its origins are glacial. Glaciers progressed down what are today river valleys leading to the coast, pushing away stone and bedrock as they forced their way forwards. As they melted, they left behind deep, U-shaped valleys that quickly filled with water as sea levels rose. One of these became the magnificent Milford Sound, which extends inland more than 15 km from the Tasman Sea. Vertical granite walls tower as high as 1,200 metres along its banks.

Milford Sound is unadulterated nature, a place where Mother Nature pulled out all the stops to create a unique landscape with unique flora and fauna. Tropical rainforests climb the steep walls of the sound, the trees grabbing hold of the stony earth with their roots. Moss and ferns thickly cover every surface. Far above the sound, steep-sided, snow-

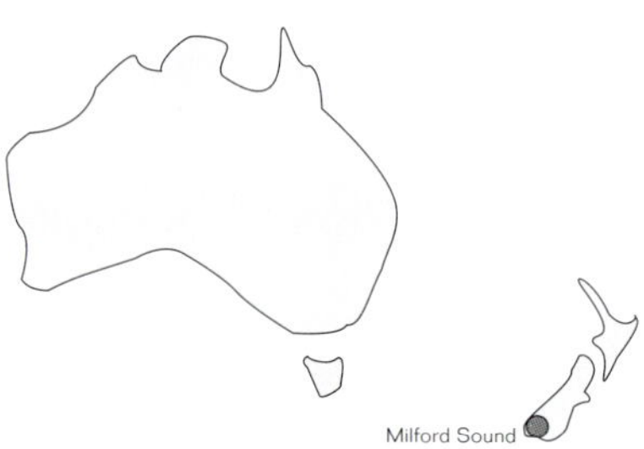

FACTS

* **Name:** Mildford Sound
* **Type:** Milford Sound is geologically categorized as a glacial fjord.
* **Size:** Surrounded by Fiordland National Park, Milford Sound is 15 km long. The total area of the national park is 1.25 million hectares.
* **Flora and fauna:** Milford Sound is a rainforest. The sea supports seals, penguins, dolphins, sharks, black corals and a large variety of birds.

Mitre Peak, 1,692 m high, is reflected in the crystal clear waters of Milford Sound. The peak is so-named because of its resemblance to a bishop's hat.

covered glacial peaks soar as high as 1,700 metres. The 1,692-metre Mitre Peak, so named because of its resemblance to a bishop's hat, is reflected in a crystal clear lake. Large and small waterfalls stream and cascade from the steep cliff walls, a product of the region's heavy rainfall. At any given moment there may be over 1,000 different waterfalls in the Milford Sound region.

The Milford Sound is one of the wettest places on Earth, receiving annual precipitation of as much as 700 cm of rain per year. It rains every single day. Visitors can count on good weather until around noon, but after lunch the clouds will quickly gather and by afternoon it is usually raining heavily.

The waters of Milford Sound are home to countless numbers of seals, penguins and dolphins. An undersea observatory called Milford Deep allows scientists and other observers to "dive" into the world beneath the water's surface. With so many prey animals assembled here, the predators are not far behind: a wide variety of sharks cruise through the fjord's waters. There are also fascinating coral reefs, some of which include the rarely seen black corals. Milford Sound is clear to a great depth, offering optimal viewing conditions. Sea plants begin to obstruct the view only in its deepest waters.

Milford Sound is mostly a climatic cool weather zone, much cooler than the rest of New Zealand. The months of May to August are the coldest, with the warmest days coming between November and February. Most tourists visit during the warmer months, not the least because of the special beauties of that season. In the southern hemisphere summer, the sun breaks through the thick clouds and impenetrable rainforest canopy to create fantastic light and shadow effects on the looming cliff faces and crystal waters of Milford Sound.

Above: It almost seems as if the mountains and cliffs arise out of Milford Sound.

Left: Clouds wreath the peaks of the fjord.

AUSTRALIA

The Sydney Opera House

THE SYDNEY OPERA HOUSE IS ONE OF THE MOST RECOGNIZABLE BUILDINGS OF THE TWENTIETH CENTURY. THIS REMARKABLE MULTI-PURPOSE STRUCTURE AND TRADEMARK OF ITS CITY IS THE MOST FREQUENTLY PHOTOGRAPHED BUILDING IN AUSTRALIA.

The opera house in Sydney Harbour is one of the most magnificent architectural wonders of the last century: it is a building and work of art at the same time. Nonetheless, soon after its dedication it had as many critics as fans. Few buildings inspire the extremes of praise and scorn heaped upon the Sydney Opera House after its opening. The London Times called it the "building of the century", but one critic who did not like its daringly atypical roof called it "a pack of French nuns playing football". The locals call their beloved opera house the "nuns (rugby) scrum" or the "oyster shells".

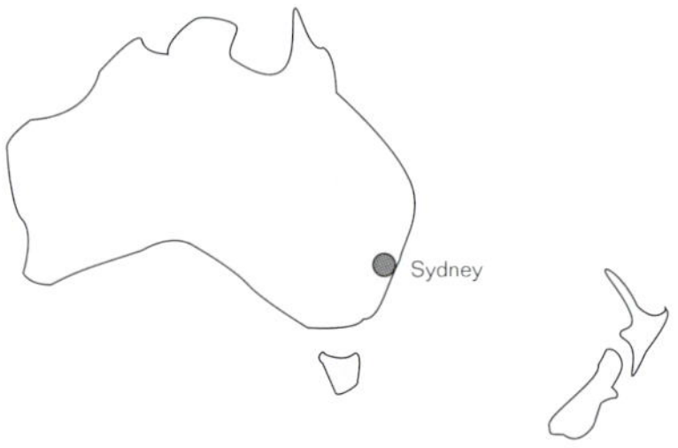

In the competition to design Sydney's new opera house, 223 architects submitted plans. In January 1957, the design by Danish architect Jorn Utzon was declared the winner, and two years later the cornerstone was laid on Bennelong Point in Sydney Harbour. First estimates called for a construction time of three or four years and a cost of $7 million. **Unfortunately, soon after construction began** it became clear that the timetable and cost projections were wildly unrealistic. In addition, the building of the unusual roof arches was plagued by major technical problems. To cover the "nun scrum", special tiles had to be made to order by a Swedish factory. Transport costs added to the soaring price tag.

The large concert hall of the Sydney Opera House seats 2,700.

FACTS

✱ Location: The Sydney Opera House sits on Bennelong Point in the harbour of Sydney, New South Wales, Australia. Its architect is Jorn Utzon.

✱ Dates: The cornerstone was laid on 2 March 1959. The first performance was on 28 September 1973, followed by the official opening on 20 October 1973. Construction took a total of 14 years and costs ran to $102 million.

✱ Size: The Sydney Opera House is 183 m long and 118 m wide with an area of over 21,500 m^2.

✱ Theatres and seats: The building houses 5 performance halls that seat a total of 5,500 people.

✱ Roof: The remarkable roof of the Sydney Opera House is covered with over 1 million ceramic tiles; 645 km of electric wiring run through the complex.

Fearing that things were getting out of hand, the government of New South Wales stopped all work at the site. New supervising architects were brought in to alter Utzon's original concept. That, the government hoped, would make the project less fraught with technical problems – and less expensive. Utzon angrily rejected the changes. Before long, the relationship between the architect and his patron could no longer be sustained. In 1966, after a particularly violent argument about the roof structure and finances, Utzon left Sydney. When a letter arrived a few years later inviting him to the opening of "his" building, the architect threw the invitation away.

A team of young Australian architects took on the task of finishing the construction. The government of New South Wales raised the necessary money with a state lottery. On 20 October 1973, the Sydney Opera House was opened with great fanfare. The planned four-year construction period had extended over 14 years, the costs to $102 million.

The Sydney Opera House is 183 metres long and 118 metres wide, enclosing an area of over 21,500 square metres. It sits on 580 concrete pillars sunk 25 metres deep in the harbour mud, and its remarkable roof rests 67 metres above it. Over a million glazed, pearl-white ceramic tiles cover the roof and its arches.

The building houses five theatres: the large concert hall seats 2,700; the theatre seats 1,500; and the smaller drama, playhouse and studio theatres seat between 350 and 500. About 1,000 additional rooms and halls can be found throughout the complex, including rehearsal studios, four restaurants and six bars. The electrical needs of five separate performance spaces, each full of complex lighting and stage machinery, required the installation of 645 km of wiring. On an evening when all five theatres are active, the Sydney Opera House uses as much electricity as a city with a population of 25,000. According to Harvard professor Bent Flyvbjerg, the real price of the project has nothing to do with its utility bill, nor with its 1,400 per cent construction cost overrun. The damage that the struggle over the opera house inflicted on the architect's reputation meant that the world would never see another building like it. The scandal associated with Utzon's resignation from the project would follow him his entire life; the great architect never again had the opportunity to design a major building.

Centre: The roof of the opera house is clad with over a million ceramic tiles.

Below: One of the best views of the Sydney Opera House is from the nearby Sydney Harbour Bridge.

NEW ZEALAND

Tongariro National Park

LOCATED IN CENTRAL NORTH ISLAND, TONGARIRO NATIONAL PARK IS NEW ZEALAND'S OLDEST NATURE RESERVE. ITS MANY VISITORS CAN TESTIFY TO THE POWER OF ITS IMPOSING LANDSCAPE AND THE MAGNIFICENT BEAUTY OF ITS NATURAL WONDERS.

How can one describe a place like Tongariro National Park? It boasts lush vegetation in one part, a desert-like high plain in another. The waters of its sparkling, crystal clear lakes lap shores of barren lava. Snow-covered volcanoes tower over it. It is no wonder the native Maori revered Tongariro as a magical, sacred place. The park's three active volcanoes – Tongariro (1,968 metres), Ngauruhoe (2,291 metres) and Ruapehu (2,797 metres) – are still an important part of Maori myths and legends.

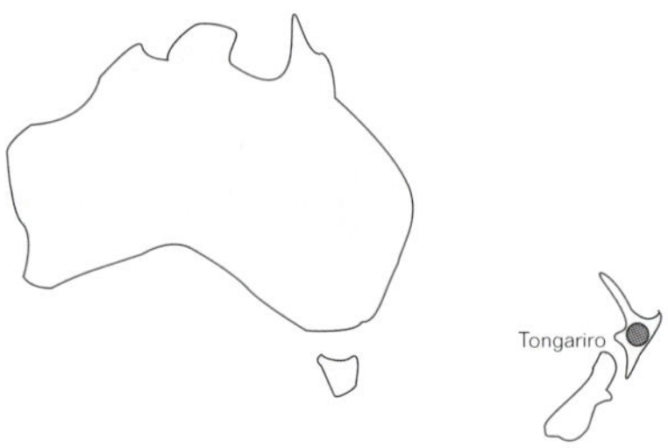

The legends tell of a Ngatoroirangi, chief of the Tuwharetoa tribe. In order to take possession of the land, Ngatoroirangi had to climb Mount Tongariro and light a fire on its peak. Accompanied only by his servant girl Ngauruhoe, the chief made his way up the mountain, where the freezing cold threatened to kill them. Desperate, Ngatoroirangi called on his sisters, who were priestesses on their home island of Hawaii. They heard their brother's desperate cry, and the Earth broke open and fire burst forth from inside the Earth. To honour the volcano god, Ngatoroirangi sacrificed his servant. Since then, the Maori call the mountain Ngauruhoe, in honour of the unfortunate victim.

Ngatoroirangi's descendants, the Tuwharetoa tribe, still live in the region around Mount Tongariro,

FACTS

*** Location and size:** Tongariro National Park is located on the North Island of New Zealand. It is New Zealand's oldest national park, founded in 1894. It has a total area of 796 km².

*** Elevations:** Elevations in the park range from 500 to 2,797 m above sea level. The volcanoes at its centre are Tongariro (1,986 m), Ngauruhoe (2,291 m) and Ruapehu (2,797 m).

*** UNESCO World Heritage:** Parts of Tongariro National Park were added to the UNESCO list of World Natural and World Cultural Heritage Sites in 1991 and 1993.

*** Maori:** Tongariro is an important sacred site to the Maori. The Maori are the indigenous people of New Zealand, who are thought to have settled there sometime between the 8th and 14th centuries, travelling from Polynesia in multiple waves of emigration.

Hot steam flows out of the crater of the 2,797-m-high Ruapehu, the most active of the three volcanoes in Tongariro National Park.

their holy mountain. In the nineteenth century, when white men were arriving in large numbers, Tuwharetoa chief Te Heuheu Tukino IV employed a diplomatic trick to undermine their efforts at exploiting tribal lands. In 1887, he made a gift of the three volcanoes to the British crown, contingent on a promise that England create a protected area around them. Thus, the sacred land became the core of Tongariro National Park, founded in 1894.

The three volcanic mountains are located in the centre of the park. Although all three are still active in geological terms, only Ruapehu erupts frequently, the last time in 1995, when it sent forth a hail of mud, ash, steam and lava over several months. The area east of Ruapehu has been transformed into a landscape resembling the surface of the moon.

Volcanic and other tectonic activity has left much of Tongariro National Park a rough terrain dotted with unstable environments. Nevertheless, lush animal and plant life is at home in the niches. Plants in particular flourish at a variety of elevations in a range of vegetation zones. Meadow grasses, lichens and high-altitude shrubs and yew trees can be found up to the snowline. The forests further down the slopes host over 50 different species of birds, including the famous kiwi bird, the emblem of New Zealand. Also found on the volcanic slopes are the park's two native mammal species – both bats.

The greatest threat to the native flora and fauna are the "introduced" species that are not native to the habitat. These range from feral house cats and ermines to the ubiquitous brown rat. Wild rabbits and red deer are also increasing in number, devouring delicate plants, some of which grow nowhere else on Earth. Protecting Tongariro from introduced species, a threat to the environment all over New Zealand, may be a problem only the volcano god can solve.

Above: Ngauruhoe rises 2,291 m above gently sloping hills.

Left: Ngauruhoe stood in as Mount Doom in the film version of *Lord of the Rings*.

AUSTRALIA

Uluru

ALSO KNOWN AS AYER'S ROCK, ULURU IS A MONOLITHIC RED STONE MASSIF IN AUSTRALIA'S NORTHERN TERRITORIES. SACRED TO THE ABORIGINES, ULURU RISES FROM THE BARREN OUTBACK STEPPE LIKE THE DORSAL FIN OF A GIANT RED WHALE.

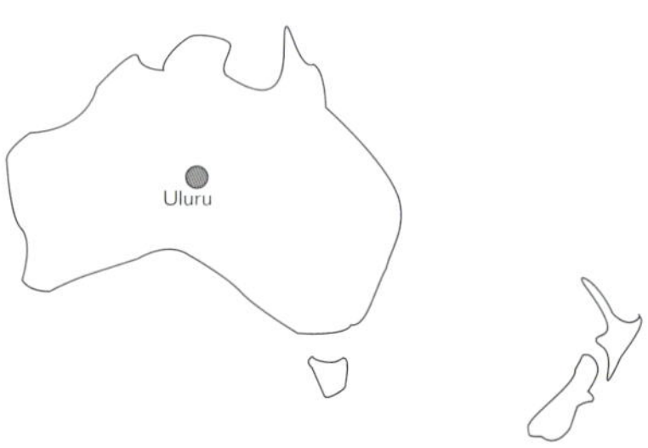

The deeply furrowed rock has a thousand stories to tell about its million years of existence. Uluru and the nearby rock formation called Kata Tjuta ("Many Heads") have been part of the Uluru-Kata Tjuta National Park since 1977. In 1985, the Australian government officially returned all of it, Uluru and Kata Tjuta included, to the local Northern Territories aboriginal peoples. The national park is their sacred land, the place where the aborigines believe all life came into being a long, long time ago.

Its tremendous size alone would make Uluru a geographical wonder. The red sandstone monolith rises 348 metres from the ground, and its maximum elevation is 869 metres above sea level. The visible part of the rock is 3.4 km long and up to 2 km wide. Its circumference is some 9 km. The red arkosic sandstone was formed some 600 million years ago, forced from the Earth under immense pressure. Mud and gravel were compressed and pushed to the surface by tectonic activity. The elemental forces at work here must have been stupendous.

Like islands floating in a barren sea, the Kata Tjuta ("Many Heads") lie about 50 km away from Uluru. Ernest Giles was the first European to see them in 1872. He called the rocks "The Olgas" in honour

Right: Lightning bathes Uluru in mysterious light.

Below: The Kata Tjuta are 36 rocky outcrops made of a conglomerate gravel with granite, gneiss and volcanic components.

of Queen Olga of Wurttemberg, who had been a great supporter of science and exploration in the nineteenth century. The Kata Tjuta are distinctly younger than Uluru, at only 300 million years. The rocks are not red sandstone, like Uluru, but coarse conglomerate gravel made up of layers of pebbles, cobbles and boulders cemented by sand and mud. Granite, gneiss and volcanic stones are present.

The local Anangu tribe considers both Uluru and Kata Tjuta to be sacred places, the ancient site of wars between different snake peoples. Their legends tell of Kuniya, the python snake woman, who journeyed to Uluru to lay her eggs. When she got there she heard that the poisonous Liru snake had killed her nephew. Hungry for revenge, she went to a place called Mutitjulu at the base of Uluru. There she met one of the Liru men. She tried to bewitch him with a dance, but he laughed at her. Enraged, she took a handful of sand and threw it on the ground. Everywhere the sand landed, the plants and trees became poisonous. Yet the Liru man still laughed. Finally, Kuniya took her digging stick (*wana*) and struck the Liru man on the head. Her rage was so great that she hit him a second time, killing him. The deep cuts that Kuniya inflicted on the Liru man can still be seen on the face of Uluru, etched deep into the rock. Kuniya and her nephew were transformed into rainbow snakes. They still live in Mutitjulu, where they watch over the Anangu tribe.

The Anangu, like most Australian aborigines, believe that all life had its origins during a creation period called 'Dreamtime' (*Tjukurpa*). During Dreamtime, the spirit ancestors walked the Earth in human and animal form. Some of these spirit ancestors crawled out of the Earth in the form of giant snakes, and it was they who gave the Earth its form. Spirit ancestors also set down laws that the Anangu and other aborigines still follow today. The ancient legends and stories are therefore the very basis of their culture. Their traditions provide answers to the universal human questions about the creation of the universe, the laws of nature and relationships between men and women. They also address the meaning of life and death and go into some detail about the afterlife. The importance of these stories to the Anangu people make Uluru, which is the setting for so many of these legends, a very sensitive area of interaction between indigenous and non-indigenous peoples. The Anangu request that no one climb the rock, though many tourists do so nonetheless. The Anangu themselves are forbidden by their traditions to set foot on it.

FACTS

* **Size:** Uluru, also known as Ayers Rock, is 3.4 km long and 2 km wide at its broadest. It has a circumference of some 9 km.
* **Height:** The visible part of Uluru rises 348 m from ground level, but over 6,000 m of the rock lie beneath the surface. Its elevation above sea level is 869 m.
* **Age:** Uluru consists of red arkosic sandstone formed 600 million years ago.
* **UNESCO World Heritage:** Uluru was placed on the UNESCO World Cultural and World Natural Heritage lists in 1987.

Finally, our tour brings us to wonders in the pole regions and the atmosphere. The seas around the permanent ice cap of Antarctica are an ecosystem rich with life in the harshest environment. The Southern Lights (Aurora Australis) are caused by particles spewed during eruptions on the surface of the sun. Then there is the high-tech wonder, the ISS, orbiting in space. That humankind could reach so far may be the greatest wonder of all.

THE POLES

AND BEYOND

ANTARCTICA

Antarctica

ANTARCTICA IS COVERED BY A PERMANENT ICE CAP SCOURED BY FROZEN WINDS AND POWERFUL STORMS. IN EVERY WAY, THE SOUTHERNMOST CONTINENT IS A LAND OF EXTREMES. IT IS THE COLDEST PLACE ON EARTH, BUT ALSO THE DRIEST AND WINDIEST.

Far from the world's trade routes, Antarctica was spared the ravages of colonization until well into the nineteenth and early twentieth centuries. Antarctica was only discovered in January 1820, when Russian Navy captain Fabian von Bellinghausen sighted the coast. The first landing took place in February 1821, after American seal hunter John Davis was blown off course from his usual hunting ground in the South Shetland Islands. **The conquest of Antarctica** began in earnest in1895. An international conference in London called on scientists from all countries to send out research expeditions. The following years are full of classic Antarctic journeys. Robert F. Scott of England came within 770 km of the pole in an expedition lasting from 1901 to 1904. The first German expedition, led by Erich von Drygalski in 1901–1903, discovered Kaiser Wilhelm Land and a volcanic outcrop called the Gaussberg. The 1907–1909 expedition of Irishman Ernest H. Shackleton came within 155 km of the South Pole before being forced to turn around. It was not until 14 December 1911 that Roald Amundsen from Norway won the race to the geographical South Pole, just beating an English team led by Robert F. Scott, who arrived there one month later. Scott and his entire team died on the way back when a monu-

FACTS

✻ Discovery: The continent of Antarctica was discovered on 16 January 1820.

✻ Area: Antarctica has a total area of 52 million km². Its highest point is Mt. Vinson, at 5,140 m. Its lowest point is the Bentley Trench at 2,538 m below sea level.

✻ Permanent ice: 90 per cent of Antarctica is covered by a permanent ice cap. 75 per cent of all fresh water in the world exists as Antarctic ice.

✻ World records: Antarctica holds many extreme world records. The coldest temperature on Earth, –89.2 °C, was measured at Russian Vostok Station. The highest sustained wind speed, 327 km/h, was measured at Dumont-d'Urville Station.

✻ Research: Antarctica has 82 research stations, of which 37 are used year-round. Depending on the season, between 1,000 and 4,000 scientists live on the continent or on offshore research vessels. This makes Antarctica the least densely settled region on Earth, with 0.0001–0.0003 inhabitants per km².

Coastal Antarctica is icy and barren, yet surrounded by some of the most nutrient-rich waters on Earth, home to a large variety of animal life.

mental storm left the explorers unable to locate food stores they had left along their route for the homeward journey. They perished from the deadly combination of cold and hunger.

The Antarctic Treaty was ratified by 44 nations on 1 December 1959. It places the continent under international protection while banning any use of Antarctica for economic gain or military purposes. As geological research continues, the need for these restrictions becomes increasingly apparent. Antarctica is a treasure trove of mineral wealth. The permanent ice cap conceals probably 45 billion barrels of oil and 115 trillion cubic metres of natural gas, in addition to extensive deposits of coal, titanium, iron, copper and uranium. There are even veins of platinum and gold beneath the icy wastes. The treaty expires in 2041. No one knows if it will be extended.

Antarctica is a landscape of climatic extremes. The annual average inland temperature is –55 °C. The lowest temperature ever recorded was measured on the Antarctic central plateau on 21 July 1983, when the thermometer read –89.2 °C. Nearly all precipitation, on average less than 4 inches per year, falls as snow. This exceedingly low figure technically makes Antarctica the world's driest, and largest, desert. From July to August there are nearly non-stop cyclonic storms. During one of them in July 1972, wind speed was measured at 327 km/hour. This is a world record for sustained wind speed.

Scientists and penguins are Antarctica's only long-term inhabitants. During the Antarctic summer, the height of the research season, as many as 4,000 scientists live on the ice cap or in offshore vessels. Penguins, seals, seabirds, squid and whales are drawn to the coastal waters, which are thick with nutrient-rich krill. The continent's nearly intact environment is thus far theirs for the taking.

Above: Kaiser and Adelie penguins are Antarctica's "natives".

Left: The American research station in Antarctica is located at the South Pole.

SPACE

International Space Station

THE CONSTRUCTION OF THE ISS IS THE LARGEST CIVIL ENGINEERING PROJECT IN ALL OF HUMAN HISTORY. AS BEFITS ITS NAME, A HOST OF NATIONS TAKE PART IN THE PROJECT, INCLUDING THE USA, RUSSIA, JAPAN, CANADA, BRAZIL AND THE EUROPEAN UNION.

It was less than forty years ago that the American astronaut Neil Armstrong became the first man to set foot on the moon on 21 July 1969. As he stepped onto the surface he made the famous statement: "One small step for man, one giant leap for mankind." Many people consider the conquest of space and investigation of its wonders to be the greatest and most exciting challenge humankind faces today. By this standard, the most extraordinary human adventure in space to date may not be Armstrong's moon landing, but the construction of the International Space Station.

In 1984, the United States government announced plans to build a space station, but cost overruns in the design and planning phase led to delays. The project began to take on a concrete form only after the end of the cold war when, in 1993, Russia decided to join the international cooperative for the construction of what is today known as the International Space Station. In 1986 the Soviet government had already begun building its own space station, the MIR (the Russian word for peace). Their know-how, but especially their experience, was crucial to the success of Project ISS. **Construction began in 1998.** First, a number of technicalities had to be ironed out so that the

Right: A 3 December 2005 photograph of Hurricane Epsilon from ISS.

Below: The Russian space station MIR was destroyed by controlled demolition on 23 March 2003.

collaboration could proceed without undue friction. This meant that the work needed to be divided in a sensible and practical manner. The American space shuttle was given the task of ferrying material back and forth to the MIR space station. On 20 November 1998, the first large piece of the ISS, a freight and control module, was "installed" in space, 350 km above the Earth. In the same year, a connecting piece, the Russian living quarters module "Svesda", was attached by means of a docking manoeuvre. From November 2000 to April 2003 the ISS was under construction with a rotating three-member crew permanently in place. Each ISS crew team spent five to seven months in space before being relieved by the next crew. After the space shuttle *Columbia* disaster in 2003, it became impossible to resupply the space station at previous levels. With all the American space shuttles grounded, the ISS crew was reduced to two members resupplied by Soviet *Soyuz* spacecraft.

The space shuttle accident slowed down progress on the ISS, and for a time all construction was stopped. In 2005 the Russians took over the larger part of the project. In 2006, the American space agency NASA was once again able to provide space shuttle flights for provisioning and materials transport. By June 2011, the ISS consisted of 15 pressurized modules. It has been a long time, however, since any of the parties involved has been prepared to commit to a binding construction schedule. Technical problems and steep increases in costs continue to cause delays. Experts outside the project now estimate that the ISS will not be complete before 2016.

When it is finished, the ISS will be a construction of gigantic dimensions, approaching the size of a football field. The solar panels will be 107 metres wide, while the habitable part of the station will be 80 metres long and weigh 450 tons. This will be by far the largest space station ever built. Thus far, with only about 40 per cent of the ISS in place, it is already the largest artificial object in space. Once finished, it should be visible with the naked eye in a clear night sky, the brightest object in the heavens.

The total costs for this fantastic project have been, so far, incalculable. During the intial planning phase, NASA estimated a total of $40 billion, and it was soon clear that this figure would have to be adjusted upwards.

FACTS

*** Beginnings:** Construction of the ISS began in 1998.

*** Size:** The ISS is 108.6 m wide at its greatest span. The habitable station will be 80 m long, weigh 450 tons and have a total area of 1,140 m^2.

*** Orbit:** The ISS sustains orbit 350–450 km above sea level. One orbit around the Earth takes approximately 90 minutes at a speed of 29,000 km/h.

*** Solar panels:** The solar panels have an area of 4,500 m^2 and generate an electrical current of 110 kW.

*** The crews:** From 2000 to 2003, a rotating crew of three were permanently stationed aboard the ISS. Since April 2003, the crew has been reduced to just two people.

*** Space flights to ISS:** As of July 2006, more than 28 space flights had docked at the ISS.

POLES

Northern Lights

THE EARLIEST ACCOUNTS OF NORTHERN LIGHTS DATE TO MORE THAN 2,000 YEARS AGO. MANY TRIBAL PEOPLES BELIEVED THEM TO BE MESSAGES FROM GODS AND SPIRITS. FOR MEDIEVAL EUROPEANS THEY WERE BAD OMENS WARNING OF COMING DISASTERS

The Northern Lights are brilliant, colourful illuminations in the sky caused when particles swept along by solar winds impact the Earth's atmosphere. They occur primarily in the polar regions. In the northern polar regions they are also called Aurora Borealis, while near the South Pole, where they are slightly less common, they are known as Aurora Australis. The farther from the poles one travels, the less likely it is that Northern Lights will appear in the sky. This means that they are extraordinarily rare over most of Europe and the continental United States.

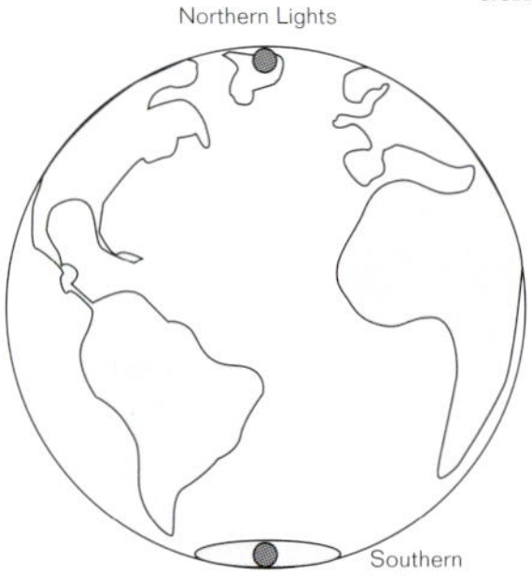

The Northern Lights result from the constant give and take between the Sun and planet Earth. Particles are released by molecular activity that takes place on the surface of the Sun. The storm of particles thus released – consisting of electrons, protons and ions – sets off what are known as solar winds. When these particles collide with atoms in the upper layer of the Earth's atmosphere, the Earth's magnetic field redirects the charged particles toward the poles, where they continue to move down through the atmosphere, illuminating air molecules along the way. The majority of Northern Lights displays appear between 65 and 400 km above the Earth's surface.

Northern Lights glimmer like tracks across the sky in northern Alaska.

FACTS

*** Name:** Northern Lights are also known as Aurora Borealis (Northern Hemisphere) and Southern Lights as Aurora Australis (Southern Hemisphere). They are most common in the polar regions.

*** Height:** The illumination occurs between 65 and 400 km above the Earth's surface.

*** Particle speed:** The particles driven into the Earth's atmosphere by solar winds are travelling at a speed of 3 million km/h. Where the Northern Lights occur, particle density is approximately 5 x 10^6 particles/m^3.

*** Distance Earth–Sun:** The Earth is 150 million km from the sun. It takes a particle storm 2 to 4 days to cover the distance.

Solar winds propel the particles at great speed, as much as 3 million km per hour. It only takes the particles four days to travel 93 million miles from the Sun to the Earth.

The frequency, duration and visibility of the Northern Lights depend on the strength of the solar winds and activity on the surface of the Sun. An active cycle, also known as a sunspot cycle, can last for eleven years. It is during these phases that Northern Lights are most commonly observed. During periods of maximum activity it may even be possible to observe Northern Lights in the middle latitudes of Europe and the continental United States.

Northern Lights are not difficult to identify. They are active, shimmering and moving through the sky. They cannot be mistaken for the Milky Way, constellations, or any other heavenly body. Each appearance is one of a kind, with its own distinct form, colour and intensity. Many times the lights fall within a clearly delineated area; other times they appear as glowing rays. Their colours span the entire spectrum. Green lights come from oxygen atoms activated by the solar particles some 60 miles above the Earth's surface; the lights are red when the oxygen is absorbed at 125 miles or higher. Nitrogen atoms produce a soft, violet light.

Tribal peoples of North America and Europe were happy to see the Northern Lights, which they interpreted as messages from gods, spirits, or ancestors. In other cultures, though, they are viewed as omens of impending disaster. The warlike Vikings of Scandinavia and the Highland clans of Scotland thought the lights meant that a huge battle was taking place somewhere in the world. Many of the names for the Northern Lights from later medieval and modern periods are charmingly descriptive. In Scandinavia they are called the Herring Flash, because the flickering lights resemble a school of fish swimming by. Finns call them Fox Fires, relating the arcs of colour to the burning tails of folklore foxes made of fire.

Modern science first began to understand the Northern Lights in the eighteenth century. The connection to the Earth's magnetic field was elaborated over the next hundred years. The theory connecting Northern Lights to solar winds and geomagnetic storms was first developed in the early twentieth century and confirmed by data gathered during the first space flights fifty years later.

Centre: The Aurora Borealis is rarely seen over central Europe. This one was observed during a period of high solar activity.

Bottom: Fantastic colours and shapes make every appearance of the Northern Lights a one-of-a-kind performance by nature.

Picture Credits

© Corbis: Peter Adams 152; Theo Allofs 34, 189 b. r., 220; Paul Almasy 115 c.; S. Andreas 113 b.; Roger Antrobus 147 t.; Archivo Iconografico 110, 141 t. r.; Bjorn Backe 233 b. 4th fr. l., 239 t., 239 b.; David Ball 143 b. l., 218 b. 2nd fr. l., 222; Gaetano Barone 120; Dave Bartruff 111 t., 207 b.; Tom Bean 201 b. l., 207 t. l., 207 t. r.; Remi Benali 64, 65 b. r.; Bettmann 47 t., 109 t., 133 b., 191 c., 203 b. r.; Jonathan Blair 30, 154; Tibor Bognár 135 b. r., 187 t. l., 219 b. 5th fr. l., 229 b. l.; John Brecher 19 t.; Richard Broadwell 201 t.; Jan Butchofsky-Houser 53 c.; David Butow 203 b. l.; Charles Philip Cangialosi 195 b. l.; Christie's Images 55 b.; Elio Ciol 130; L. Clarke 219 b. 4th fr. l., 226, 227 c.; Claudius 33 t. l.; Ralph A. Clevenger 223 b.; Brandon D. Cole 223 t. l.; Sheldan Collins 99 c.; Dean Conger 31 b. l., 31 b. r., 102; W. Perry Conway 193 t.; Joel Creed 169 b.; Marco Cristofori 126; Fridmar Damm 10, 65 t., 77 t.; James Davis 164, 169 c.; Tim Davis 165 t. r., 232 b. 2nd fr. l., 235 b. r.; Dennis Degnan 144, 145 b.; DAJ 98; Ric Ergenbright 125 b., 127 t.; Robert Essel 41 b. l.; Macduff Everton 163 M., 229 b. r.; Eye Ubiquitous 8 b. 2nd fr. l., 21 t., 173 t.; Randy Faris 181 t.; Kevin Fleming 194; David Forman 88; Owen Franken 63 c., 167 b. l.; Free Agents Limited 55 t. r., 103 t., 103 b. r., 115 t., 135 b. l., 197 b., 209 b. l.; Michael Freeman 71 c., 71 b., 99 t., 99 b., 171 t. r.; Franz Marc Frei 193 b. l., 195 t.; Stephen Frink 81 t. r., 221 t. l.; Arvind Garg 161 b. l.; Mark E. Gibson 163 b.; S. P. Gillette 85 b.; Todd Gipstein 101 t. l., 101 t. r.; Richard Glover 5 t., 198; Farrell Grehan 192; Annie Griffiths Belt 73 t. l., 73 b.; Darrell Gulin 213 t. r.; Karl-Heinz Haenel 133 c., 224; Derek Hall 183 t. l.; Richard Hamilton Smith 239 c.; Robert Harding 51 b. l., 89 t. l., 125 t. l.; Paul Hardy 123 t.; Roger De La Harpe 36; Blaine Harrington III 204, 206; Thomas Hartwell 31 t.; Martin Harvey 8 b. far l., 12, 13 b. l., 21 b.; Jason Hawkes 150; Dallas and John Heaton 53 t., 57 b. l., 60; Lindsay Hebberd 78, 79 t., 91 c.; Chris Hellier 69, 117 t., 117 b. l., 117 b. r.; John Heseltine 132, 151 t.; Jon Hicks 71 t., 93 b. l.; Historical Picture Archive 83 b. r.; Robert Holmes 212; Angelo Hornak 180; Eric and David Hosking 211 b.; Dave G. Houser 127 M., 171 t. l.; Rob Howard 94; Hulton-Deutsch Collection 37 t.; Hanan Isachar 72, 74, 75 t. l.; Ladislav Janicek 106/107, 108, 225 b. r.; Gavriel Jecan 13 b. r.; Lalage Johnstone 188, 189 t.; Dean Francis Joseph 138, 139 t., 139 b. l., 139 b. r.; Ray Juno 107 b. 5th fr. l., 148; Wolfgang Kaehler 29 c., 61 b., 91 t., 111 b. l., 131 b. r., 155 t., 175 b.; Catherine Karnow 62, 63 t.; Karen Kasmauski 55 t. l.; Steve Kaufman 158/159 b. 3rd fr. l., 178, 179 b. l.; Richard Klune 106 b. far l., 119 b.; Earl & Nazima Kowall 54; Frank Krahmer 179 b. r., 213 b.; Wilfried Krecichwost 225 b. l.; Bob Krist 142, 153 t. r.; Simon Kwong 96; Otto Lang 50; Mark Laricchia 231 t. r.; Patrice Latron 86, 87 t.; Lester Lefkowitz 205 t., 205 b. l., 205 b. r.; Danny Lehman 66, 177 b.; Frans Lemmens 27 t. r., 158 b. far l., 170; Charles & Josette Lenars 43 b., 52, 53 b., 79 c., 61 t. l., 119 t. l., 163 t., 183 t. r., 183 b.; Francois Lenoir 119 t. r.; Michael S. Lewis 85 c.; Liu Liqun 58, 59 b. r.; Chris Lisle 42; Massimo Listri 49 c., 115 b., 157 b. l.; Craig Lovell 171 b.; Benjamin Lowy 25 t. l., 25 t. r., 25 b.; Araldo de Luca 133 t., 141 t. l., 143 b. r.; Frank Lukasseck 201 b. r.; Ludovic Maisant 13 t., 49 t.; Lawrence Manning 17 t. l., 69 t. l.; William Manning 145 c., 155 c., 155 b.; Gunter Marx 184/185 b. 3rd fr. l., 200; Massimo Mastrorillo 218/219; Michael St. Maur Sheil 125 t. r.; Wally McNamee 104; Mike McQueen 105 t.; Manfred Mehlig 87 b. r.; John and Lisa Merrill 4, 141 b.; Hans Peter Merten 149 b.; Gail Mooney 196; Kevin R. Morris 43 t., 43 M.; David Muench 189 b. l.; Francoise de Mulder 46, 47 b. r.; Amos Nachoum 218 b. far l., 221 t. r.; NASA 165 t. l., 176, 233 b. 5th fr. l., 232/233 b. 3rd fr. l., 236, 237 t. l., 237 t. r., 238; Tom Nebbia 28; Michael Nicholson 35 t. l., 73 t. r.; Kazuyoshi Nomachi 8/9, 19 b. l., 27 t. l., 27 b., 82, 83 t., 143 t.; John D. Norman 21 c.; Richard T. Nowitz 23 b. l., 75 b., 146, 174; Oliviero Olivieri 116; Charles O'Rear 109 b. l., 134, 199 b., 211 c.; Gianni Dagli Orti 47 b. l., 111 b. r., 181 b.; Douglas Peebles 215 t. l., 215 t. r.; Paul C. Pet 35 b., 182; Sergio Pitamitz 20, 93 b. r.; José F. Poblete 89 b.; Louie Psihoyos 97 t., 97 b. l., 97 b. r., 122; Carl & Ann Purcell 18; Jose Fuste Raga 6/7, 8/9 b. 3rd fr. l., 11 t. r., 11 b., 15 t., 26, 35 t. r., 38/39, 76, 77 b. l., 77 b. r., 91 b., 93 t., 106/107 b. 3rd fr. l., 118, 145 t., 156, 177 t. l., 187 b., 216, 218/219 b. 3rd fr. l., 225 t.; Chris Rainier 11 t. l.; J. Ramid 160; James Randklev 210, 217 b. r., 232/233; Vittoriano Rastelli 140; Carmen Redondo 17 b., 33 t. r., 90; Roger Ressmeyer 22, 214, 158/159, 199 t., 237 b.; David Samuel Robbins 95 b., Fulvio Roiter 181 c.; Bill Ross 157 b. r., 217 t.; Guenter Rossenbach 16, 128, 129 b. r., 131 t., 149 t. r.; Charles E. Rotkin 191 b.; Galen Rowell 84, 95 t. l., 193 b. r., 195 b. r., 217 b. l., 235 b. l.; S P 63 b.; Sakamoto Photo 70; Kevin Schafer 159 b. 5th fr. l., 167 t., 173 b. r., 175 c.; Alan Schein 184 b. 2nd fr. l., 190, 191 t.; Michael T. Sedam 213 t. l.; ML Sinibaldi 45 b.; H. Sitton 57 b. r.; Joseph Sohm 208, 209 b. r.; Paul A. Souders 51 t., 59 t., 59 b. l., 109 b. r., 121 c., 136, 137 b., 153 t. l., 177 t. r., 221 b., 231 b., 235 t.; Roman Soumar 45 t. l.; Jon Sparks 228, 229 t.; James Sparshatt 147 b. r.; Herbert Spichtinger 37 b., 69 b., 121 b., 199 c., 227 t.; Ted Spiegel 153 b.; Hubert Stadler 158 b. 2nd fr. l., 175 t.; Mark L Stephenson 197 t. r.; Christopher Stevenson 186; Kurt Stier 83 b. l.; Stock Photos 231 t. l.; Keren Su 5 b., 48, 56, 57 t., 61 t. r., 65 b. l., 105 c., 105 b., 172, 173 b. l., 184/185, 232 b. far l., 234; Jim Sugar 185 b. 4th fr. l., 215 b.; Svenja-Foto 107 b. 4th fr. l., 129 t., 129 b. l., 147 b. l.; Torleif Svensson 19 b. r.; Chase Swift 185 b. 5th fr. l., 211 t.; Swim Ink 2, LLC 123 b. r.; Murat Taner 39 b. 4th fr. l., 40, 92, 202; Luca I. Tettoni 38 b. far l., 44, 45 t. r., 49 b.; The Art Archive 157 t.; Paul Thompson 184 b. far l., 187 t. r.; Vanni Archive 127 b.; Sandro Vannini 23 b. r., 39 b. 4th fr. l., 75 t. r., 124; Brian A. Vikander 29 t., 29 b., 79 b., 95 t. r., 103 b. l.; Ian Walker 112; Patrick Ward 113 t. r.; Julia Waterlow 168; Anna Watson 131 b. l.; Karl Weatherly 113 t. l.; Anthony John West 179 t.; K. M. Westermann 17 t. r.; Michele Westmorland 159 b. 4th fr. l., 162; Stuart Westmorland 223 t. r.; Nik Wheeler 37 c., 87 b. l., 151 b. l.; Lee White 100, 101 b.; Wild Country 85 t.; Peter M. Wilson 137 t. r.; Nick Wiseman 135 t.; Roger Wood 9 b. 4th fr. l., 14, 15 c., 15 b., 32, 33 b., 203 t.; Adam Woolfitt 67 t. l., 80, 151 b. r.; Alison Wright 38 b. 2nd fr. l., 67 b.; Michael S. Yamashita 24, 41 t., 41 b. r., 209 t.; Jon P. Yeager 169 t.

© Gerhard Klimmer: 51 b. r.

© MEV: 23 t., 38/39 b. 3rd fr. l., 67 t. r., 68, 81 t. l., 81 b., 89 t. r., 106 b. 2nd fr. l., 114, 121 t., 123 b. l., 137 t. l., 149 t. l., 161 t., 161 b. r., 165 b., 166, 167 b. r., 197 t. l., 227 b., 230

© Thomas Uhlig: 9 b. 5th fr. l.